THE HEART
OF AN
EXECUTIVE

THE HEART
OF AN
EXECUTIVE

*Lessons on
Leadership from the Life
of King David*

RICHARD D. PHILLIPS

Doubleday
New York London Toronto Sydney Auckland

PUBLISHED BY DOUBLEDAY
a division of Random House, Inc.
1540 Broadway, New York, New York 10036

DOUBLEDAY and the portrayal of an anchor with a dolphin are trademarks of Doubleday, a division of Random House, Inc.

BOOK DESIGN BY RENATO STANISIC
MAP DESIGNED BY JEFFREY L. WARD

Library of Congress Cataloging-in-Publication Data

Phillips, Richard D. (Richard D.), 1960–
    The heart of an executive: lessons on leadership from the life of
King David / Richard D. Phillips.
      p. cm.
    1. Leadership—Religious aspects—Christianity.   2. David, King of
Israel. I. Title.
HD57.7.P495   1999
658.4'092—dc21
                                  98-21259
                                     CIP

To my father

The shepherd of my youth,
The model for my manhood

and

To the Good Shepherd

Who laid down His life for the sheep,
and sits upon the throne
of His father David

CONTENTS

PREFACE

This book is not written for organizations but for the men and women who inhabit them, who indeed *are* the organizations we are so concerned about today. We are living in a time when change and new forms of effectiveness are required at a dizzying pace. Reengineering, reorganization, and "right-sizing" are but a few of the means employed to turn around an organization's sagging performance. But how often our efforts at change fail to address the real and underlying issues at hand. Ours is not a failure of structure or alignment, but something that runs much deeper. Our main concern should be with the state of leadership today and with the passions and principles that inform that leadership. Yet leadership is seldom found in a consultant's briefing packet. My conviction and the conviction of this book is that organizational change requires individual change and growth, first and foremost among our leaders. For leadership takes place first and foremost in the human heart, and change must first reside there if it is to make a credible and enduring impact on ourselves and our organizations.

The story of David, Israel's greatest king and hero of the Bible's Old Testament, is the story of an executive. That may sound strange in a time when executives are, generally speaking, anything but heroes. But David was not typical of executives, then or now. David was not a typical anything. He and his story call us to reconsider our vision not of what is or what was, but what *ought* to be and indeed *can* be. Through his life he sets before us not only different answers but different questions as well, challenging us to raise the line of our sight and aspiration.

David's story is that of a career, an executive career. His story is like that of so many others, preparation leading to advancement, trials and challenges serving to build character and hone skills, advancement leading to achievement, and finally the passing on of the torch to others. At the same time, David's story is like no other: it comes down to us out of the centuries as an inspiring challenge, a rallying cry for the wearied heart, and a reminder that all dreams need not fall short of their realization.

David's story is essentially a story of contrasts. We start with the contrast between David and Goliath, the names themselves serving as a metaphor for the little guy standing up to the bruiser. The start-up company against the Fortune 500. David's success in this early encounter leads us to the conflict between David and King Saul, the change-agent visionary versus the paragon of self-serving power. Then, just when we think we have left conflict behind, we enter into the real struggle of this story, that which takes place within David himself. In all these conflicts and contrasts we encounter challenges familiar to our own time, most dramatically when David is forced to reckon with the mixed reality of his own heart.

David's story is not moral or myth, any more than David was himself. David was a leader and executive, a man whose capacity for both greatness and folly is staggering. Therefore, the colors that so boldly comprise his portrait are the very ones that must make up our own. In David's story today's manager and leader will see his own challenges, her own frustrations and dreams. *The Heart of an Executive* tells a real but far from commonplace story; David's life challenges all of us today who would be called leaders, and kindles the fire of hearts grown weary. My hope, then, is that you will join me in this story, this life, and in this living lesson sent to us by the Bible and its heavenly Author, to look within the heart of David—and thereby into your own as well—there to gaze upon the heart of an executive.

As a final note, I wish to explain my use of male and female pronouns in this book. All of the major characters in this story are men; such was the Israel of 1000 B.C. But since matters of the heart transcend gender distinctions, I have consciously applied lessons for the modern-day audience to both men and women, both of whom are challenged to reckon with the formidable task of leadership as so vividly depicted in David's life and career. Here is yet another instance in which the central theme of his life is so relevant to us: "The Lord looks at the heart."

I have much to be grateful for in connection with this book and many friends to thank for their part in it. I think first of my friends and colleagues on the leadership faculty of the United States Military Academy at West Point, who like iron on iron have honed my understanding of this great subject. Particularly, I think with love and appreciation of the late Colonel Jeff McNally, a master teacher of the art and science of leadership and a friend who nurtured and inspired my own efforts. I especially wish to thank Greg Hiebert, my dear friend, colleague, and mentor, who has so enriched and enlarged my own journey. To him, and my many friends at BellSouth Corporation, I am greatly indebted for much love and learning. Similarly, I am indebted to my brothers and sisters at Tenth Presbyterian Church in Philadelphia for their love and encouragement. I am most grateful to Charles Morris and Scott Waxman for their vision and support in this wonderful project, as well as to my editor, Eric Major of Doubleday, for his graciousness and skill.

Finally, I thank my wife Sharon with love and a special gratitude, for her steadfast endurance and irreplaceable participation in this wonderful labor. You are my true friend and my heart's true home.

ISRAEL IN THE TIME OF KING DAVID

SYRIA

Damascus •

Great Sea

Tyre •

Phoenicians

Ramah •

Sea of Galilee

Mt. Tabor

I S R A E L

• Jabesh-gilead

River Jordan

Mahanaim •

Gilgal •   P E R E A

Gibeah •

Nob •   *Ammonites*

• Ekron

Ashdod •   *Valley of Elah*   ◉ Jerusalem

Ashkelon •   P   • Gath   Bethlehem •

• Adullam

H   Keilah •

Gaza •   I   Hebron •   *Dead Sea*

S

T

I

A

Masada •

Rabbah •   N

• Ziklag

Moabites

©1998 Jeffrey L. Ward

| 0 | MILES | 30 |

| 0 | KILOMETERS | 30 |

PROLOGUE

THE SHEPHERD

הרעה

David's career started out early and lonely, not on summits of power and achievement, but in lowly fields of service, in a time of preparation for later fulfillment. Like so many others, David practiced on a micro-scale the skills with which he would later write large. But most impor-tantly, David's early life shaped the principles that would guide him on the extraordinary journey that lay ahead, the like of which no novelist would dare to invent.

As is so often the case among the truly great, David's origins were humble. He was a shepherd, a most demanding calling then and now, one that yields rewards only after the expenditure of much effort and skill. It was in these fields, in the pastures amid the flocks of his father Jesse, that David received his first lessons in the art of leading and in the disci-plines of the executive.

Being a shepherd is exhausting. For one thing, the shepherd leads the flocks out into lands filled with danger: predators, hostile weather, starvation, and disease. For another, sheep are just about the most inept followers imaginable. Besides being plain stupid, they are easily panicked and annoyed and debilitated. Unable to defend themselves against wolves, they also need protecting from themselves; sheep are notorious for wandering off good pastures or away from sources of water, for destroying what good grass is available, and for placing themselves in one irretrievable situation after another.

> *It was not the shaping of hands, but the shaping of his heart: the aspirations, the dreams, the definition of success and the passion . . .*

As a result, David's experiences as a shepherd were many and varied. A shepherd has to think. He has to watch and plan and anticipate, making rapid decisions and taking quick and determined action, all valuable skills for the executive-in-training. The shepherd defends the flock from predators, and this requires anticipation and watchfulness. He guides the sheep on their way, directing them to green pastures and fresh waters. He watches closely for strife and conflicts that lead to disorder and confusion within the flock. The shepherd prepares fields in advance of the flock and calculates likely pitfalls and dangers. When they are rooted in one place too long he prods them forward; when they rush off heedlessly, the shepherd gathers them in.

Yet it was not mainly the skills that the boy David honed in those fields that so marked him for later glory. It was not the shaping of his hands, but the shaping of his heart. How true this is for us all. For while skills are essential, what sets apart the true leader is the heart. The aspirations. The dreams. The definition of success and the passion that drives him forward. David gained plenty of experience in those early years, but it was in his reflections upon that experience that his heart was molded and he was set apart from the crowd.

Reflection and meditation are things we seldom do today. In our early years of preparation, we are often too focused on making contacts and winning sterling evaluations, not realizing that the real task of these early challenges is to set first principles into place. How few reflect on the implications and lessons taught in the events of the working day and week and year. How few challenge their own decisions and draw conclusions, establishing parameters to guide future encounters. Diaries and journals are a thing of the past; quiet reflection, it seems, has been pushed aside by recreation and networking. And so experience leads just as easily to mindless patterns as it does to wisdom and understanding.

Perhaps it was because David had nowhere else to go in the few

moments of relaxation that his busy to-do list afforded, but it is clear that
he did indeed reflect. In fact, David's thoughts soared while his feet trod
the Judean hills and his shoulders rested on the shepherd's crook. Furthermore, his reflections are not lost, for David took most careful notes
that have come down to us. We know them as the psalms of the Old
Testament, which are not only a record of David's emotional and spiritual
journey but also finely crafted works of poetic art. They were set to music
and sung by generations of his people, though their tunes are long lost to
us now. No doubt David's voice filled the silence of evenings with poetic
music, songs profound and penetrating and inspiring. And in those
psalms we see his heart laid bare.

Undoubtedly, David's best-known psalm is his Twenty-third, one of
the most well-loved pieces of literature ever penned. Though the time of
its writing is unknown to us, there is little question that its origin comes
from the hills where Jesse's flock roamed and David stood beneath vast
skies. Psalm 23 opens a wide door into David's heart. It offers a penetrating glimpse into his life of faith, but is also a catalog of what he learned
guiding those sheep and a record of his critical thinking on the task of
leadership. Here we see David the follower of God, the lamb delighting
in the care of his Heavenly Shepherd. Echoed in David's delight in the
Lord's care over him is his own reflection on the task of the shepherd-
leader.

The Lord is my shepherd, I shall not be in want.
He makes me lie down in green pastures,
he leads me beside quiet waters,
    he restores my soul.
He guides me in paths of righteousness
    for his name's sake.

Even though I walk
    through the valley of the shadow of death,
I will fear no evil,
    for you are with me;
your rod and your staff,
    they comfort me.

You prepare a table before me
    in the presence of my enemies.
You anoint my head with oil;
    my cup overflows.
Surely goodness and love will follow me
    all the days of my life,
and I will dwell in the house of the Lord
    forever.

Psalm 23

There are few more comforting images than "the Lord is my shepherd." It evokes a feeling of security, and reassures us that God is interested and involved and in control of our lives. No human, of course, can fill God's shoes, but captured in these stanzas is David's conception of those blessings true leadership offers. The shepherd lives among the sheep. He identifies with them in his heart and takes note of them on his weekly planner. The shepherd shares the hardships the sheep must face, the risks and the dangers as well. Indeed, the shepherd stands among the sheep both figuratively and literally, leading through personal presence and intimate acquaintance.

Hidden in the words "The Lord is my shepherd" is a concept that has radical implications regarding our understanding of leadership and the heart of the shepherd-executive. In the mind of the shepherd, the goal of his leadership, the result of all his planning and effort, that outcome for which he is responsible, is *the followers themselves*. Not a cluttered list of stakeholders—though like any other executive, the shepherd has many. Not a sophisticated index of ratios. It is the sheep that are his preoccupation, his burden, and his joy. This is the thought that made David delight in the leadership of his God, and it is evident that this was his understanding of his own role as shepherd.

> *The shepherd . . . identifies with the sheep, shares their hardships, risks, and dangers . . . leading through personal presence and intimate acquaintance . . . The followers are themselves the goal of his leadership.*

To put this in slightly different terms, how did David conceive of the organization over which he served? For years, American corporations have been conceived of primarily as *financial* entities. Profit and loss, cash flow, debt-to-equity ratios, and stock price do not merely describe the organization; these are what the organization *is*. This view of the company is dominant today (and we wonder why so few are inspired by our leadership!). More recently, much productive thinking in the realm of quality management presented the corporation primarily as a collection of *systems*. Different processes, all interconnected, define what the organization is.

But for David, the organization was defined by flesh and blood relationships. What we will find all through his career is that he conceived of every organization he served and led as a living entity, one in which men and women learned and dreamed, sacrificed and rejoiced. For young David, his little company was defined by relationships. Trust between sheep and shepherd, sheep and fellow-sheep. Close affection and mutual commitment. These were the dynamics of success for young David, and they became hallmarks for all his life and achievements.

What a radical conception of the organization and the role of executive! For the shepherd, the product *is* the follower. Not profits, not market share—these are the products of *their* labor. The followers themselves are the product of the shepherd's efforts. When the sheep grow strong, when they survive the hazards of the journey, when they return to the village transformed from lambs into strong rams, then the shepherd has faithfully and successfully discharged his duty. Yes, the sheep who followed David must be led and cajoled and motivated for performance. But it was they who filled his thoughts as he slipped into sleep at night and for them that his eyes searched when first light signaled each new day. *The shepherd is the servant of the sheep*; it is their growth and nurture that define his task and set the agenda for his success.

I believe that it is in just this way that David is a model for those executives today who seek not just to carve out success for themselves, but also to achieve a lasting and meaningful legacy. It is the executive who acts as a shepherd over an organization, seen first and foremost as a human community, who will capture the hearts of employee and customer alike, and who will in turn achieve what no leader could ever command.

The life of the shepherd is given for the sheep. The results of his planning and implementation, of her passion and sacrifice, are seen primarily in those who follow. Success is evidenced in the followers' inspiration, their growing confidence, new capabilities, and fresh achievements. Experience leadership today does not itself produce sales or production. It produces committed and capable followers, who themselves make the sales and deliver the goods. *How easily this insight is missed*—but David captures its essence in these brief words, "The Lord is my shepherd." Being a shepherd is all about the guidance and nurture and protection of the sheep. So it is for true executives; their role is very much like the shepherd's, however rarely it may be conceived of in this way.

The executive as shepherd, then, captures what was in the heart of young David, poised at the start of his epic career. In the rest of the Twenty-third Psalm, he goes on to sketch implications as to the tasks thus required.

First, he turns his pen to the task of *direction*. Because of his own Shepherd, David rejoices, "I shall not be in want." For sheep, of course, the issue is safe and rich grazing grounds, and the availability of fresh water. "He makes me lie down in green pastures, he leads me beside quiet waters." So the executive must make decisions and communicate effective plans, monitoring and intervening along the way. Thereby, David muses, "he restores my soul. He guides me in paths of righteousness." To the shepherd, this is the finest reward—that his knowledge and experience and insight direct the flock in the right way—and so he guides them "for his name's sake."

"I will fear no evil, for you are with me" . . . Every effective leader instills confidence and assurance in times of threat and turmoil.

Second, David learned in those fields the importance of the leader's presence in *instilling confidence*. He sings, "Even though I walk through the valley of the shadow of death, I will fear no evil, for you are with me." In the journeys through the hills, the flocks often had to pass through narrow valleys—places of danger that rightly unsettled the sheep and endangered the whole enterprise. In the shadows of the passes lurked wild animals, and the valleys were the sites of sudden storms and floods. There was menace in the changing scenery, as there often is on today's shifting corporate landscape. The flock thus recoiled in apprehension, instinctively casting their eyes about for a sight of the shepherd. His personal presence gave the sheep assurance, calming and moving them forward because of their trust in his watchful care. This need for trust is the same in human organizations; David's early experience would be repeated over and over, proving that every effective leader must learn to instill confidence and assurance in times of threat and turmoil.

How insightful are David's words that follow: "Your rod and your staff, they comfort me." These were the tools of the shepherd's trade and the ever-present symbols of his authority. Indeed, the staff is emblematic of the shepherd himself. It is what he rests his weight upon in weariness and plants in the dirt before each step. Its purpose is primarily for supervising the sheep themselves: the crooked end was bent just so in order to slip around the wayward neck, coaxing the stray back onto the right path. How familiar are the sheep with the sight and the feel of the shepherd's staff. It comforts them, for it assures them that there is someone watching over and drawing them back from the error and folly.

The staff is the *authority* the shepherd wields over the sheep. David's thought here is keen: he himself is comforted by the fact that God wields the staff over him with the care and authority of a shepherd. Followers expect the executive to exercise authority in order to rightly shape behavior, to nudge this one to the left and yank that one back to the right. Especially in times of danger or uncertainty, the follower is comforted by the leader who assertively and wisely wields authority. So too must he wield the *rod*, a short and blunt weapon. Just as sheep were comforted in the valley of shadows to see the shepherd ready to strike and defend, so also do men and women today look to the executive to wield power to protect and defend. "Your rod and your staff," David reflects, "they comfort me."

> *Followers expect the executive to exercise authority to rightly shape behavior . . . Especially in times of danger or uncertainty, the follower is comforted by the leader who assertively and wisely wields authority . . . "Your rod and your staff, they comfort me."*

These, then, were the first reflections of young David upon his experience in the fields. The shepherd stands among the sheep, making the journey with them, providing direction, wielding authority, and exercising might for their defense.

Two more reflections will complete the psalm, the first of which is that the shepherd provides recognition and reward to the sheep. "You prepare a table before me in the presence of my enemies." The banquet table was prepared for celebrations and commemorations. There, the faithful servant was commended publicly and thus vindicated before those who would oppose him.

It is interesting how David has now expanded the scope of his psalm far beyond the needs of the animals he himself was serving. Enlarging on his theme, he expresses a distinctively human need, one so vital that he turns to God for its fulfillment. No doubt, this was what he was trusting the Lord to do—to vindicate and recognize the faithful service of His follower, so overlooked and despised among those of his fellow men who looked down on the lowly state of a mere shepherd. Followers *do* look to the leader for vindication and recognition, even so large-hearted a follower as David.

> *At the heart of working men and women is the longing—though oft forgotten and sadly despaired of—to participate in something greater than themselves, to belong to a cause that is meaningful and to share in a legacy that endures.*

Along the same line, David sings, "You anoint my head with oil; my cup overflows." In the dry and dusty Palestine of the ancient world, sooth-ing oil for the face and head was a blessing rarely bestowed. So also the cup which overflowed with wine, refreshing the parched throat of the sojourner. Rewards do matter (the Bible consistently speaks of faithful service being *rewarded*) and for David this payment served to validate and appreciate his hard-earned achievement. But it was not merely the reward that was given, but the Giver of the reward that mattered above all. "*You* anoint my head," he sings, and it is a relationship that he celebrates as much as the reward itself.

Finally, David's great psalm closes with a hope that is widely shared by men and women of all ages: "Surely goodness and love will follow me all the days of my life, and I will dwell in the house of the Lord forever." David turns to his own Shepherd with the hope of belonging, of membership in something worthy and meaningful and enduring. It is not David alone whose thoughts rise to such heights. For it is true that people will work for wages and are motivated by recognition and reward. But at the heart of working men and women is the longing—though oft forgotten and sadly despaired of—to participate in something greater than themselves, to belong to a cause that is meaningful and to share in a legacy that endures. David as shepherd could offer his sheep little of this, but turning to the Shepherd of men and women he dared to dream of so great a prospect for himself. This, to David, was the centerpiece of these early and formative reflections on the task of the leader, and it is the highest calling for all those who, like God, stand at the head, not of beasts, but of soul-bearing women and men.

It is David who introduces this theme of the leader as shepherd to the pages of Scripture, one that is picked up by many subsequent biblical writers. But it is in the work and words of Jesus that what David began reaches its crescendo. Jesus said of Himself, "I am the good shepherd; I know my sheep and my sheep know me . . . and I lay down my life for the sheep" (John 10:14, 15). Here all that David pointed to is narrowed to these mighty essentials: *The shepherd knows and is known by the sheep, and he offers himself for their sake.*

For Jesus, as for David, leadership is defined by these two principles: it is personal, and it is sacrificial service. Personal leadership does not always demand contact with each individual follower, particularly from those executives entrusted with a large organization. But the shepherd knows the sheep and the sheep know him. They are not, to him, a faceless mass. They are not human resources, but people. The leader knows his people—he understands their frustrations and fears, perceives their weak-

nesses and their strengths; she knows when they must be prodded forward
and when they must be brought along still waters. To them he is not a
distant calculator of numbers, an obscure maker of policy, but rather their
shepherd, their leader. They know his dreams and the principles he holds
dear, and they are themselves being shaped by his character and personality.

This, above all, is what they know about the shepherd-executive: He
lays it down for the sheep. She spends herself for their sake. He can be
trusted and believed in because he
sacrifices himself for their sake.

> *For Jesus, as for David,
> leadership is personal and it
> is sacrificial. The shepherd
> knows the sheep and the
> sheep know him. And above
> all, the shepherd can be
> trusted and believed in
> because he sacrifices himself
> for their sake.*

Here, then, is the young David
whom God found and saw as the man
after His own heart. Here in Psalm 23
we see him longing not just for success, but also for purpose and meaning; peering within his heart we see
both love and self-sacrifice. How
strongly would the imprint of these
poetic words, this stunning aspiration,
be evidenced in the years to follow. No doubt David often fell short of it,
particularly in those early days of trial and test. But we can see him singing, softly and intently, words that shaped the self-consciousness of the
leader he would later become: "The Lord is my shepherd, I shall not be
in want . . . I will dwell in the house of the Lord forever."

Chapter 1

WHILE SHEPHERDS WATCHED THEIR FIELDS

"GIVE US A KING!"

תנה־לנך מלך

David was a man defined by his heart, but he was also a man defined by his times. Like all historical figures, he is inseparably linked to a history and to a cause. Far from the free agent of today, who hopes to build a career through an arm's-length commitment, David shared the fate and the strggle of his people, Israel. Accordingly, it is in light of the pressures and challenges facing this larger organization that David comes down to us in history. And there were stiff challenges indeed, at the heart of which was a choice. It was a choice regarding leadership, made both by the people and by God.

It was the turning of the first millennium B.C. and the situation was grave for Israel. For the several hundred years the nation had dwelt in Palestine, the Promised Land, invading neighbors had continually harassed and sometimes subjugated the people. This period, covered in the Bible's *Book of Judges*, was most turbulent. During this time, Israel followed a downward spiral of immorality and rebellion against God, a pattern that resulted in His withdrawal from their midst and subsequent disaster, usually in the form of foreign domination and oppression. But occasionally the people repented of their sins and called upon the Lord. During these times God provided deliverance from their trials through the all-purpose military, political, and religious leaders called the judges. Often accompanied by supernatural means of support, the judges provided temporary respites amid these centuries of darkness.

Threats of hostile invasion reappeared as David's story prepared to unfold. At the time, the judge ruling over Israel was Samuel, an exceptionally able and faithful leader. Samuel is one of those quintessential transition figures in the Bible: born through the devotion and prayer of his once-barren mother, Hannah, raised among a corrupt generation of priests, Samuel emerged as a role model and guide, directing the wayward people back to their legacy of faith. Samuel was everything you could ask for in a judge of Israel: He was effective in battle and in speech, in war and in peace, serving honestly and capably.

But now, late in Samuel's life, crisis loomed again. To the west, the Philistines were pressing in once more, and to the east the Ammonites— age-old enemies, though cousins of the Israelites—were on the move. In response to these external threats, the people became uneasy and concern began to spread.

As is always the case, these external forces served to highlight the leadership crisis that had long been simmering in Israel. Established through Moses as a theocracy, Israel was to stand apart from the surrounding nations by the fact it had no king but God Himself. In place of a palace was the Ark of the Covenant, the gilded container in which Moses had placed the tablets of the Ten Commandments. It was the throne of God on earth, or rather the footstool of His heavenly throne, and Israel was its home. Whereas other nations had a human king to lead them into battle, Israel went forth with priests parading the Ark. This arrangement provided omnipotent power for Israel against her enemies: the problem was that when the Lord was angered by the people's disobedience, He removed His power from Israel and they were left leaderless and vulnerable. To many, Moses' arrangement seemed odd and ineffective.

So their concern was this: "What kind of leadership will lead us forward into the uncertain and dangerous future?" This question is no doubt familiar to anyone concerned with the external threats facing our corporations and nations today. Competition increases and old patterns seem inadequate, just as was the case for Israel. It is the external threats that catch our attention, yet the real issues are these: "Who and what kind of leader will navigate these waters safely and successfully?" "Who are we and what must we become in order to fulfill our destiny?" "What are our basic convictions regarding our business and ourselves?" "What do we believe is right, and will work?" Just as these are the pressing issues for so many corporations today, they were also at the heart of Israel's crisis.

Samuel, who represented God's rule in Israel, had never failed them, except in this: He had grown old, and his sons, perhaps raised with too little time and attention, were not the kind of successors who inspired confidence. The Bible tells us,

> But his sons did not walk in his ways. They turned aside after
> dishonest gain and accepted bribes and perverted justice.
>
> (1 Samuel 8:3)

This was on the minds of the elders of the tribes when they came to Samuel and confronted him with the situation:

> "You are old, and your sons do not walk in your ways; now
> appoint a King to lead us, such as all the other nations have."
>
> (1 Samuel 8:5)

Seldom have more fateful words been spoken. For the whole point of what set Israel apart, what made it special and formed its particular identity, was this: *Israel did not have a king like the other nations.* God was its king; the judges and the priests were not despots but were His administrators, accountable to His just laws.

The Bible loves to teach by means of comparisons and contrasts, and this is just what unfolds as Samuel stands

> *The real issues are these: "What kind of leadership will navigate these waters safely and successfully?" "Who are we and what must we become?" "What are our basic convictions?" "In what are we to trust?"*

before the demands of the people. Samuel was shocked by the words put to him—which amounted to a betrayal of all he had stood for and a repudiation of his whole career. The words were a rejection of the very Lord who had delivered Israel from slavery in Egypt and shepherded it over the centuries. Samuel's faith in God is contrasted with the elders' trust in worldly ways—"We have been looking around at the nations and want to do what they are doing," they were saying. The episode that follows, then, can be read in terms of the conflict between faith and apostasy.

There was something additional happening, however, that is fundamental to our understanding of the nature of leadership, something that has recurred time and again even in our own day. Both Samuel and the elders were looking into an uncertain and dangerous future and reckoning with real challenges in the present—but they were seeing entirely different things. On what were they basing their respective visions? Samuel's vision for the future arose from his understanding of Israel's distinct identity—its past, its legacy, its particular capabilities and calling. The people's vision, however, was framed by the fears of the present; not by a critical examination of their hearts, but by a desire to conform to whatever seemed to be working well for others. One was motivated by courage and conviction, the others by fear and conformity.

The elders were benchmarking not merely the methods and approaches of the surrounding nations, but their very identity. That is the one thing that can never be discovered through an industry survey. *An organization must have its own identity*, not that of another, just as it has its own past, its own legacy, and its own particular place within an industry and in the world.

It is not easy standing alone before a multitude, though this is sometimes required of an executive. Samuel, shaken and beside himself, took the matter to the Lord. The Lord consoled him.

"It is not you they have rejected, but they have rejected
me as their king."
(1 Samuel 8:7)

So God gave instructions to Samuel, and they were words of the worst sort of punishment: He told Samuel to give them what they asked for. Israel would have a king like the other nations. Centuries later, other prophets would point back to this day, bemoaning the consequences of this decision,[1] just as scores of businesses look back on similar choices as the root of many troubles.

Samuel's stand against the elders provides us with a contrast from which we are meant to profit: a contrast between courageous leadership based on faith and conviction, versus the weak and vacillating expediency that is so willing to compromise all that an organization is and has been. Samuel, it seems, lost out before the others' mass flight from principle, yet in support of his faith God allowed him to explain to them just what they were getting into. Then He took action to install a king over the people who would provide the very sort of leadership they had demanded.

According to the practice of the Canaanites, the neighboring peoples to whom the elders had pointed, the king was the direct representative of God in such a way that he himself was regarded as a semi-deity. This was a marked contrast from the Israelite system, in which God's law was the rule. Not only did the Canaanite king have an incredible salary and stock option, as well as a palatial and inaccessible office, but he ruled with an arbitrary and absolute power. Therefore, Samuel gave this warning:

> "This is what the king who will reign over you will do: He will
> take your sons and make them serve with his chariots and horses,
> and they will run in front of his chariots . . . He will take your
> daughters to be perfumers and cooks and bakers. He will take
> the best of your fields and vineyards and olive groves and give
> them to his attendants . . . He will take a tenth of your flocks,
> and you yourselves will become his slaves. When that day comes,
> you will cry out for relief from the king you have chosen, and
> the Lord will not answer you in that day."
>
> (1 Samuel 8:11–18)

How loudly his words resound in our ears today! Do we hear the message? Here is the challenge: "Do you want to serve expediency rather than a sense of purpose? Do you want the mental and emotional ease of conformity to the latest trend? Do you want, above every dream of

---

1. *Hosea 13:11 and Ezekiel 20:32, 33 are two excellent examples of this.*

achievement and meaning, to be ensconced in your suburban lifestyle? Then this is the kind of leader for you . . . Just bear in mind that the price is your being used like fodder before the royal chariots. The price is slavery. And when the day of reckoning comes there will be no one to rescue you, and God will leave you to experience the consequences of your actions."

These may be pretty strong words, but they were exactly what Samuel was saying to the elders. How amazing, and illustrative, was their response:

> "No!" they said. "We want a king over us. Then we will be like
> all the other nations, with a king to lead us and to go out before
> us and fight our battles."
> (1 Samuel 8:19–20)

Not wanting to bear their share of responsibility for the future of their children, they sought a king to do all the thinking and planning and fighting for them. They didn't want a leader to ask them what they thought, to inspire sacrifice and commitment in them, or to expect participation and creativity from the ranks. They wanted a magical leader to usher in an age of fantasy, not one of purpose and achievement. And for this, they were prepared to offer themselves and their children upon his altar.

How very far from the ideal of leadership set down for the nation by God when Moses sent the tribes into the land of promise. The executive was to be a servant of the people, a shepherd for the sheep. A king was not to demand exorbitant riches or to establish opulent courts. He was not to be a law unto himself, following different rules than those of the masses, but to "revere the Lord his God and follow carefully all the words of [His] law . . . and not consider himself better than his brothers" (Deuteronomy 17:19–20).

Samuel's heart must have sunk as he listened to the elders' demand. He quietly acquiesced, and then sent the people home to await their new king.

Where do you go to find the kind of leader the people were demanding? What do you look for? Surely, this king must come from a family of prominence. He must be physically imposing and impressive in stance. Was there such a man available in Israel? There certainly was—there always is—and his name was Saul. Saul, we are told, was the son of Kish, a man of standing, and he himself was "an impressive young man without equal among the Israelites—a head taller than any of the others" (1 Samuel 9:2). God had sent Samuel to explain to the people just what it was they were choosing; now he sent them Saul to provide a more eloquent demonstration.

They wanted a magical leader to usher in not an age of purpose and achievement but of fantasy . . . The price was slavery.

It would be easy, and perhaps comfortable, to demonize Saul. Certainly, many unpleasant things will be seen in and through him before this story is done. Yet he is not a wooden villain. Nor did God openly oppose this king who will serve as the antithesis of our story's hero. Rather, both God and Samuel invested a great deal in Saul, and shared their sorrow over what was to come. Yet, in answer to the question, "What kind of leadership must we have?" Saul provides an answer intended to stand in stark contrast to the kind of healer David would be.

It was a dramatic moment when Samuel gathered the nation for the installation of this new king. There, to all the twelve tribes, Samuel cried out,

"But you have now rejected your God, who saves you out of all your calamities and distresses. And you have said, 'No, set a king over us.' So now present yourselves before the Lord by your tribes and clans."
(1 Samuel 10:19)

Ceremoniously, then, he called out the tribe of Benjamin; the king would be a descendant of the last of Jacob's twelve sons. Next came the name of Saul's clan, then that of his family. Finally, and surely attended by baited breath as the elders eagerly waited to behold their savior, "Saul, son of Kish" was called out.

Eyes were straining, hearts were pounding. Here was the man to whom they would sell themselves! His name was called—"Saul"—but there was no one striding forth. "Where is the king? Where is our savior?" It was God who broke the silence: "He has hidden himself among the baggage."

What a comical sight, and one fraught with meaning. The leader they so desired, the king to rule like that of the other nations, has taken the stage, and it is empty. So they ran to the baggage train where Saul was hiding. No grand speech, no stirring vision statement, no steely-eyed gaze filled with purpose. But as he finally stepped out from under the wagon, they saw that "he was a head taller than any of the others." Just then the clearly disgusted Samuel came up, and he declared to them,

"Do you see the man the Lord has chosen? There is no one like
him among all the people."
Then the people shouted, "Long live the king!"
(1 Samuel 10:24)

Just what are we to make of this? The biblical account lets this incident pass without comment. But there are, I think, two ways of understanding this scene. One is to look at Saul himself. Surely he had some idea of what he was getting into. Sent by God to provide a living example of ineffective leadership, he at least had not asked for it. What had driven him to the place of refuge among the baggage? It is not unlikely that it was the look on the faces of the people as they awaited their save-the-day executive. Eyes without sight, ears all too ready to shut out the clamor of the difficulties. They might have been sheep, but they were not a flock longing to follow their shepherd out into the fields; rather they were sheep who expected to stay snug in their pens while the new king went out to face the wolves alone. It's hard, then, to blame Saul for hiding.

> *Eyes without sight, ears all too ready to shut out the clamor of the difficulties . . . It's hard to blame Saul for hiding.*

On the other hand, we see the elders in their rush to fawn over this reluctant but superficially appealing king. Despite his behavior, Saul was the kind of person who looked wonderful, who could strike a fine portrait pose, who could give off an immediate aura of confidence—if you were only looking skin deep. How many men and women today occupy a similar place among us today! They bear the look we expect, and like Saul, they have the requisite credentials. After all, he had the prophet's anointing and they come from the best schools and prior postings. Saul was just what they were looking for.

The scene closes with both God and Samuel lending a hand to poor Saul. The prophet, for his part, sat the people down and explained the rules for having such a king. He wrote all this down as a sort of constitution, before sending them back home again. God helped out by touching the heart of a number of warriors, so they would join up with Saul and form his bodyguard. All in all, it wasn't a complete disaster for the new king—and with his situation he would need all the help he could get.

The passage, however, closes with a warning:

> But some troublemakers said, "How can this fellow save us?"
> They despised him and brought him no gifts.
> (1 Samuel 10:27)

Are we surprised that so many Israelites were less than inspired by the prospect of having Saul for a king? We ought not be, for this sort of coronation takes place time and again in our own day. The kind of leader they sought would not engage the heart of the organization, instill purpose, provide clarity to convictions and principles, or invite investment and ownership. They wanted a leader who would make their troubles go away, for the time being at least—and already the prospects appeared bleak to many.

There were no tears that day, though not that many cheers either. But surely, as we draw our thoughts away from this scene—the families heading back to their homes, the king off to set up his court, and poor Samuel left standing alone—we can only imagine that rain began to fall softly, anticipating the regret that would surely follow.

THE PROPHET AND
THE KING

הנביא והמלך

In Saul, as we have seen, the Bible is setting forth one side of a contrast. But even though the Israelites' demand for a king was an act of rebellion, God's purpose included more than simple punishment. He was teaching them, just as His story is teaching us, about the dynamics of both leadership and followership. In the terms of modern management practice, God was instilling a readiness for change among His people. He was like the executive today who knows what commitments the people must ultimately make, but who also knows they are far from ready to make them. Thus, the hard lessons to be learned under Saul's leadership were intended not only to make His people feel the error of their ways but also to prepare them to follow the kind of leader God intended for them, a leader like the shepherd David.

No sooner was Saul installed as king than a crisis presented itself. Perhaps having heard of this new leader, an Ammonite chief, named Nahash, decided to put the strength of Israel to the test. Striking in the lands on the opposite side of the Jordan river, where the Israelite dwellers were naturally isolated and vulnerable, Nahash laid siege to the town of Jabesh Gilead. His terms were pretty simple: If they surrendered he would spare their lives and *only* gouge out the *right* eye of all the men. His intent was very clear—"bring disgrace on all Israel" (1 Samuel 11:2), meaning, of course, the new king Saul. Somehow not overwhelmed at this offer, the leaders of Jabesh decided to seek Saul's aid, promising to give in to Nahash if no relief came in seven days.

Critical incidents like this are always both a threat and an opportunity to the executive, particularly for the newly installed one. They are a danger because, as in this case, an early failure can undermine his or her whole position. They are an opportunity in that they serve as a vivid means for rallying the troops and, perhaps more important, making clear what the priorities and values really are. In this sense, a critical incident is worth twenty policy statements and stump speeches.

To his credit, Saul did not fail to see the importance of his response. Indeed, the news spun him into a rage. Immediately, he ordered that two oxen be brought in and slaughtered, their pieces to be parceled to the twelve tribes. It doesn't take an ancient Hebrew scholar to figure out what this meant! In any case, he sent along a message to make it all clear:

> "This is what will be done to the oxen of anyone who does not
> follow Saul and Samuel."
>
> (1 Samuel 11:7)

The result was as the new king intended:

> Then the terror of the Lord fell upon the people.
>
> (1 Samuel 11:7)

Then, sending word ahead to the men of Jabesh Gilead, Saul rapidly marched his warriors so as to catch the enemy unawares. Breaking into the Ammonite camp at night, his forces scattered them and then cut them down all during the next day.

It must have felt good for Saul, earlier so reluctant, to have proved successful in his first battle. Indeed, the victory certainly made the people feel good, for they rallied to his banner, hailing him and offering to slay those who had earlier bad-mouthed his coronation. Magnanimously, Saul forbade such action and gave the credit for his victory to the Lord. At this juncture, Samuel, anxious again to give Saul all the momentum he could muster for him, called the people back to Gilgal, so they might voice their unanimous support for their king.

> *Critical incidents are both a threat and an opportunity to the executive . . . An opportunity to rally the troops and make clear what the values and priorities really are. In this sense, a critical incident is worth twenty policy statements and stump speeches.*

All told, things were starting out pretty well for the new king. He could have ignored the crisis or lost the battle. Yet, for the thoughtful observer, there is still an unsettling feeling. Saul had handled the threat admirably, showing skill and aggressiveness. But the handling of his followers left something to be desired. What an opportunity this was to draw the tribes, who had been long indifferent to one another, together in order to build cohesion and a national sense of identity. But, perhaps instinctively, Saul immediately turned to coercion. True, Saul's urgent situation required quick action, and yet it is clear that what he was concerned about were his followers' feet and hands, and not their hearts.

Samuel clearly picked up on this. We can imagine his anxiety as he regathered the people around Saul after this success. "Will he rise to the occasion? Will he speak to the hearts of the men and women here, pointing out not just the victory but its significance and the new opportunities it inspired?" What an opportunity this was to make a dramatic impact on the organization, to link a crisis averted to a renewed call to change and reform! How disappointed Samuel must have been when, after receiving the accolades and offering the obligatory sacrifices to God, Saul bypassed the opportunity and went straight to his own merriment.

Samuel, however, was a resourceful man. He had led the nation since his youth and knew a thing or two about what it takes to shape and guide a large organization like this. Who knows how long he watched, tapping his foot, to see if Saul would seize the day. When he could wait no longer, Samuel decided now would be a good time for his farewell speech.

As always, there was a lesson in Samuel's action. First, he called upon the people to acknowledge that, though he had faithfully and honestly served them, the mantle of leadership had now passed to Saul. Then he reminded them that it was God who had shepherded them faithfully through generations past. He had brought them out of slavery in Egypt. God had helped Jacob, their forefather, and settled their ancestors in this Promised Land. During the years of the judges, God had allowed their waywardness to lead them into trouble, but He always sent a rescuer to save them. In response, they had faced the challenge of their own time by rejecting Him and demanding a king like that of the nations.

> "Now here is the king you have chosen, the one you asked for;
> see, the Lord has set a king over you. If you fear the Lord and
> serve and obey him and do not rebel against his commands,
> and if both you and the king who reigns over you follow
> the Lord your God—good! . . .
> Yet if you persist in doing evil, both you and your king
> will be swept away."
> (1 Samuel 12:13–15, 25)

What was Samuel's point? "This is not about one strong man! This is about your calling as a people, and as an organization!" Unlike Saul, Samuel recognized the need for more than a strong and impressive leader. He knew how important a sense of purpose, an inspiring identity, and an acceptance of calling were. So he set before them the legacy of their forefathers, and the distinct purpose God had established for their nation: They were to be a nation serving God with all its heart, making Him known to the surrounding nations and walking in His light.

Thus Samuel walked away again from the stage of official public life. He would retire to focus his energies on just being a prophet of the Lord. He promised to pray for the people and to continue to set an example and to teach them. We are not told what Saul was doing as all this unfolded, and his silence is deafening.

One more episode from Saul's early reign will make clear what these events are saying about the nature of leadership. Once again, it was a crisis in the form of foreign invasion, this time from the Philistines in the east.

> *Unlike Saul, Samuel recognized the need for a sense of purpose, an inspiring identity, a sense of calling. Saul's silence is deafening.*

In the time after his enthronement, Saul had made one organizational innovation. He established a standing army, gathering three thousand warriors to his banner and placing them in a central location. Part of the motivation for this seems to have been the presence of Philistine garrisons deep in Israelite land. Indeed, just outside Saul's own hometown of Gibeah there was an important enemy stronghold. Furthermore, these garrisons were difficult to displace, being strategically on dominant high ground. Finally, and worst of all, the Philistines were a technologically superior culture. They had progressed into the Iron Age, while Israel had yet to advance beyond bronze weapons and implements. This tremendous advantage meant that Philistine swords could break the weapons Saul's soldiers used. It was in response to this situation that Saul drew together his new army.

The action commenced near Gibeah, where Saul's son, Jonathan, was in command of one of Saul's battalions. Jonathan shared Saul's military prowess, but otherwise had little in common with his father. Faithful to God and intensely committed to Israel's higher calling, the young leader used the thousand soldiers at his command to drive the Philistines from the area surrounding his home. When word of this achievement spread, the uneasy truce that had existed between Israel and the Philistines was broken and the two enemies prepared to battle in earnest. Summoning the reserves, Saul assembled the warriors of Israel at Gilgal to meet this threat.

What happened next illustrates the weakness of Saul's style of leadership. When he was able to rout the relatively small army of Nahash the Ammonite, the people gathered around him and cheered. But when the Philistine war machine began to make its appearance, with its thousands of chariots and "soldiers as numerous as the sand on the seashore," quite a different response occurred. Far from rallying to their chosen king's cause, multitudes fled to hide in caves and wells or to escape across the Jordan river. Even those who stayed with Saul "were quaking with fear" (1 Samuel 13:5–7).

How many executives over the centuries have been faced with this situation! Those leaders who rely on the power to coerce, who encourage followers to avoid risk and investment, will often find that they have bred instincts that produce panic and flight when that leader is himself threatened from without.

Things were unraveling for Saul, so we should not be surprised to see Samuel back on the scene again. Samuel was not only an ex-judge, he was also a prophet of the Lord. Therefore he had access to privileged information—such as what God planned to do in this dire situation. So here, again, was another critical incident, and Samuel seized upon it, seeking to direct the hearts of the people to their true calling. Furthermore, the prophet was putting their king to the test.

To this end, Samuel sent word that Saul was to wait with the army for seven days, at which point the prophet would make an offering and beseech the Lord for His help. What long days these were as Saul waited! Surely he had his gaze fixed on the enemy advance, with their initial maneuvers beginning to be unveiled—though outgunned as he was, there was not much that he could do about it. Forced by the prophet to exercise the personal, inspiring leadership needed to hold his force together during this tense period of waiting, Saul did nothing of the kind and was a complete failure. While he stewed, his numbers dwindled daily, until finally the seventh day came.

Samuel did not come, however, at least not while Saul impatiently stared down the road on which he was expected. The soldiers who remained, knowing well the situation, had staked their all on divine intervention. The point of the burnt offering, for which they awaited the prophet, was to dedicate the men to the Lord and thus secure His favor in battle. But the offering had to be offered by a priest, which Samuel was and Saul was not. Meanwhile, the king's scouts informed him of the enemy advance, which now threatened to cut off all routes of escape.

What would a man like Saul do in this situation? We know very well. Demanding that the offering be brought to him, he himself made the sacrifice in Samuel's place. "Let's get this silly business over," he must have muttered. Yet making an offering to God was central to the identity of Saul's organization, as well as to their strategy. It was not at all something to be taken lightly, particularly since God had shown time and again that His help would overthrow even the most powerful of enemies.

No sooner was this accomplished than up came the prophet, furious to learn what Saul had done. Saul replied, " 'When I saw that the men were scattering, and that you did not come at the set time, and that the Philistines were assembling . . . I felt compelled to offer the burnt offering' " (1 Samuel 13:11, 12).

The cultic rituals of ancient Israel seem strange to the modern reader, and it is hard for us to understand how all this could possibly relate to the modern executive. But the point is that here was a leader focused only on the externals. Was their established strategy to outmaneuver or outfight the Philistines? Not at all, and there was not a man among them who thought this possible. Their strategy was to rely on the Lord, drawing strength from Him and following the instructions He passed down. But when the crunch came, Saul could not do it. It did not dawn on him to consider the effects of his actions on his followers, or to recognize that his actions conflicted with the principles that governed his organization. So when Samuel stalked off in anger and Saul turned to view his followers, he was stunned to find only six hundred soldiers left.

How many executives today make bold statements about the principles that will guide us into the future, the strategies and the capabilities needed for success—only to throw them all out the window at the first sign of danger or difficulty. Then we wonder why our leadership fails to inspire commitment, just as Saul surely wondered. The issue is that of credibility—is what we are asking of our people credible? Are our words reliable beyond the next voice mail? Do we show ourselves to be committed to the principles and values we publicly espouse?

How many initiatives for customer satisfaction have been undermined by an unwillingness to yield on revenue goals? How many employee empowerment programs have gone the way of King Saul's sacrifice when leaders showed not the slightest willingness to share power? The same thing happens with our statements about employee loyalty, and training and ethics. We, like Saul, wonder where everyone has gone when the dust has cleared—why they aren't showing commitment and a willingness to make sacrifices for the organization. For when executives only pay lip service to the essential values and aspirations for which the company stands, it is no wonder that men and women start looking for a place to hide.

In his beautiful Psalm 23, we saw that David viewed the organization as a human organism, made up of flesh and blood relationships. But now we see that for Saul it was something entirely different. For Saul, the only reality was the pressures bearing down upon him, the threats and immediate dangers, the obligations of the moment. Few people will offer their hearts, their souls, and their lives to this view of reality. Sense of purpose, credibility, trust—it is these that make for commitment and passion and sacrifice. And it was as hope for these dwindled that Saul's ranks also began to fade away.

> *Here is a lesson for leaders: You cannot fake it. You have to be in order to do.*

Here is a lesson for leaders: You cannot fake it. You have to be in order to do. In order to inspire the hearts of others you must first have a passion for an ideal greater than yourself and a sense of purpose that extends beyond the pressures of the day. Only then will you be credible under fire, and only then will you look around and find your ranks holding firm—indeed, gaining strength.

A Change of Heart

מנחם־לבב

Even this early in the story, we are starting to see an apt description of the Sauls of this world. Saul does not, on his own, possess a sense of purpose for his people, a vision for the direction he would lead them. What does he envision? Cleaning off his to-do list, and managing the crisis of the day. From the start, Saul's great concern was his own prestige, his own popularity, his own grip on the reigns of power. As we will see, these concerns progressively dominated his thinking so that ultimately he will dream only of seeing himself ensconced at the head of the board-room table. Though frightened at first to be king, and for good reason, Saul got used to the executive mantle soon enough. But it was the trap-pings of power and not the calling that fueled his imagination.

Saul possessed that horrible, but all too familiar, talent for carrying the air of executive leadership, while not having the first clue about long-range strategic issues. He could identify a bona fide crisis and respond, but he could not handle the lulls between the storms. The biblical ac-count of his reign, which covered forty-two years, tells us next to nothing about these periods: Apparently, there was little to say. He was, indeed, the king the people had demanded.

It was not that Saul did not *know* how to lead, but rather that any sense of obligation to his followers, to his organization as a living entity, never seems to have entered his mind. Quite in contrast from the shepherd of David's psalm, Saul simply did not view the state of his sheep as something significant to him. His focus, as executive, was upon himself and his perks and his problems, not upon those who had hailed his ascension and now looked to him for something of inspiration.

During Saul's long reign he would mainly serve as a military chief dealing with sporadic external threats. As such he was largely successful. God did indeed rescue him from the Philistine threat looming at Gilgal, but it was through the daring of Saul's virtuous son, Jonathan, rather than through the king's leadership. Jonathan had seized the opportunity to launch a bold and unexpected assault, and God used this to spread an unnatural panic through the Philistine ranks. As the years passed, there would be other threats and other successes, and Saul's throne grew secure. Increasingly, however, his reign stood in the way of any real progress for Israel. This is the hallmark of the Sauls in our midst—they neither perceive nor achieve any purpose beyond personal prestige.

One result of Saul's conception of leadership was that faithful Samuel never got to enjoy his retirement. Indeed, his relationship with the king became progressively confrontational. When, as we saw earlier, Saul violated the religious mores by making the burnt offering at Gilgal himself, Samuel had bad news to give him: God would not sanction such a king, though He would continue to support His people. God's edict was that Saul would be denied a dynasty to follow after him. The king could stay in office, but no heir of his would succeed him. "The Lord has sought out a man after his own heart" (1 Samuel 13:14), said the prophet, a heart not governed by expedience and self-absorption. The message was clear: Saul was on probation with God.

The leopard, however, seldom changes his spots. Continuing to define reality in terms of personal success rather than corporate achievement, it was inevitable that Saul would cross the line again. This happened, some years later, on the occasion of a holy war with the archenemies of Israel, the Amalekites.

The principle of holy war was central to Israel's religion, and it accounts for the Israelites' incredible rise from slavery in Egypt to ownership of the land of promise. It was this that defined them as a people; Egypt might have Pharaoh for its general, Canaan had its commander-kings, but it was the living God who led Israel into battle and won for them the victory. God was present with them and was to be looked to, prayed to, and followed for success. This is why Samuel so opposed the selection of a human king. Israel was not to turn to compromise, not to negotiate with the enemies of God, not to put its trust in diplomatic maneuvers or to make ill-begotten alliances.

We are not surprised, however, to see that these are exactly the things Saul did. It was what he was hired for, after all. He not only employed the means typical of other kings but conspired to draw attention to himself and away from the Lord. You could count on Saul to follow the path of least resistance, of short-term success, and particularly, of self-aggrandizement. He truly had lived up to the people's expectations.

> *Saul possessed that horrible, but all too familiar, talent for carrying the air of executive leadership, while not having the first clue about long-range strategic issues. This is the hallmark of the Sauls in our midst: they neither perceive nor achieve any purpose beyond personal prestige.*

All this came to a head when Samuel visited Saul's camp after one particularly great victory. The nation Israel was fighting had earned the anger of the Lord, and so God had commanded not only that no one be spared but also that no booty be taken—the principle being, "Even your cattle are anathema to us!" Similarly, the enemy king, a war criminal of the worst kind, was to be executed rather than bargained with. But as Samuel looked over the scene of Saul's victory, he saw the herds of the enemy in Saul's pens and the Amalekite king, alive and unmolested. Saul, flushed with triumph, rushed out to greet the prophet, hoping to celebrate his defeat of the Lord's enemies. But the look on Samuel's face brought him up short:

> But Samuel said, "What then is this bleating of sheep in my ears? What is this lowing of cattle that I hear?"
>
> (1 Samuel 15:14)

The jig was up. Saul could not be counted on to pursue the purposes of God, but only to serve his own. Not knowing how to follow, he could not be trusted to lead. Samuel's response to what he was seeing was direct:

> "You have rejected the word of the Lord, and the Lord has
> rejected you as king over Israel!"
> (1 Samuel 15:26)

The way a person responds to rebuke or punishment is always a mark of his or her character, and here Saul's is laid bare. First he replied, " 'I have sinned. I violated the Lord's command and your instructions' " (1 Samuel 15:24). The evidence, after all, was eating grass right in front of them. But, then, ever the blame-shifter, he went on,

> "I was afraid of the people and so I gave in to them. Now I beg
> you, forgive my sin and come back with me, so that
> I may worship the Lord."
> (1 Samuel 15:24–25)

"Look," he was saying, in effect, "what's the big deal? We'll sacrifice some offerings to the board of directors, put a slick spin on what has happened, and move on with business!" But Samuel was not buying this, and instead retorted with this classic rebuke:

> "To obey is better than sacrifice,
> and to heed is better than the fat of rams."
> (1 Samuel 15:22)

"If you want to please the Lord, Saul," he was saying, "then quit doing whatever seems best to you at the moment. Quit serving your own self-interest. Live by God's principles, if you want to worship Him. But if not, don't think you can make up by burning a few calves!"

Indeed, Saul's excuse is most illustrative: "I was afraid of the people and so I gave in to them." How familiar this Saul is to us today! Whether taking a hard and demanding line, or acquiescing to the voice of the ranks, he never gets it right, never comes across with any credibility. Why?

Because it was clear to all that *his* prestige, *his* stock option, *his* reputation, and not the greater good, were driving the train. But in Samuel, the prophet who bore the message of God, the majority stock owner of Saul's little enterprise, Saul encountered someone who would not back away from the truth. So when Saul pleaded, "Forgive my sin and come back with me," Samuel curtly replied, "I will not go with you . . . you are rejected," and that was the final word.

Devastated, Saul fell to his knees and tore the skirt of Samuel's robe, as both he and any hope of God's blessing departed for good. Samuel merely looked down and pronounced the final verdict:

> "The Lord has torn the kingdom of Israel from you today and
> has given it to one of your neighbors—to one better than you."
> (1 Samuel 15:28)

Saul was rejected as the leader of Israel, but he was not done pleading. There was something more important to him than leadership and in the logic of his final plea we see what made him so unworthy to bear authority over men and women:

> "I have sinned. But please honor me before the elders of my
> people and before Israel."
> (1 Samuel 15:30)

Notice what he did not say: "Give me one more chance to get the job done." Not, "But I so badly want to lead my people." The modern equivalent of his plea would go something like this: "Can I keep my sky-box at Yankee Stadium? Will you still keep my portrait up in the lobby?"

Surely Samuel was a man who understood his own times. He saw beyond the events before him. He deduced principles and recognized the calling set before his people. We can easily imagine the frustration he felt not only observing the sordid progression of events but reluctantly participating in them. The people had asked for this kind of king to lead them. Did they understand what they were asking, the prophet had wondered? Did they not recognize that it is the heart that makes the executive effective, not merely the skills, the credentials, the appearance?

I think Samuel would understand our times as well, and have felt much the same concern. He would have seen the way able men and women give their energies, not to *make something of* themselves, or their company, or the people who follow— but to *get something for* themselves. And usually it is things that do not last and are left behind when we pass on that they pursue.

Saul was an image man, first and last. He was a monument builder— and the monuments were to himself. For such executives, character and purpose have no place in their vision of leadership. They see only the cease-

Whether taking a hard and demanding line, or acquiescing to the ranks, Saul never gets it right, never comes across with any credibility. Why? Because it is clear to all that his prestige, his stock option, his reputation, and not the greater good, were driving the train.

less managing of perceptions and the manipulation of human beings.

Thus Samuel faced the end of his days a bitterly disappointed man. He had longed for the man after God's own heart, the shepherd he knew could inspire the hearts of men and women. But now he went home, never to see Saul again, only to mourn over this king and the people.

Samuel wasn't the only one whose heart was breaking. For the final line of the biblical account of this episode is as remarkable as it is instructive:

And the Lord was grieved that he had made Saul king over Israel.
(1 Samuel 15:35)

God had given Saul to the people as a judgment upon their lack of faith—and yet it pained His heart to see this kind of leadership. His pur-pose was ultimately constructive, to create a readiness for the true leader-ship that was to come. But it *is* painful to observe, then and now, men and women placed in the executive's chair—a seat of possibility and meaning and importance—only to squander it all over tawdry ambition and shortsighted gain. How hard it is to see the servant's place taken by the charlatan.

And the Lord was grieved that he had made Saul king over Israel.

It is difficult, in a translation, to convey the strength of this statement as it is rendered in the original Hebrew text. God was sorry, He repented, He turned away from what He had done. But, as the Bible itself is so zealous to point out, God is the unchangeable One. As Samuel himself had insisted about the Lord,

> "He who is the Glory of Israel does not lie or change his mind;
> for he is not a man, that he should change his mind."
> (1 Samuel 15:29)

And yet this is exactly what we see God doing. Instructively, the Hebrew verb is the same as that used to convey God's sorrow over having installed this Saul in the first place. God does not, cannot, change His mind or repent—but when He looks upon this king, He does. What are we to make of this? Here is God, who by His nature cannot change or be mistaken, who knows all things in advance and infallibly—yet here He is sorry about what He has done! God repents!

Clearly, a major point is being made. The Bible, in order to present the unfathomable God to the minds of men, often pictures Him in human terms. It speaks of His "hands," His "long arm," etc. And here it speaks of the eternal, unchanging God "repenting" of what He has done. The point is abundantly clear: The counterfeit leader is reprehensible in the extreme. He is an abomination. He is just as burdensome to the heart of God as he is to the backs of men.

> *How can God repent of what He has done? The point is clear: The counterfeit leader is reprehensible in the extreme, just as burdensome to the heart of God as he is to the backs of men.*

Would that we had the same revulsion both Samuel and God showed over Saul, the self-serving executive. Our generation feels the effects of such leadership, surely as in any other time. Would that we too would repent.

But even this was not to be quite the last word. For as David would later write, "The Lord is compassionate and gracious." So God spoke to Samuel again, sending him on one more mission:

"Fill your horn with oil and be on your way; I am sending you
to Jesse of Bethlehem. I have chosen one of his sons to be king."
(1 Samuel 16:1)

Though dispirited and fearful of Saul's reprisal, Samuel went and,
according to God's instructions, he arrived at the house of Jesse. There
he stood as Jesse's sons paraded before him one after another. First came
Eliab, the oldest, and Samuel thought, "Surely the Lord's anointed stands
here before the Lord" (1 Samuel 16:6). But God replied,

"Do not consider his appearance or his height, for I have
rejected him. The Lord does not look at the things man looks at.
Man looks at the outward appearance, but the Lord
looks at the heart."
(1 Samuel 16:7)

How embarrassing for Samuel, to be rebuked for committing the
same sin his people committed. "Teacher! Instruct thyself!" How easy it
is for appearances to control our assessments, even for a seasoned veteran
like Samuel! Next came Abinadab, then Shammah, then the rest of the
seven sons Jesse brought with him. None were chosen by God.

"Is this it?" asked Samuel. " 'There is still the youngest,' Jesse an-
swered, 'but he is tending the sheep.' " You get the message: That one is
of no account . . . Don't waste your time on him. What does he know
about leadership . . . living in the wilds with animals, dreaming dreams
and singing songs. What could he learn out there to prepare him to be
king? "Samuel said, 'Send for him; we will not sit down until he arrives.' "

So out they went to get the boy. When he arrived Samuel saw that
he too was handsome, but no doubt in desperate need of a bath and some
fresh clothes.

Then the Lord said, "Rise and anoint him; he is the one."
(1 Samuel 16:12)

It reads like a fairy tale. But what God arranged in such a fantastic
fashion is intended to convey an everyday meaning: Men look at the
outward appearance, but what really matters is the heart.

I have always been fascinated by the expression, "The first impression is what really matters." I do not doubt that there is practical truth to this statement. But first impressions are necessarily shallow, external. The cut of the clothing, the posture and gestures, the enthusiasm in the eye—I assure you that Saul can do these better than David, at least for thirty minutes. But the corollary to the principle of first impressions is this: *You get just what you are looking for.*

What are you looking for, then, as you interview prospective leaders? What do your questions aim for? Matters of the heart or only those things we wear on the outside? Perhaps if we valued such hidden, inner qualities as courage and candor, character and compassion, our questions and our assessments, and finally our organizations, might be very different than they are now.

It was an enormous challenge for the people of Samuel's time, even for Jesse and, indeed, the prophet himself, to believe that something beneath the surface counts for more than what meets the eye. Even Samuel, so disgusted with the shallow strength of Saul, found it hard to see beyond the résumé, the charm, the *look*.

> *What are you looking for, then, as you interview prospective leaders? Perhaps if we valued such hidden, inner qualities as courage and candor, character and compassion, our organizations might be very different than they are now.*

Let us not mistake the message of this story. For there is a clear choice before us, for our organizations and, more importantly, for ourselves. What fields will we cultivate? Those of the hands and the head only, or first and foremost that of the heart? It is a question we must each answer, and it is an urgent one. Our time is crying out for leaders like David, the men and women after God's own heart. We need the leader who is defined not by his or her own greatness, but by the greatness of the followers. Not the leader who celebrates his own abilities, who gleefully puts her marvelous decisions on display, but the leader who rejoices in the character and ability being cultivated in the precious human lives entrusted to him. Our generation is thirsting for the shepherds, those who will watch over and lead the flock.

There is a message for us as individuals, too. In broad terms, there is a choice before you—a choice between Saul's path and the path taken by David.

And yet our eyes are more accustomed to the sordid sight of Saul, self-seeking and self-serving. He is the forerunner of all who view the executive chair as little more than a means for financial and career success. Saul does not inspire, he demands; he does not lead, he dictates and he cajoles; he does not build for the future but reacts to the crises of the day. Saul was not loved, though his abilities were admired by many. He had authority, but little influence. *Saul was a king, but he was not a leader.*

Who is the real leader? The real leader is the servant and the shepherd, the man "after God's own heart." The one who guides and nurtures, who guards and tends the flock God has entrusted to him. The leader is the one who sees his people not as a means to an end, but as his trophy and his joy, the legacy she leaves after herself. The true executive is the man or the woman motivated not by skyline offices or shiny insignia or fat bonuses, but by the service to and through those people whose lives are so deeply affected.

God had compassion on faithful Samuel, and let him rest his eyes on the shepherd who would fulfill his longing. This was the challenge, the question of his time: "What will be the heart of the executive?" God's answer was a young man named David. Would that He would so grace our own time, our own nation, our own corporations. That is His job, and so we ought to pray as Samuel did for mercy and grace. But for us there is a calling and an obligation—to seek the path less chosen, to value and cultivate the things of the heart, to lead and to serve as shepherds.

> *Our time is crying out for leaders like David . . . Not the leader who celebrates his own abilities, but the leader who rejoices in the character and ability being cultivated in the precious human lives entrusted to him. Our generation is thirsting for the shepherds, men and women of heart.*

IN THE SHADOW
OF GIANTS

The Day of
Reckoning

יום־מספר

B. F. Westcott once remarked, "Great occasions do not make heroes or cowards; they simply unveil them to the eyes of men. Silently and imperceptibly, as we wake or sleep, we grow strong or we grow weak, and at last some crisis shows us what we have become."[1]

Saul had been growing weaker, slowly but perceptively, and the crisis finally arrived at the Valley of Elah. His name was Goliath.

Saul's leadership had been rejected by God, but that did not mean he was no longer king. It simply meant that God would no longer throw His support behind his cause. No more would God fight Saul's battles, for His favor had gone to another. Perhaps they were both relieved at the new arrangement. Meanwhile, Saul's regime continued to enforce the status quo even as the world outside changed. One of these changes was

---
1. C.f. Cyril J. Barber, The Books of Samuel, vol. 1, Neptune, N.J.: Loizeaux, 1994, p. 151.

a renewal of vigor within the nation of Philistia, Israel's western neighbor, a vigor that found expression in yet another invasion of Israelite soil.

Thus we turn to one of the most familiar stories of the Bible, indeed one of the most well-known confrontations of all history and literature. The Philistines' need for living space predictably launched them out from their five coastline cities. To match this threat, Saul assembled his forces on one side of a great canyon, the Valley of Elah. This site has been identified today by historians and archaeologists, and seen in its center is a deep ravine where winter rains flood. Some twenty feet in width, with steep banks ten to twelve feet high, this natural obstacle provided an ideal defensive position. Here Saul brought his army to stand against the invaders.

This battle would prove to be a watershed event for Saul. No longer the servant of the Lord, he could not count on divine intervention; instead he would have to rely on his own strength and skill. Perhaps Saul was pleased with this prospect, but then he did not reckon on the giant.

You have to give the Philistines credit: Unlike Saul, they knew how to reconsider a strategy. They had tried overwhelming numbers, but to no avail. Superior technology had also failed. So now they recruited the giant Goliath to lead them into battle. This time, when the battle lines were drawn, the massive warrior stepped forth.

What a spectacle this must have been! There were the two armies drawn up on opposite banks of a formidable ravine. The soldiers of both sides would have been thrusting and parrying up to the edge of the ravine, trying to taunt the enemy into a foolhardy attack across this strong defensive terrain. Insults and catcalls filled the air, and yet the situation was a stalemate.

Then the din began to subside as the Philistine ranks parted and Goliath stepped out. Into this quiet came the clanking of heavy armor, rattling with the long and awkward steps of the giant warrior. Forward to the edge of the ravine, and then down into the ditch he came, easily the largest man the Israelites had ever seen. Before him went his shield bearer, and the shield itself was impossibly large.

If we read the ancient measurements correctly, then Goliath stood over nine feet tall. He wore a coat of scale armor, a massive bronze helmet, and greaves covering the long expanse of his shins. For his weapon,

Goliath carried a spear—more like a harpoon—the head of which weighed more than fifteen pounds and could thus penetrate the strongest armor. Perhaps there is some literary embellishing going on here, or perhaps he was just a freak anomaly. But we get the message: This was the biggest, baddest warrior anybody had ever laid eyes on, or likely ever would.

The Philistine strategy is not specified, but it is not difficult to sort out. Anxious to avoid the high casualties of assaulting such favorable defensive ground, perhaps also attuned to the psychological dimension of war that had earlier aided Jonathan's bold forays, they sent out the giant to undo their hated enemy. With Goliath on their side, the Philistines were finally going to get even with Saul and the men of Israel.

We can see the look on the defenders' faces as Goliath cast down his gauntlet and lifted up his face, full of arrogance and ridicule:

> "Why do you come out and line up for battle? Am I not a
> Philistine, and are you not the servants of Saul? Choose a man
> and have him come down to me. If he is able to fight and kill
> me, we will become your subjects; but if I overcome him and
> kill him, you will become our subjects and serve us. . . .
> This day I defy the ranks of Israel! Give me a man and
> let us fight each other."
> (1 Samuel 17:8–10)

There are, no doubt, a couple of messages here. Primarily, Saul is learning a lesson for disobeying God. He was the king of Israel, not of Ammon or Egypt or Moab—and Israel existed for the glory of God. It's a bit suspicious, therefore, that just when Saul is rejected by the Lord, the Philistines come up with Goliath.

On a more mundane level, however, there is this: The executive who stands pat, whose thinking is dominated by today's to-do list, who can only relate to the pressures facing him this week or month or quarter, is bound to wake up to find some fearsome giant standing before him in the valley. Competition means the target is moving, is thinking, is changing and adapting. One day, sooner or later, the opposition's ranks part, and out walks a Goliath. Perhaps it is a new product line or a novel arrangement for reaching the market. Unfortunately, it is not the short-sighted executive alone who pays the price. First there will come the kind of downsizing Goliath intended to enforce on Saul's army.

The idea of deciding a battle through individual combat was not a new one in the ancient world, but it achieved a new meaning with the arrival of a man like Goliath. One man against the other, the fate of thousands in the balance. There was something neat and attractive about the idea—my cause against your cause, my god against your god, trial by combat—but especially so for the Philistines! Thus as Goliath's gauntlet of challenge thudded to the ground, the future darkened for the hosts of Israel.

But long odds do not ensure defeat, nor was this the first or the last time a nation or people were faced with discouraging odds. We think of the Miltiades' Greeks at Marathon, Scipio's Romans against the juggernaut of Hannibal, George Washington at Valley Force, and are reminded that few are the challenges that valor, energy, and sacrifice cannot overcome. But then Saul does not really fit in with this group of heroic champions, does he? The Bible's narrative sums up the Israelite response neatly:

> On hearing the Philistine's words, Saul and all the Israelites were
> dismayed and terrified.
> **(1 Samuel 17:11)**

There was no champion, therefore, no one bold or zealous enough to step forward and pick up Goliath's gauntlet. The result was ignominious stalemate.

The days rolled by, then weeks, and the standoff continued. What a humiliation for Saul as each day the giant came forth, threw down the glove, and spit insults at the king, his people, and his God. It was evident now that Saul's leadership would not bring God's intervention, and so the matter was left to his own ability. Was not Saul the man of stature in Israel? Did he not stand taller than everyone else? But now he shrank before the specter of this giant, a parable for all who place their trust solely in their own capabilities, only to find themselves unable to live up to a mighty challenge.

The biggest indicator of Saul's failing leadership was the unwilling-ness of any of his followers to answer the challenge, day after day, morn-ing and evening, as Goliath wounded their collective pride. Saul himself was well advanced in years, so perhaps he could not be expected to an-swer the call. But what of Jonathan? Was Saul holding the prince back or was there something else? What about the commanders of the army, the heroes of earlier fights? As the great military theorist and historian J. F. C. Fuller once wrote, "What the leaders are, that, as a rule, will the men below them be."[2] So it was in the ranks of Saul's army.

We have a lot of negative things to say about Saul, but this is too much! Standing there glassy-eyed, his warriors feeding off his giant list-lessness. If nothing else, Saul had a willingness to act, though often thoughtless action. The one thing Saul had always been able to do was look a crisis in the eye and fight for all he was worth. Had the man no heart left at all? Had Samuel's and God's rejection stolen his confidence? Was his conscience plaguing him this badly? To understand, we must go back just a bit in the story.

If it hasn't already become clear, the demands of leadership were not making Saul a better man. The com-promises and coldhearted calculations he made had chipped away at his heart until there was little of worth left. It is no different today. Leaders who betray their basic values, who brush aside the principles they publicly espouse, pay a heavy cost with the passage of time. With every compromise of principle, the principle itself has less power over us. Before long a pattern emerges, ultimately solidifying into a habit. Further down the line, the habit becomes ingrained and a new aspect has alloyed itself into the character. Our lives are this way. We are constantly engaged in the work of making and remaking ourselves—like it or not—by means of the choices we make day to day.

The Bible expresses what had happened this way:

> *The executive who stands pat, whose thinking is dominated by only the pressures facing him this week or month or quarter, is bound to wake up someday to find some fearsome giant standing before him in the valley.*

2. *J. F. C. Fuller,* Alexander the Great, *New Brunswick, N.J.: Da Capo Press, 1960, p. 79.*

> Now the Spirit of the Lord had departed from Saul, and an evil
> spirit from the Lord tormented him.
>
> (1 Samuel 16:14)

We need to understand that the Bible is not letting Saul off the hook, any more than you or I can blame God for the misfortunes we bring upon ourselves. Furthermore, it is a general rule in Scripture that God never opposes someone who has not first rejected and opposed Him. But the point is clear: Saul's past misdeeds were dogging him, and God was not about to let him brush them off this time.

So Saul, the man noted for his striking appearance, began to take on a new image. An ugly image. Before long, even his sheepish attendants took note and cautiously broached the issue with their king:

> "See, an evil spirit from God is tormenting you. Let our lord
> command his servants here to search for someone who can play
> the harp. He will play when the evil spirit from God comes upon
> you, and you will feel better."
>
> (1 Samuel 16:15–16)

It is noteworthy that these attendants are unnamed in the account. Where, we might ask, are the characters of substance, like Saul's son Jonathan or the general, Abner? Saul had driven them away, threatened by their popularity and strength. Now he was left with unnamed sycophants, anxious to tend to his affliction but never to address its cause.

It is always a sign of trouble when an executive surrounds himself or herself with courtiers unable and unwilling to offer anything but praise and adoration. Such people always seem to be available, quick to work themselves into favor through ingratiating servitude. The leader who welcomes them is avoiding, consciously or not, the truth about himself. In the years before, Saul had seen his soldiers desert him, and so now he settled for those insects who gravitate to the light that power radiates. They, at least, would not abandon him. In his misdeeds, he had seen his authority challenged by those men like Samuel and Jonathan who cared more about their cause than their career. So now he would surround himself only with spineless creatures with slippery tongues. "You are so right, my king!" "That is a brilliant idea, my lord! Right on target, chief!" Saul came to value these consoling voices more than painful words of truth.

Perhaps Saul was just lonely, feeling sorry for himself, and so he desired supportive companions. But, as the old commentator, Matthew Henry, tells us: "How much better friends had they been to him if they had advised him, since the evil spirit was from the Lord, to give all diligence to make his peace with God by true repentance, to send for Samuel to pray with him and to intercede with God for him! Then might he not only have had some present relief, but the good Spirit would have returned to him."[3]

One of the greatest arrows in any leader's quiver is the ability to say these words: "I was wrong." "Forgive me." "Thank you for challenging my decision." Far from exhibiting weakness, such words show that the executive is still alive. He is still a man; she still has a beating heart. Be wary, then, of resenting those who dare to sit down, look you in the eyes, call you to account. Perhaps they are old friends or colleagues. A valued and trustworthy subordinate. These are the companions we should seek, and the sometimes unpleasant words to which we should offer our ear.

It is always a sign of trouble when an executive surrounds himself or herself with courtiers unable and unwilling to offer anything but praise and adoration . . . who are quick to work themselves into favor through ingratiating servitude . . . insects who gravitate to the light.

It is much easier, however, to defend yourself than to listen. "He's just jealous of my success," says a voice in our mind. "She's just trying to throw me off balance, to make herself look good." Beware of the impulse to quickly lift the shield, or close the door on the voice of candor and real concern. Beware of the effects of a heart grown lazy by idleness, grown hard through frequent misuse. For there are moments, turning points in the life of every Saul, when he could easily have turned back onto a better path and restored his heart. But surely there also comes a time—and such

---

3. *Matthew Henry,* Commentary on the Whole Bible, *vol. 2. Peabody, Mass.: Hendrickson, 1991, p. 288.*

a time did come for Saul—when his heart had become so callused, so hard and impenetrable, that there could be no turning back.

Are we surprised, then, to see this king utterly impotent on the day of reckoning? Are we shocked to watch his jaw drop and his face slacken when the reality he had long betrayed faced him in the form of the Philistine giant?

A younger Saul might have raced into the ravine and snatched up the gauntlet of challenge himself. A more faithful Saul might have turned to the prophet Samuel for God's assistance, or to God Himself in prayer and plea. A Saul more alive might have defended the name and the cause of his people, lifting his voice to catch upon the wind, beckoning younger arms and livelier legs to sacrifice their lives for the costly prize of the Philistine champion's head.

> *One of the greatest arrows in any leader's quiver is the ability to say these words: "I was wrong." "Forgive me" . . . "Thank you for challenging me." Be wary of resenting those who dare to sit down, look you in the eyes, and call you to account.*

Instead we see the wheels spinning, hear the deadly voice speaking in his mind: "I can't trust these people to fight for me . . . Look at the fear on that captain's face—he never really was loyal to me . . . Look at that band of warriors shuffling their feet—I bet they're going to bolt any moment now . . . Why didn't they tell me about the giant . . . ?"

Saul was a dead man, even though he still breathed. He had been dying for some time now. And for forty days, as Goliath taunted Israel's and Saul's army morning and evening, his life and his reign slowly faded.

"Your Servant
Will Go"

עבדך ילך

There can't have been very many skilled musicians around in 1000
B.C., and so Saul's attendants may have been hard-pressed to come up
with one on short notice. But since it was their idea that some music
might relieve Saul's tortured spirit, a musician had to be found. Fortu-
nately, one of the attendants remembered a young shepherd from down
near Bethlehem who could play the harp.

> "I have seen a son of Jesse of Bethlehem who knows how to play
> the harp. He is a brave man and a warrior. He speaks well and is
> a fine-looking man. And the Lord is with him."
> (1 Samuel 16:18)

Among his other talents, David was a lyre player. Surely he had
honed this skill during quiet nights alone in the fields, having an appre-
ciative, if uncritical, audience in the ewes and rams. Now he would play
on the national stage, in the court of the king—quite a rapid promotion.

Jesse must have felt his head spinning with all the attention he was getting. First his eighth and youngest son was anointed by the prophet, and now the king had called him to the court to attend on him personally.

Thus began David's life on the public stage. The people of this time believed that music soothed mental anguish and aided in the healing process, a conclusion now clinically documented. In this way, David made quite an impression on Saul. His playing did indeed relieve the tormented king, and whenever the evil spirit came upon Saul, David would come out and play for him.

We have to wonder just what the Lord was cooking up with this odd and providential crossing of paths. All along, God has been pressing His point by setting a contrast before us; surely the same is taking place now. Indeed, the description of David that Saul received from his assistants hints at just this:

> "He is a brave man and a warrior. He speaks well and is a fine-
> looking man. And the Lord is with him."
>
> **(1 Samuel 16:18)**

Not a bad recommendation! David, it may seem, is much like Saul. He is a brave warrior (fighting raiders was an unavoidable part of being a shepherd in those dangerous days), and furthermore he was noticeably handsome. "Just like you, Saul." There was one thing, however, that turned this comparison into a striking contrast: "And the Lord is with him."

We can see what a loaded statement that was. The Lord had departed from Saul, but He was with David. Saul was a tormented and inwardly turbulent man, whereas David's fellowship with God brought him peace. And just as the courtiers had plainly observed the king's struggles, so also had David's bliss been obvious enough for them to mention. Despite the external similarity, the contrast between David and Saul would have been more than evident to those who served in the court of the king.

David served faithfully and well under Saul. This was young David's idea of networking and self-promotion: to answer the call when it came, work diligently at the task given to you, and serve with all your heart. David had not manipulated his summoning to the executive suite, and once in the king's service he did not feel the need to weave himself into the intrigues of the court. How striking this is when we remember that David had been anointed by the prophet as a sort of counter-king. But the very things that made him fit to be a king also made him faithful as a servant.

Later on, it will be important for us to note that at Saul's first encounter with David he thought very highly of the young man, and it was not until later that the jealousy would emerge. Saul's replacement had arrived in his own court and, as is so often the case among those possessed of real character, he came as one willing to loyally serve.

Saul's musical reverie, however, did not last long. When the Philistine attack broke on Israel's western flank, the king had more pressing business and so David was left with time on his hands. A teenager, he was ineligible to fight in the army. Besides, as the eighth son, he would likely be passed over for the honor of fighting for his country. What an excellent opportunity for a little time off and recreation, we might think! But David went back to Bethlehem to tend the sheep he had been forced to neglect.

The three oldest of Jesse's sons were serving up at the front lines and Jesse, now too old for traveling, longed for news of their safety. The battle lines having been drawn for some weeks, Jesse would have heard of the situation, though it seems that David, back out in the fields, had not. Therefore, Jesse sent his youngest, and least important, son with some bread for his brothers, some cheeses for their commander, and instructions to bring back news of their condition.

It was early in the day when David arrived at the valley, just as the morning routine was taking place. Up ran the soldiers from each side, taunting and shouting their battle cries, but careful not to fall into the deep ravine and thus come within range of their enemies' spears. What a sight for a teenage boy, sheltered from the world as he was! Dropping off his supplies, David ran to the front, searching until he discovered the unit where his three older brothers were lined up. As he began to greet them, however, something happened that was sadly routine to them but shocking to David:

> As he was talking with them, Goliath, the Philistine champion
> from Gath, stepped out from his lines and shouted his usual

> defiance, and David heard it. When the Israelites saw the man,
> they all ran from him in great fear.
>
> (1 Samuel 17:23, 24)

Imagine the effect of this upon such a young, inexperienced patriot. It would be like a boy getting to serve as batboy for the baseball team he most admires, only to discover that the team is throwing the game. Where are the mighty ones of Israel! Where are the victorious hosts of Saul, ready to throw down their lives for hearth, for home, and for God?

Once the racket subsided, the brothers condescended to fill in their bewildered little brother:

> "Do you see how this man keeps coming out? He comes out to
> defy Israel. The king will give great wealth to the man who kills
> him. He will also give him his daughter in marriage and will
> exempt his father's family from taxes in Israel."
>
> (1 Samuel 17:25)

That's it. No concern over the state of their army, no shame for their craven avoidance of duty. Just this: "Hey, if you're looking to make it big, now's your chance!" And quite an incentive it was that Saul had offered! How like the embittered leader to seek to purchase what he could no longer inspire. How like Saul to think he could just buy the loyalty and sacrifice of his people with a loaded incentive plan. Here is yet another mark of the empty-hearted executive, the instinctive use of the carrot and the stick. Attendance you can buy, acceptable and sometimes even excellent performance you can purchase, but that's about it. You don't get people to take on Goliath for a reward they may well never get to enjoy! To get truly selfless service and commitment, the executive must be prepared to trade in a different currency: trust, love, a personal example, an inspiring sense of purpose. And of these, Saul's account was now empty. Devoid of leadership, there was no one among the warriors willing to risk his own neck, even for the royal purse. Young David was clearly surprised, but we should not be.

Seemingly unable to absorb what he was confronted with, David turned to others nearby, hoping for something more encouraging.

"What will be done for the man who kills this Philistine and
removes this disgrace from Israel? Who is this uncircumcised[1]
Philistine that he should defy the armies of the living God?"
(1 Samuel 17:26)

Notice the completely different tone of David's inquiry from that of
his brothers. At the heart of his statement are the principles at stake, not
the prizes. David's mind was not cap-
tured by the opportunity for person
gain, and his bearing was not shaken
by the sorry example of the king.
Rather, it was his heart that was affected, and it was broken by the disgrace being visited upon his people
and his God. Obviously hoping to encourage or shame these trained, veteran warriors to their duty, David's
words fell upon deaf ears.

*How like Saul to think he
could just buy the loyalty
and sacrifice of his people
with a loaded incentive plan
. . . To get truly selfless
service and commitment, the
executive must be prepared
to trade in a different
currency: trust, love, a
personal example, an
inspiring sense of purpose.*

There David was, a mere shepherd, berating and cajoling the sea-
soned warriors. It was more than his arrogant older brothers could stomach.
What could he know about battle? Who was he to hassle them about something everyone else, after all, was doing? They weren't the only ones afraid
to rise and meet Goliath's challenge. They had seen the giant and been
through the drill for forty straight days, and they were not about to let this
snotty little shepherd kid give them a hard time about it. So Eliab, the
eldest, jerked the shepherd David around and hotly berated him:

"Why have you come down here? And with whom did you leave
those few sheep in the desert? I know how conceited you are and
how wicked your heart is; you came down only to
watch the battle."
(1 Samuel 17:28)

---

1. *The circumcision of males was the mark that set Israel apart from all other nations. Thus, to be
uncircumcised was to be estranged from the people and presence of God, something that was
anathema to every true Israelite.*

We remember that this, the eldest son, was the one Samuel had been so impressed by, only to be rejected by the Lord as lacking the true stuff of kings. So Eliab may well have held a grudge against his youngest brother. But in any case, any one who has ever been a little brother knows exactly what was behind those words. "Hey, you little runt! What do you know? . . . Shouldn't you be back with your little sheep? . . . You always get me in trouble, you brat . . ."

Let's not pass this by, however, without making some observations on the effects of stagnation in an organization, for there is more going on here than the insecurity of a bullying older brother. There is, first of all, the frustration of blatantly ineffective methods repeated over and over again, the poison of repeated and mounting humiliation. We get an indication of this by what is said here of Goliath. At first, you remember, the giant dared to jump down into the ditch with his shield-bearer, there to lob his jeers. But by the time David had arrived, it was said, "Do you see this man who keeps *coming out?*"[2] (1 Samuel 17:25). Goliath was now not merely entering the ravine, but was laboriously making his way up the Israelite's side without being challenged, then taunting them right to their faces. Like little pygmies, the valiant ones of Israel scurried away from his spear. So the military situation here was not quite at a standstill, but was in fact deteriorating substantially. One giant and the whole Israelite position was falling apart, just as one competitor's product innovation can make an entire company crash.

Worst of all, however, was the fact that Saul had no response to this situation. This was abundantly clear to his soldiers, who must have felt like rats caught in a sinking ship. The frustration and the malignant passivity had spread deep within the ranks. This is just one example of the trickle-down effect of stagnant executive leadership.

So the brothers were not exactly thrilled to see David, or to listen to his exhortations. It was precisely because David was right, that he had correctly diagnosed the situation, that they so despised him and his words. There are indeed times when talk will simply get you nowhere. David,

2. Although The NIV Study Bible *translates this as* "coming out," *the Hebrew text is closer to* "coming up."

for sure, was not getting very far—that is, not until a group of soldiers decided the person this young orator needed to exhort was not them, but the king himself.

A lesser man would have regretted opening his big fat mouth. Quite a few, I imagine, would have backed away and discreetly piped down. But David was not one to keep unpopular opinions to himself. His words were not a bluff, nor were they intended to mock. They came directly from his heart, and they directed David straight to the king. Already we see an audacity in David that is striking; we should prepare ourselves for one of those remarkable incidents where history stands still, and all heaven's eyes are watching.

The scene is easy to picture: Saul was probably seated among sullen officers, his face no longer even angry, just weary, his uniform no longer gleaming and his weapons bearing the look of disuse. Up strides the shepherd boy, a spring in his steps like a basketball player just entering the game in the fourth quarter. And this is not the only reason he looks out of place, for he is not even dressed as a warrior, but carries a lowly shepherd's pack slung over his shoulder. Nonetheless, he must have exuded a zeal and confidence that overcame his appearance. Matthew Henry says it well: "A little shepherd, come but this morning from keeping asleep, has more courage than all the mighty men of Israel."[3]

So once again, David came before the King of Israel. There must have been just a moment of mutual discomfort at this strange and awkward scene, before the young servant broke the ice:

> "Let no one lose heart on account of this Philistine; your servant
> will go and fight him."
> (1 Samuel 17:32)

What does a mighty king say to such as this! Saul, not one to be easily encouraged, merely replied:

3. Commentary on the Whole Bible, vol. 2, p. 293.

"You are not able to go out against this Philistine and fight him;
you are only a boy, and he has been a fighting man
from his youth."
(1 Samuel 17:33)

There are several things for us to take note of here. First, there is
David, and his faith-driven heart, which protected him from the fears and
doubts that held the others captive. There is also his failure to mention
anything about Saul's great reward. No "and by the way." No "and while
we're at it, can I check out this daughter of yours?" Does David not care
about money and women? It is obvious that David cares much more for
the God he had come to know in shepherds' fields and the principles to
which he was bound than for material rewards. David believed in a cause,
as all true champions must. *Faith in-
spires what riches and rewards could
never motivate.*

> *What strikes us is his failure
> to mention anything about
> Saul's great reward. No "and
> by the way . . ." No "can I
> check out this daughter of
> yours?" . . . Faith inspires
> what riches and rewards
> could never motivate.*

What about King Saul? For one
thing it is obvious that he does not recognize this harpist who had so recently
been important to him. He had not
taken note of him then, since he was
only a useful tool, and so now he was
just another strange person wasting his
time. Perhaps he was slightly touched by the foolish yet honest valor of
the shepherd boy, and his words carry at least an inkling of this. And yet
once again we see Saul considering only the outward appearance, notic-
ing none of the signs of a living, beating heart. How difficult old habits
are to break! Like a groove in his psyche, Saul possessed an utter inability
to look beneath the surface. He will not, and cannot, change his paradigm, and so he listlessly sits before the one who must supplant him.
David does not *look* the part of a hero, and so he must not *be* one. No
matter that there are no other candidates. Saul discards David's words
according to the pattern engraved on his dying heart. "Champions are
tall, like me." "Champions wear costly armor, as I do." But being like
Saul was not exactly a strong recommendation on that day.

Saul and David are brought together in this story to instruct, so let us listen well. We have, of course, the obvious contrast between Saul, the man of appearances, and David, the man of heart. But there is another contrast at this point in the story, a contrast in their manner of perception. How does a captain, a leader of war or of industry, perceive the challenges before him? What is his mode of seeing? What does an executive, for instance, see when customer expectations have

> *Saul possessed an utter inability to look beneath the surface. David does not look the part of a hero, and so he must not be one.*

risen, or when technical advances make his best-selling product obsolete? Is it a threat to short-term profits or a chance for the company's true identity to shine? Does it produce panic or inspiration? The difference, as Saul and David show us, is in the *manner* in which such challenges are *seen*. The only backdrop against which Saul viewed Goliath was the landscape of the present. But David looked back into his own past and into his people's history, and he saw something beyond the giant Goliath. He saw a vision of what Israel was all about, a vision that beckoned him forward, that turned the valor of yesterday into tomorrow's possibility. He saw God in his life and in the life of his people, and he saw the capacity for change and new vitality. Therefore, he saw Goliath not as a menace or a deadly threat, but as a mandate for the expression of faith.

Most important to David's thought progression was his knowledge that God is present with His people in their times of trial. His faith in himself, and his faith in Israel's long dormant potential, rested squarely upon his faith in a delivering God. As he would later write in one of his better-known psalms:

> *O Lord, how many are my foes!*
> *How many rise up against me!*
> *Many are saying of me,*
> *"God will not deliver him."*
> *But you are a shield around me, O Lord;*
> *you bestow glory on me and lift up my head . . .*
> *I will not fear the tens of thousands drawn up against me on*
> *   every side.*

Psalm 3:1–3, 6

In light of such a God, perceived by faith, how small seemed the warrior-giant, Goliath. But Saul, his gaze restricted to the earth, saw no hand moving the events of his own or anybody else's history. He saw no pattern to the cosmos, no principles to which he could dedicate his life. As Saul saw it, he stood alone before Goliath, and how menacing was the sight.

Just what is it, we may wonder, that inspires these few gilded champions, like David, to rise above the trials of this earthly life? The apostle Paul, writing in 2 Corinthians, gives this explanation, "We live by faith, not by sight" (2 Corinthians 5:7). What else besides faith could possibly empower men and women to stand tall in the face of seemingly invincible power? What else sustains the lonely executive who gazes upon the status quo and cries, "I dare to chart a different course. I dare to walk by faith and to stand alone if necessary"? What else motivates the whistle-blower in her lonely stand against a corrupt hierarchy? Faith is not mere wishful thinking. Rather, faith is confidence in a principle, a person, or, as in David's case, in God. Faith gave David certainty despite the demoralizing impotence of Israel's army and king, and despite the giant Goliath himself. Faith is acknowledging a higher power and a higher accountability, trusting in more than the sword, or the powers that be, or the mighty dollar.

> *What is it that inspires the few who rise above the trials of this life? What is it that empowers, that impels, that sustains? A higher power, a higher accountability, than the sword or the dollar.*

David must surely have been bewildered as Saul brushed aside his offer to battle the giant. But he pressed his case, arguing not so much on his own strength, but on the willingness of God to respond to the faith of His people. We can imagine Saul's face changing as David pleaded his case. Perhaps there was a faint smile of remembrance, when he too had possessed such daring and zeal. Perhaps there was a reluctant nod, unimpressed but willing to relent. In any case, relent he did:

Saul said to David, "Go, and the Lord be with you."
Then Saul dressed David in his own tunic. He put a coat of armor on him and a bronze helmet on his head. David fastened

on his sword over the tunic and tried walking around, because
he was not used to them.
"I cannot go in these," he said to Saul, "because I am not used
to them." So he took them off.

(1 Samuel 17:37–39)

Here is one of the classic scenes of all literature, a masterpiece of symbolism and subtlety truly worthy of its Author.

"Go," said Saul, "and the Lord be with you." The irony in these words is palpable, for the Lord had already gone with and to David. It was this that accounted for his courage.

Then comes a poignant scene, as the weak and heartless Saul removes his own personal armor and offers it to David for his duel with Goliath. "Here, let me help you," Saul seems to be saying, with all the nobility left in him. "Let me give you *my* seal of authority—discredited though it is. Take *my* weapons—useless as they have shown themselves. Go forth in *my* name—though it is a curse on the lips of every man in the army."

So David, gracious and loyal to a fault, tries it all on. But, of course, it just doesn't fit. It was too big, too bulky, too ill-suited for a man with a different source of strength. After all, the trappings of personal privilege and bureaucratic authority just don't rest well on the shoulders of a true champion. This scene is both a lesson for leaders today and a great and defining moment in the life of our model. How easy it might have been for David, despite his selfless motives, to take on the garb of the sordid Saul. But David has to be himself and go his own way, even when, *particularly* when, the stakes are so high. He knows that wearing Saul's armor will not only drag him down but will undermine all that makes him strong, corrupting who and what he is. He may try it on and walk around for practice, but in the end he must walk back and simply say, "Sorry, it just doesn't fit."

How closely this strikes at the heart of a challenge felt by many a true leader today. In company after company, a new day is dawning with a demand for new, more genuine leaders: executives who speak to the

heart, who stand like a shepherd among the sheep, not merely demanding high performance but inspiring it. So does it make sense to fall into
the old patterns, assume the old trap-
pings and incentives, and go on dedi-
cating ourselves to a discredited logic?
Surely we must say to the Sauls who
inhabit our own palaces, "I'm sorry,
but this won't fit me. The way you
stayed hidden in your office does not
fit my priorities. Your emphasis on
short-term efficiency over long-term
capability does not support my plans.
The way you made employees feel
vulnerable and dispensable cannot
continue if I am to truly lead." Per-
haps it was this, returning Saul's proud armor, that demanded the most
courage from David, more so than even the prospect of fighting Goliath.

> *Does it make sense to fall into the old patterns, assume the old trappings and incentives, and go on dedicating ourselves to a discredited logic? Surely we must say to the Sauls who inhabit our own palaces, "I'm sorry, but this won't fit me. Perhaps it is this that demands the most courage.*

"I cannot go in these," he said to Saul, "because I am not used
to them." So he took them off. Then he took his staff in his
hand, chose five smooth stones from the stream, put them in the
pouch of his shepherd's bag and, with his sling in his hand,
approached the Philistine.

(1 Samuel 17:39–40)

This is what makes a champion. Not strength of arms, not wizardry
at spreadsheets, not a charismatic speaking style, but strength of heart,
conviction, and passionate faith. These things don't just come overnight,
and they cannot be purchased at the nearest graduate school any more
than they can be motivated by Saul's great treasure.

"Man looks at the outward appearance, but the Lord looks at the
heart." There are indeed times when it all comes down to just this. But
those are the times that matter, the times when new beginnings are born.

KING OF HEARTS

מֶלֶךְ־לִבִּים

It all must have happened pretty quickly. One minute an onlooker would have seen this odd shepherd boy petitioning the king, the next the strange scene of Saul's armor first offered then rejected. There were, though this would not be revealed until later, two kings there upon the valley. The king of trappings and privilege, who was in fact no king at all, and the true king about to be revealed, the king of hearts.

Here is how it happened: Without fanfare or ceremony, the puny-looking youth bounded down the slope and jumped down into the ravine where Goliath stood. The heads of onlookers began to turn, their arms pointing, and the lungs of two whole armies were filled with baited breath.

David directly got on with his business:

> Then he took his staff in his hand, chose five smooth stones from
> the stream, put them in the pouch of his shepherd's bag and,
> with his sling in his hand, approached the Philistine.
>
> (1 Samuel 17:40)

The scene is a classic one, David versus Goliath—the original. And the first thing it teaches us is a lesson in courage.

Ernest Hemingway is the one who defined courage as "grace under pressure."[1] Of this, David is one of history's first great exemplars. Let's not kid ourselves and think he didn't feel the pressure. There was real pressure, in the form of a nine-foot giant heading David's way:

> He looked David over and saw that he was only a boy, ruddy and handsome, and he despised him. He said to David, "Am I a dog, that you come at me with sticks?" And the Philistine cursed David by his gods. "Come here," he said, "and I'll give your flesh to the birds of the air and the beasts of the field!"
>
> (1 Samuel 17:42–44)

So David had very good reasons to be frightened by what he was getting into.

William Tecumseh Sherman, the Civil War commander, gave this as his definition of courage: "A perfect sensibility of the measure of danger, and a mental willingness to incur it, rather than the insensibility to danger of which I have heard far more than I have seen."[2] How well this description fits David's actions! For it was not ignorance of the danger that led him forward, but a particular estimate of it, a clear understanding of his strengths and weaknesses, and upon which he risked his all.

In short, David's courage was grounded in his faith in something greater than himself. There was something David cared about more than himself, a power, a principle which he embraced with steadfast commitment; in David's case, that something was the Lord his God. So armed, he went forward knowing the odds but confident of success.

Let's listen to his own explanation, as David responded to Goliath's threatening words:

> "You come against me with sword and spear and javelin, but I come against you in the name of the Lord Almighty, the God of

---

1. *Quoted in the* New York Times, *November 24, 1963.*
2. *William S. McFeely, ed.,* The Memoirs of General William T. Sherman, *vol. 2, New York: Da Capo Press, 1984, p. 395.*

the armies of Israel, whom you have defied. This day the Lord
will hand you over to me, and I'll strike you down and cut off
your head. Today I will give the carcasses of the Philistine army
to the birds of the air and the beasts of the earth, and the whole
world will know that there is a God in Israel."

(1 Samuel 17:45, 46)

What a contrast to the attitude displayed by Saul, who fought only
for his *own* prestige, his *own* program. He had shown courage in days
past, no doubt, particularly when danger was accompanied by good prospects of success. Yet how impotent this left him in the face of a clearly
superior enemy! Paralyzed by his self-serving motives in the face of overwhelming force, Saul could go neither forward nor back, like a mouse
trapped in a corner.

There are so many today who feel Saul's predicament. They feel
trapped in no-win situations, faced with oppressive work situations, with
superiors who are often unethical, misguided, or abusive. And yet, unwilling to risk a loss, holding no flame for which they are willing to risk
it all, they are thereby disarmed and stripped of power.

Let's not minimize the real chance, indeed the seeming likelihood,
that David would lose this fight. Surely such an encounter should not be
entered into lightly. Yet, in considering David's stand against Goliath, the
question that must be asked is this: Is there anything you are willing to go
down in flames for? Or, as in David's case, to have your head chopped
off for? When it comes right down to it, is there anything to which you
are more committed than self-preservation, however defined? Is there
anything that will empower you to withstand a threat to your performance
appraisal without cringing in surrender, regardless of the cost? If the answer is no, then you, like Saul, have been reduced to a slave. If no, then
both you and your boss know that, like Saul before Goliath, you have
been reduced to a captive. Pinstripes or royal robes, both can easily become a prison uniform.

In contrast, David comes forth as a model for what faith and genuine
freedom are all about. On the one hand, he is perfectly willing to be
struck down rather than betray the God he trusts, or to shrink back from
the principles he holds so dear. On the other, and this is perhaps the most

striking thing, he is absolutely convinced that he will not go down in flames. His final words, as he came close to wage battle, are these:

> "All those gathered here will know that it is not by sword or spear
> that the Lord saves; for the battle is the Lord's, and he will give
> all of you into our hands."
>
> (1 Samuel 17:47)

The New Testament's Book of Hebrews says this, "Now faith is being sure of what we hope for, and certain of what we do not see" (Hebrews 11:1). This is exactly what we find with David. He perceived his situation in light of a reality no one else saw, and he trusted himself to the unseen God he knew to be real. Armed with faith, David believed that with God's help he would win a fight that was otherwise hopeless, precisely because he believed this was His fight.

> "Now faith is being sure of what we hope for, and certain of what we do not see." *David perceived his situation in light of a reality no one else saw, and he trusted himself to the unseen God he knew to be real.*

David's example here does not license us to recklessly engage in foolish causes, nor to oppose our boss at every turn. The situation he was in happens rarely, perhaps a few times in any person's life. Yet it is those crossroads events that largely shape the character of our lives.

At the same time, David's courage in battling Goliath also depicts a daily pattern of faith and dignity, precisely because of his principled motives. Consider the implications for the area of ethics as just one example. When faced with an ethical challenge, we often hear nothing better than a utilitarian emphasis. Why is insider trading wrong? "Because the market system won't work well if confidence is eroded." Why should companies avoid polluting the environment? "Because there are many stakeholders who can exert negative pressure." Why should we pay a good wage? "Because it will lessen the likelihood of union organizing." But how impotent such approaches are in the face of our own greed and in the presence of competitors who cheat and get away with it.

David's response to the ethical temptations of our time would un-

doubtedly be this: "You are accountable to God, both now and in the end."
And so the way of faith is that of trusting in Him, precisely when the world
points the other way. With this fixed in his heart David was set free to
follow the course he knew to be right. Through faith David found courage,
and through courage, much in contrast to Saul and his followers, he found
freedom instead of fear. Faith produces freedom in a way that legislation
never can, giving us liberty to pursue the course we are convinced is right.

David, having mastered his own heart, now turned his focus upon
the task at hand. There he stood, unarmored before the hulking warrior,
carefully placing a stone into his slingshot. Eyeing the oncoming Goliath,
with a shield-bearer before him and armor covering almost his entire
body, David would have seen precious little margin for error.

Picture little David standing before the giant and imagine that you
are a strategy consultant giving him advice. Looking over the opponent
you would conclude that in a battle of raw strength, David was a goner.
But, you observe, if he can move quickly, staying out of the Philistine's
reach, if he can use the greater range of his own weapon to good effect,
then he might just have a chance. It would, of course, take a truly great
shot. While David had five stones, he probably would have had time for
only one or two shots before the giant was upon him.

David took his shot, and what happened amazed all the eyewitnesses.
Whirring the sling around his head he sent the stone straight for the
giant's head. Goliath's servant, reacting to the threat, lifted up the great
shield, but too late. Then with a crack, the stone impacted the great giant
right in the forehead, just beneath the rim of his helmet. "The bigger
they are, the harder they fall," it is said. And Goliath's fall must have
been a mighty one. Tottering back and forth, then accelerating toward
the ground, he finally crashed with all his great mass in one great, loud
heap. Little David had slain great Goliath!

So David triumphed over the Philistine with a sling and a stone;
without a sword in his hand he struck down the Philistine
and killed him.
David ran and stood over him. He took hold of the Philistine's

sword and drew it from the scabbard. After he killed him, he cut
off his head with the sword.
When the Philistines saw that their hero was dead,
they turned and ran.

(1 Samuel 17:50, 51)

How are we to account for so great a victory? Will we say that God
gave it to David? Undoubtedly, this is what David would say, but all who
watched saw it was David's hand that sent the stone flying. David was
fortified by his faith in God, and strengthened by the hand of the Almighty, and he triumphed against the odds.

Nor, in retrospect, can we call this a freak chance of luck. David
should have beaten Goliath, *if* he could make the shot. Once he was dead
everyone could see his weakness: he was really a big, strong, and slow
opponent, easily overcome by skill and speed. Indeed, Goliath's strength
had lain in the fear he inspired. Once this was overcome, Goliath was
not a very tough opponent.

Are such stunning triumphs possible for *you*, or are they only possible
for the great of every age, the heroes of history? Victories like David's
are won every day, mostly by little men and little women, who, though
unheralded by history, are just as pleasing in the sight of God. If you can
believe, then you can stand in David's shoes; if you win a triumph like
his, it will be with a hand trained for battle and a heart fortified by faith
in the God of victory. Indeed, this is how God wins His battles, by raising
up men and women of faith and therefore of valor; and it is their hands
that He is pleased to guide to success. David's skill was acquired in the
fields of practice, but his courage came by seeing God going before him
into the struggle. He wrote:

I have set the Lord always before me.
  Because he is at my right hand,
I will not be shaken.
Therefore my heart is glad and my tongue rejoices;
  my body also will rest secure,
because you will not abandon me to the grave.

Psalm 16:8–10

David's triumph over Goliath serves as a metaphor for every little guy who overcomes the fearsome bully. Think of the many start-up companies that have prevailed against the established powers. Generally, they did it just the way David did. They employed weapons suited to the situation, weapons Goliath or Saul would never think to use but which were perfectly fitted to their particular background and training.

How many times did David shoot stones out of that sling at curious predators drawing near his sheep? How many times had he made his dinner out of a hare or a bird felled by stones from his sling? David made that shot because he had practiced it thousands of times in the fields around Bethlehem. So while no sword-wielding warrior could ever have taken down Goliath, the shepherd boy was equipped with the perfect tools for a winning and innovative strategy.

Where do new and stunningly effective strategies and approaches come from? How does an individual or a company sow the seeds of innovation? The same way David prepared for that once-in-a-lifetime slingshot. By drawing upon the distinct skills and experiences that have shaped our own past, and by applying them to new areas where no one could possibly have anticipated their success. We are innovative when we are true to who we are, and when we are willing to risk it all with passion and purpose.

> *How do we sow the seeds of innovation? The same way David prepared for that once-in-a-lifetime slingshot. By drawing upon the distinct skills and experiences that have shaped our own past, and by applying them to new areas where no one could possibly have anticipated their success.*

In this sense, David's triumph resulted from preparation and practice. No one had watched, much less applauded, on those lonely nights when he fended off mountain lions and drove away the wolves. But those unheralded battles counted, just as the formative years of the executive-to-be yield their fruit when later tests come.

David's faithfulness in small things had brought triumph on the larger stage, so his time of preparation was now abruptly cut short. For after this great and heroic day he would no longer labor in obscurity. He was an overnight success of the kind that is years in the making, years in which courage, faith, and skill are fused together to produce a champion.

As we stand back and gaze with wonder on this great tale of valor and conquest, there is one more lesson still. A lesson not just about victory, but more centrally regarding the nature of genuine leadership: *The only true king is the king of hearts*. Here is the greatest calling for the executive, and the greatest challenge, too: to master his own heart, so as to inspire the hearts of others.

David stands up to Goliath and strikes him down, with faith, courage, and skill. Isn't that what leadership is all about? Isn't that what leaders ought to envision for themselves? There they were, the hosts of Israel's army—discouraged, helpless, defeated already in their hearts. But up strides the real leader and all this is swept away in one bold, inspiring stroke. Isn't this what we long for in a champion? One who risks himself to defend a cause and point the way for others. "The good shepherd lays down his life for the sheep" (John 10:11), Jesus taught; in the valley of the giant, David wonderfully prefigures Him.

Thus we add another image to our portrait of the executive leader. He must first be a shepherd and then a champion. The opportunities for such leadership abound. The company is faced with making a necessary, but drastic, organizational change, and everyone is sure it cannot work, it will not work, it's not worth making work. Then up comes the leader, and she sets the pace, challenging herself, making the sacrifices needed, boldly demonstrating by her actions what words so often fail to express. And suddenly the change can work, it will work, and it is worth making work.

> The only true king is the king of hearts. *Here is the greatest calling for the executive, and the greatest challenge, too: to master his own heart, so as to inspire the hearts of others.*

Or perhaps we are faced with a cost-cutting mandate, and all are afraid that it, like Goliath's sword, will surely undo all we have built. But then the executive stands up and declares, "The cost-cutting starts with me, with my expense account, and my bonus, and my salary, if necessary." And suddenly what was once an insidious threat becomes a noble crusade for everyone involved. The true executive, shepherd and champion, can make the impossible happen.

In just this way, when David struck down Goliath, all Israel sprang up into action. Soldiers who were terrified only moments before now found fearless blood in their veins. The enemies, once proud and boastful, went running for their lives, casting their weapons into the dirt.

This is the kind of executive who will set an organization on fire. "Man! Did you see what he just did! Did you see him stand up for what is right! Did you see the courage, the audacity!" Those are the words every leader should long to hear spoken about himself or herself. Isn't this what leaders are for, to win the battle of the heart, which is after all the real battle? A leader had been found for Israel, from the most unlikely of places, but possessing the one thing that makes a true leader, a true heart.

| *Chapter* |
| **3** |

MORNING STAR, EVENING SUN

WEAVING THE
STRANDS

מארג החוטים

Recently I saw an interview with a professional golfer who had won his first U.S. Open. He was talking about how this one event had changed his life forever. Suddenly he was known by thousands of people and the product endorsements were rolling in. But at the same time, he found his privacy slipping away, his life seeming to take a course all its own.

David's victory over Goliath was like this, only more so. By removing this threat to the nation and by setting such a remarkable example of valor, the shepherd boy captured the nation's heart with one stone's throw. No longer would he enjoy quiet nights tending the sheep; David's pasture would be growing rapidly, bringing both opportunity and danger, joy and sorrow. As is so often the case for those who achieve sudden fame, David found success quite a bit harder to swallow than hardship. David's great victory did not lead him beside still waters, but sent him swimming into the rapids of intrigue and deceit.

One immediate result of David's triumph, however, was that it got him into contact with Jonathan, King Saul's son and heir apparent to the throne. Jonathan was one of those rare individuals who stand out in his or her own time. He was a man of great courage and vision, maintaining a tenuous relationship with his father. In an earlier Philistine war, it was Jonathan's bold leadership that saved the nation. And though Saul was rescued by his son, his own force having largely deserted, we don't get the feeling this was much appreciated. Later on, in another battle, Jonathan unknowingly violated Saul's orders. When the king brought him forward to be executed, as Saul had promised for any transgressors, the army had rebelled and demanded the young prince's release. Despite his un-doubted loyalty and valor, and the bonds of blood that still held them together, Jonathan's deeds earned resentment from his father. In this, he would not be alone.

We are, indeed, tempted to view Jonathan as something of a tragic hero. His heart was in the right place, but having Saul for his father destined him for trouble. Jonathan would not have seen it this way, how-ever, instead counting it a privilege to offer his life to his people, his family, and his friends. Jonathan was pure inspiration, and the sight of David's victory over Goliath won his heart to the shepherd of Bethlehem forever.

> Jonathan became one in spirit with David, and he loved him as
> himself . . . And Jonathan made a covenant with David because
> he loved him as himself. Jonathan took off the robe he was
> wearing and gave it to David, along with his tunic, and even his
> sword, his bow and his belt.
>
> (1 Samuel 18:1–4)

How often, after we have climbed ladders to success, we fail to ap-preciate the joy and importance of genuine friendships, the true bond of shared purpose and conviction and faith. Foolishly thinking that our lives consist mainly of goals and obligations, plans and achievements, we easily neglect the precious relationships that are essential for the well-being of any heart. It is often said that no one will look back on his deathbed and wish he had worked one more item off his to-do list. But many will look back and sadly reflect on precious friendships neglected and left to wither. Genuine brotherly love, sisterly companionship, is absolutely essential for all who would pursue a path of purpose and meaning.

Here in the relationship between Jonathan and David begins one of the greatest stories of friendship of all time, a kinship shared by two bold and visionary leaders who drew strength and refreshment from each other. The story starts in the heart of Jonathan, a man who might have seen a threat to all his dreams of success in the brash young conqueror. He was the king's own son, the darling of the army, and heir to all his father's kingdom. Yet what had David's stand against Goliath done if not discredit this king and his house? Furthermore, with David on the scene Jonathan would no longer be the ideal by which every man measured himself. With one well-placed stone, David had vaulted to a position Jonathan had taken many years, many battles to attain. And yet, to the enduring credit of this genuinely heroic man, we can detect not a trace of envy or resentment in any of his words or actions. David was not a threat to Jonathan's hopes and dreams, for these had been given to something greater than mere ambition. It is here that we see the true stature of Jonathan's greatness.

We are not given many details of their first meeting, but we can imagine some of the dynamics. Jonathan was many years older than David, probably in the prime of his life. Indeed, it is not at all improbable that Jonathan was a hero to the provincial teenager. How awkward it must have been for David, when first he found himself on somewhat equal footing with this veteran champion.

Jonathan was undeterred by the many barriers that might have naturally dampened such a relationship, such as the difference in their age and social status. Approaching this newly forged leader, he fully and unreservedly embraced him to his heart. The Bible says that Jonathan "made a covenant with David." A covenant is the most sacred and binding relationship one can enter into—our marriage ceremony is an exercise in covenant-making. Imagine, then, the tenseness that might have been in the air as the great prince approached the young hero, his veteran soldiers looking on. "Will there be friction? Will they battle to see who will be top dog?" But then Jonathan breaches the space in a second, grasping his junior by the arms and exclaiming, "I will be your friend forever. I will love you as I love myself."

In case we might think there is a touch of ingenuousness in the prince's behavior, his next actions remove any doubt. Taking off his robe, his symbol of rank as prince, he draped it around David's shoulders. This was quite an amazing gesture! Was Jonathan cloaking David with the protection of his own position, perhaps anticipating trouble between David and Saul, or was he going so far as to acknowledge that this shepherd was the true heir? It's hard to tell. Either way, however, it is an extraordinary demonstration of friendship. Additionally, Jonathan arrayed young David with his military tunic, his sword, his bow, and his belt, thus expressing his sponsorship of the young hero and legitimizing him before the army.

David had no qualifications for such honor, save the quality of his heart, but it was this that Jonathan was looking for in others. How much we have to learn from this extraordinary man! He had the freedom to love and to honor the things that are true, right, and excellent, for he had overcome his own ambition and pride. He, like David, had found something greater than himself and he cast his heart into it, finding the true stature of greatness in the process.

The lessons here are many. The first is the badly needed reminder that friendships are vitally important to the executive. David found sponsorship in a time of transition; support and encouragement in a time of dizzying change. But he would receive many more wonderful gifts from Jonathan as time passed by. He would have Jonathan's prayers and heartfelt support. Through their friendship the champions would fan the flames of faith and purpose, providing each other the encouragement every leader needs to see clearly through trials and temptations. The Scripture says the soul of Jonathan was *knitted* with the soul of David, and it is the woven strands that are made truly strong and firm, and the isolated, hanging cords that are most easily cut off.

Years later, when David learned of Jonathan's death on the field of battle, he cried out, " 'I grieve for you, Jonathan my brother;/you were very dear to me./Your love for me was wonderful' " (2 Samuel 1:26). True friendship is indeed a special treasure, surpassing many things. It certainly surpasses the worth of promotions and bonuses and stock options. Yet how many people foolishly cast the living wealth of friendship into the furnace of personal ambition, sacrificing meaningful relationships for things that neither last nor satisfy the heart.

Finally, here in this grand and genuine gesture of Jonathan, the prince of Israel, we see again that love is the most powerful creative force imaginable. Much was changed that day because one man rejoiced in the achievement of another. One man loved his nation, his God, the cause that was at stake, and the truth to which he was committed, and that love transformed threat into possibilities, envy into admiration, rivalry into holy alliance. It is only those people who, like Jonathan, have given themselves away to something greater than themselves, who possess such freedom to love. So it is that love cannot be truly born except where faith has made its cradle; or as the New Testament puts it, "The only thing that counts is faith expressing itself through love" (Galatians 5:6). What a powerful principle for leaders, then and now.

David, for his part, would never forget the love and support given in a dangerous and uncertain time. And after all the glory and triumph of his later years, it was this friendship that he found most wonderful. David's son, Solomon, would later offer his reflection on the gift of true friendship, perhaps shaped by the experience of his father:

> *Two are better than one,*
>> *because they have a good return for their work:*
> *If one falls down,*
>> *his friend can help him up.*
> *But pity the man who falls*
>> *and has no one to help him up!*
> *Also, if two lie down together, they will keep warm.*
>> *But how can one keep warm alone?*
> *Though one may be overpowered,*
>> *two can defend themselves. A cord of three strands is not*
>> *quickly broken.*
>
> (Ecclesiastes 4:9–12)

David's triumph over Goliath, followed by the flight and destruction of the Philistine army, caused quite a sensation in the towns of Israel. As Saul's soldiers streamed back to their villages, their wives and children gave joyous welcome at the threshold of the home, parents came running for joy and from relief, and old friends reunited for rest and congratulations. The scenes were no different from those replayed down the ages when the specter of war is banished by the pealing bells of victory and peace.

Love is the most powerful creative force imaginable. Much was changed that day because one man rejoiced in the achievement of another. Love transformed threat into possibilities, envy into admiration, rivalry into holy alliance.

For his part, King Saul was off the hook, his long-feared defeat averted. Returning to the heart of his land, he was greeted by praise and celebration, and beaming faces of happy women and the awe-filled gazes of children. And yet it was not long before his heart, initially cheered by this praise, was turned to yet a darker shade of gray:

> When the men were returning home after David had killed the Philistine, the women came out from all the towns of Israel to meet King Saul with singing and dancing, with joyful songs and with tambourines and lutes. As they danced, they sang:

> *"Saul has slain his thousands,*
> *and David his tens of thousands."*
> (1 Samuel 18:6, 7)

It's not hard to track Saul's descent into hatred toward David. At first, relieved by the slaying of Goliath, Saul had given David high rank in the kingdom as a sign of his pleasure. But as David's name spilled off the lips of the admiring people, envy began to fester in Saul's heart. To him, they ascribed the defeat of thousands, but to David, tens of thousands. These of course do not reflect actual body counts, rather the people's estimate of their relative portion of the triumph. Saul had so long cherished, and felt he deserved, the embrace of the people, and now even this was shadowed by the young upstart!

> Saul was very angry; this refrain galled him. "They have credited
> David with tens of thousands," he thought, "but me with only
> thousands. What more can he get but the kingdom?" And from
> that time on Saul kept a jealous eye on David.
> (1 Samuel 18:8, 9)

Envy and insecurity, here were the twin pillars of Saul's restless heart, and their synergy would be more than terrible. We are told that David served with continuing success in Saul's administration, earning him the approval of the other officials, and this too undercut Saul's sense of comfort. David was the morning star and Saul the setting sun; the brighter David shined, the hotter Saul burned.

It is noteworthy, in comparing Saul's response to his son Jonathan's, that the latter had far more to lose in David's rise. Saul saw in him a potential, even inevitable successor; to Jonathan he was the replacement who would cut short his own rise. How much more poignant, then, is the contrast. All that Jonathan had given away, Saul clung to for his very life. One rejoiced and found love for the rising hero, the other only wretched loathing.

It would be a mistake, in light of this comparison, to say that Saul's anger stemmed from a lack of faith. Saul had faith all right. There were plenty of things he placed his trust in. He trusted his prestige, he trusted a firm grip on power, and he trusted the glory of his own name. Saul's identity was bound up in these things, as were his sense of security and his hope for the future. It is not, therefore, faith itself, but rather the *object* toward which faith is directed that shapes the heart.

It is the same for executives today. Do we trust the smiling faces of stock analysts, the approving reports from pundits, the glowing figures of short-term success? If so, these will shape our attitude toward our organization and its members, and give a particular tilt to our hearts. But if we put our trust in a shared credo, a set of guiding principles, a calling for our contribution in this world, then our hearts will be set on a more productive course.

On the individual level, each of us must face the question: "What do you trust?" "What are your hopes, your identity, and sense of security set on?" If our faith is in a certain level of income, a degree of status, or our grip on the rod of power, then ambition for these things will necessarily guide us. No wonder, then, that we communicate so little affection to colleagues and subordinates. No wonder we leave our spouses feeling empty and alone. No wonder that despite genuinely warm feelings for our children, so many resent them as often as love them. "For where your treasure is," Jesus taught, "there your heart will be also" (Matthew 6:21). So it is that what we love is what we are becoming.

> *If our faith is in a certain level of income, a degree of status, or our grip on the rod of power, then ambition for these things will necessarily guide us. . . . "For where your treasure is," Jesus taught, "there your heart will be also." So it is that what we love is what we are becoming.*

Jonathan put his faith in God, in His cause and the cause of his own people, and these were his treasures. With this faith he wove golden strands of strength and love. Saul trusted himself and the cause of his own petty ambition; out of that faith the silky black strands of loathing and intrigue were woven. Saul's jealousy would be a deadly poison, springing from the wells of his self-absorption, poison both for David and for himself.

SCHEMES OF THE WICKED

מזמות־הרעים

Almost everyone knows what it's like to be resented and disliked. There was that kid in school who just would not let up, who could not be turned from his meanness. Or, as many of us have known, there was the boss who obviously got a bad first impression, or perhaps sees something unknown but offensive in you. Nobody likes to be hated; it is unnerving at worst and unsettling at best. Imagine, then, having to face the animosity of a despotic king, one who controls the armies and the spies, who has the ability to twist justice and pronounce sentence. This disturbing situation is what David found himself in as he entered into King Saul's service.

Saul's malignant attitude found expression in two major ways. The first, and most direct, was an impulsive and embarrassing attempt to kill the young champion. God, it seems, had responded to Saul's hatred for David by renewing his spiritual torment and, as a result, the brooding king was once again seen behaving erratically.

> He was prophesying in his house, while David was playing the
> harp, as he usually did. Saul had a spear in his hand and he
> hurled it, saying to himself, "I'll pin David to the wall." But
> David eluded him twice.
>
> (1 Samuel 18:10, 11)

The term "prophesy" in the Old Testament has a wide range of meanings, depending on the context. Here it most likely serves as a negative characterization of Saul's ranting. Remarkably, in came David again, despite his newly gained high rank, to take up the servant's position and soothe his king with music. Based on the past, everyone must have expected things to take a turn for the better when, all of a sudden, Saul's royal spear came flying toward the harpist.

I'm sure there are quite a few musicians who have more than a little experience they can relate to David's! Certainly, there are numerous rising young executives who have dodged the boss's barbs as they have unexpectedly flown across the conference table. Like everyone else who has had such an experience and learned from it, David surely kept his eyes open, eluding Saul's missile on two separate occasions.

Gathering his wits somewhat, Saul then devised a subtle but well-worn tactic. "I'll send him off to die in battle," he thought; for if the rising star cannot be eliminated outright, then perhaps he can be ruined by other means. Saul's motive and intention are laid bare before us. He saw David as an outright threat to his throne and was scrambling to do him in:

> Saul was afraid of David, because the Lord was with David but
> had left Saul. So he sent David away from him and gave him
> command over a thousand men, and David led the troops in
> their campaigns.
>
> (1 Samuel 18:12, 13)

There was a problem with this strategy, however, for when the Lord is with the would-be victim, everything he does works out for his good! Each mission David was given, each greater challenge, brought him to higher levels of achievement and fame. The biblical narrator makes clear the secret to David's success, saying, "the Lord was with him." But there is also no doubt that, as this drama played out, David was simply head and shoulders above all others when it came to leadership. It is, after all, common that a rising executive whose reputation is based not on gimmicks or political workings, but on a clearer understanding of the tasks at hand and a firmer commitment to the demands of leadership, simply thrives where many had hoped he would flounder. The true executive flourishes on responsibility coupled with challenge. Indeed, when Saul sent David away from the jaded environment of the palace staff, he was doing him a favor. There, in a position of independent authority, David had ample opportunity to demonstrate his superior abilities.

How easy it would have been for Saul to blame God for his frustrations, and he probably did so on numerous occasions. But the fact of the matter is that if God was against the king's hand, it was because his was a hand directed by self-serving opportunism. And if the Lord was with David, it was a heart like His own He supported. A lesson learned and forgotten and relearned throughout time: *Wickedness simply does not pay.* Oh, it may seem to have its immediate usefulness, but in the end, in a universe ruled by a moral God, it just does not pay. Or, as David reflected it in sacred song:

> *He who is pregnant with evil*
> *   and conceives trouble gives birth to disillusionment.*
> *He who digs a hole and scoops it out*
> *   falls into the pit he has made.*
> *The trouble he causes recoils on himself;*
> *   his violence comes down on his own head.*
>
> **Psalm 7:14–16**

The more Saul hung David out to dry, the more the sun shone upon him. The worst way, it turns out, to get rid of a real leader is to put him on the front lines:

> When Saul saw how successful he was, he was afraid of him.
> But all Israel and Judah loved David, because he led them
> in their campaigns.
>
> (1 Samuel 18:15, 16)

You have to respect Saul's persistence, however, as he responded to his failure. Thrusting David into dangerous settings had clearly proved counterproductive to his plans, but he also could not afford to kill his rival outright. Well, he reasoned, if you can't beat them, get them to join you! Thus, Saul turned to the second classic maneuver in thwarting the rise of the unbeatable champion: He sought to co-opt David, this time through the offer of his daughter's hand in marriage.

> Wickedness simply does not pay *in a universe ruled by a moral God . . . The more Saul hung David out to dry, the more the sun shone upon him.*

There are a couple of interesting points to take note of in this turn of events. First of all, the daughter being offered to David now was the very one Saul had offered to whoever would kill Goliath, and yet here she is, available as a pawn once more. Is Saul such an unreliable leader now that he openly reneges on promised rewards? Or, perhaps, had David sensed the danger of too close an alliance with this king and let the matter go?

The second thing that is increasingly evident is Saul's growing preoccupation with establishing a dynasty. No longer interested in his own personal contributions to Israel, he simply wanted his name to live on in a line of future kings. If such a line must go through David, so be it. It is striking how familiar this is to the modern landscape; instead of familial bloodlines, it is often a generation of "old school" managers that long for self-preservation. But the motive is always the same: "I want my name to live on in honor after I am gone." In Saul's mind, as is often the case today, this end (which is a perfectly natural one) justified any means that might prove successful.

David's response to this offer shows clarity of thought, along with keen sensitivity to this dangerous threat. His reply was this:

> "Who am I, and what is my family or my father's clan in Israel, that I should become the king's son-in-law?" So when the time came for Merab, Saul's daughter, to be given to David, she was given in marriage to Adriel of Meholah.
>
> (1 Samuel 18:18, 19)

David was swimming in deep waters, indeed. David was faced with a situation that could lead him into open conflict with Saul. After all, what could be more offensive to the king than having his daughter's hand in marriage refused. However, to fall into this trap would mean falling into Saul's circle of influence. It would place Saul's name and Saul's mantle on the young champion who wanted to be anything but another Saul. To win the hand of Saul's daughter meant losing the war of hearts, and so David took the humblest route he could find and simply declined the offer.

This trap, though successfully evaded by David, would quickly be replaced by another. For Saul had one more daughter left, by the name of Michal, and this one had a crush on David. Now the king sent one of his courtiers, in a scene straight out of *Business Week* or daytime TV, who whispered into David's ear:

> "Look, the king is pleased with you, and his attendants all like
> you; now become his son-in-law."
>
> (1 Samuel 18:22)

You get it: "We'll make this easy for you; just join our team and things will work out wonderfully for you . . ." How bewildering it must have been to Saul and his courtiers (integrity and a sense of calling are always incomprehensible to such creatures) when David brushed aside this new suggestion, objecting that he had no proper bride-price to pay. This was quite a clever response, for according to the customs of the day Saul could hardly shame his daughter and his house by letting her go cheaply. But ever up to this sort of game, Saul struck back with an offer truly worthy of his sordid heart:

> When Saul's servants told him what David had said, Saul
> replied, "Say to David, 'The king wants no other price for the
> bride than a hundred Philistine foreskins, to take revenge
> on his enemies.' " Saul's plan was to have David fall by the
> hands of the Philistines.
>
> (1 Samuel 18:24, 25)

Now here is the wedding gift you just can't go out and buy at the mall! And oh, how the Philistines would love to get their hands on David! How they had waited, striking out from their fortified homeland, for a chance at the young hero. Even David appreciated the quality of Saul's maneuver, but he could hardly back down now. To make things harder, Saul set a time limit for David's gift, so the budding war leader would have to work quickly and thus dangerously. Saul knew that in order to win this kind of bride-price David would have to stick his neck out quite far indeed, perhaps too far.

Since time immemorial, there has been a scene played and replayed, a touching and humorous picture of the young suitor applying to the father for the hand of his lovely daughter. Saul sat waiting by the door, watching the timepiece, and before long up came David to claim his bride. Some suitors might bring flowers for the mother, others might bear credentials showing a solid reputation and good paycheck. David brought none of these, instead pouring into the outstretched hands of Saul not one hundred, but two hundred Philistine foreskins. Do not try this trick at home!

We are not told just what the king did with this bride-price, but it is likely it did not receive an honored place in Saul's home. Indeed, the Scripture's account is brief and modest, yet to the point: "Then Saul gave him his daughter Michal in marriage." No kidding. David's victory gained him not only Saul's daughter but also kept him free from the cage Saul had designed for him.

So David has had his coming-out party, and a challenging one it has been. Indeed, we may see this period as David's organizational coming-of-age. The sad fact is that one generally needs more than high aspirations and a sterling character to navigate such waters; one also needs a fair portion of organizational savvy. Young David received a rapid, but high-quality graduate education in the school of King Saul.

Yet, frankly noting David's ability to discern between goodness and foolish naïveté, it is essential that we once again observe the description that best defined his time in Saul's court; David served faithfully and exceptionally well. His heart continued to be set on the polestar established by his faith and purpose, and we can be sure that if this were not so, the biblical writer would have taken note. "God was with David," even if, sadly, his superior thought of nothing other than seeing him fail. These words, with which the Bible narrator sums this period up, are the bottom line on this chapter of David's life:

> David met with more success than the rest of Saul's officers, and
> his name became well known.
>
> (1 Samuel 18:30)

Sometimes there is no other safety than in a good performance. This was such a time for David, and even his success brought peril. But performance always pays, at least over time, and when coupled with a true and uplifted heart, it usually inspires as well. The sad fact is that to live by principle, to follow the path of a cause and not just a career, will often lead the rising star into the path of the setting sun. We will serve unjust superiors, insecure and frightened creatures who long for nothing more than our destruction, despite even our selfless service. But for those who dance, like David, amid the schemes of the wicked, he leaves not just his example, but these words of wisdom in sacred song:

> *Be still before the Lord and wait patiently for him;*
> *do not fret when men succeed in their ways,*
> *when they carry out their wicked schemes.*
> *Refrain from anger and turn from wrath;*
> *do not fret—it leads only to evil.*
> *For evil men will be cut off,*
> *but those who hope in the Lord will inherit the land.*
> *A little while, and the wicked will be no more;*
> *though you look for them, they will not be found.*
> *But the meek will inherit the land*
> *and enjoy great peace.*
>
> **Psalm 37:7–11**

DAVID, CHANGE AGENT

דוד שׂר־הפך

When David was summoned to serve as an executive officer in Saul's court, he embarked on a major transition in his career. For him this elevation came most suddenly. Knocking off Goliath allowed him to skip numerous middle-management positions that would otherwise have been mandatory. Now he found himself in that most tenuous and challenging of positions, and one that most rising executives will face at least once in their careers. David was now a change agent.

"Change Agent." These two words send shivers down the pinstriped backs of rising managerial stars. Definition: "a woman or man with too much responsibility, too little authority, and a willingness to embrace career disaster that is all too often rewarded with success." Change agency means skirting the line between hungry masses and nervous chieftains. Change agents often end up losing their heads, as the history of revolutions shows, and find safety only in success. But change agents are also heroes to those who desperately need new answers and new questions. They are heroes who have dared to love and, if necessary, to have lost. It is no surprise, then, to find that many, if not all, truly outstanding executives were by necessity change agents once or many times.

Even in the admirable company of change agents, David stands out as one of the all-time greats. Indeed, right from the start of his time in Saul's regime there is strong evidence that David methodically, thoughtfully, and boldly engaged in a program designed to challenge the existing paradigm. Though ultimately failing to engineer change from within Saul's regime, David the change champion planted the seeds that he would later harvest from outside the king's corrupt court.

> *Change Agent:* "*A woman or man with too much responsibility, too little authority, and a willingness to embrace career disaster that is all too often rewarded with success.*"

The first incident that clues us in to David's ambition to change the political situation in Israel has to do, unpleasantly, with Goliath's head. It seems that David kept this with him for some time, though not as a kind of perverse souvenir. Here is what happened in the immediate aftermath of David's victory:

> Then the men of Israel and Judah surged forward with a shout
> and pursued the Philistines to the entrance of Gath and to the
> gates of Ekron. Their dead were strewn along the Shaaraim road
> to Gath and Ekron. When the Israelites returned from chasing
> the Philistines, they plundered their camp. David took the
> Philistine's head and brought it to Jerusalem, and he put the
> Philistine's weapons in his own tent.
>
> (1 Samuel 17:52–54)

To understand the significance of David's strange actions we need to turn a few pages backward in Israel's history. Our first stop is to the time when a young Samuel was leading Israel. Back then, on this same turf, Samuel the judge had won a great victory against the Philistines, so that the "towns from Ekron to Gath that the Philistines had captured from Israel were restored to her" (1 Samuel 7:14). Does that sound familiar? Exactly the scene after the more recent defeat of the Philistines. David, perhaps alone of the exuberant victors, realized that this triumph did not exactly represent a new day in the history of Israel. The nation had been down this road before, literally. David perceived that unless this victory served to inaugurate a wholly new chapter of history, a fresh new opportunity for the nation, then his own triumph was destined to be just one high point in an endless back-and-forth struggle. Surely it was this thought that led David to the gates of Jerusalem, Goliath's bulky head in tow.

But why Jerusalem? In our day, as for the past three thousand years, the name Jerusalem is synonymous with that of Israel. It is the capital and the glory of Judaism. But in young David's day, Jerusalem was something of an embarrassment.

When the Israelites entered into the Promised Land, their task was to drive out the Canaanite nations who lived there and who were the incurable enemies of God. Although these nations were generally stronger than the people of God, by trusting in Him the Israelites felt confident of victory. The Book of Joshua recounts a golden age of triumph for the army-nation of Israel, advancing from success to success with the Ark of the Covenant of the Lord leading the way.

Joshua not only describes the seizure of the Promised Land but also its distribution to the twelve tribes of Israel. Interestingly, Jerusalem was allotted to two tribes—Benjamin (Saul's tribe) and Judah (David's tribe). Located on the border of these two tribes, Jerusalem was assigned to both and thus, both were responsible for driving out the pagan occupants, the Canaanite people called Jebusites.[1]

Of all the towns and cities given to Israel, Jerusalem was one of the few examples of the Israelites failing to drive out the Canaanite occupants. Joshua 15:63 tells us this:

> Judah could not dislodge the Jebusites, who were living in
> Jerusalem; to this day the Jebusites live there with the
> people of Judah.

The whole point of driving out these nations was to keep them from dwelling among the Israelites, and thereby corrupting this holy nation through their idol worship and gross immorality. And yet, there they were,

---

1. *Joshua 15:8 assigns Jerusalem to the Judahites, 18:28 to the Benjaminites.*

right in the midst of Israel down even to David's own day. This was not the only example, but it was the most glaring instance of the past failure and the present malaise. Instead of separating themselves from the pagans and their ways, David's people had begun to intermarry with the Jebusites, to pick up their customs, and thereby to fall away from the God, who was their protector.

Now we see what David was doing at Jerusalem. He was serving notice that this cancerous problem would be dealt with, on the basis of his God-empowered victory over Goliath and on behalf of the nation he did not even lead yet. Henceforth, he challenged, both to his countrymen and their enemies, Israel would return to its legacy and its strength; Israel would seek the Lord and thus receive His help as in days of old. And Israel would fulfill its given purpose.

How does this relate to the present-day change agent? In every way, for change is a commitment to a future based on principles and aspirations. David was reminding a forgetful people of their own espoused values and their present-day implications. Think of Martin Luther King and his stand against racism and segregation. It was precisely because he pointed to America's own espoused values, liberty and justice for all, that his words shook the nation. It is the same in the corporate environment. "Are we to compete on customer service?" the change agent asks. "If so, what are the implications of this for the kind of company we want to be, for how we must develop and manage those in our ranks who will provide that service, for how we must measure progress and dole out rewards?" Change agents lead not on the basis of power or position, but on the force of their arguments. They challenge the status quo, not on the grounds of their own revolutionary dreams but with the very values and principles that define the organization. It was with these motives, then, that David staked Goliath's head before the walls of Jerusalem.

> *Change is commitment to a future based on principles and aspirations . . . Change agents lead not on the basis of power or position, but on the force of their arguments. They challenge the status quo . . . with the very values and principles that define the organization.*

Therefore, the first qualification for the role of change agent is *vision*.

Not the sort of pointless slogans and wall-cluttering posters that pass for vision today, but a clear perception of the factors that must shape the future. A change agent is a visionary and a dreamer, but not a starry-eyed over-optimist. She is one with the *courage,* and that is the second prerequisite, to face the music today so there may be singing tomorrow. He speaks out against our inertia-driven methodologies and politically-minded priorities. She explains, persuades, and cajoles, unafraid to be challenged in return or to commit herself to the mandates of her own program. The change agent acts not just out of a conviction that the message is right, but that it is essential, that the very future hangs upon the thread of today's decisions.

It was pretty brash of David, a teenager of only recent fame and achievement, to single-handedly throw down the gauntlet before both the ancient thorn-in-the-side Jebusites, and his own people's negligent leaders. But, then, David was a *believer,* a passionate and driven believer, and that is the most important qualification for the change agent.

Being a believer, however, does not require that the change agent be a martyr. Let's be clear about this: David was a zealot, he was willing to go down for his convictions, but David also had no intention of achieving a glorious martyrdom. So in company with his passion and courage, he demonstrated the kind of exceptional judgment so greatly needed by the agent of change. *Excellent judgment,* then, is the final qualification David showed for the job of change agent.

> *The four qualifications David showed for being a change agent:* Vision, Courage, Passionate Belief, *and* Excellent Judgment.

David stands out as a change agent in these four qualifications. But there were also four things that David deliberately *did* that also stand out as a model for today's change champions. The first is that he walked the tightrope between challenging the leadership and *not confronting the leaders themselves.* How tempting it is to point a finger at the higher executive who can't make a decision or never gets his hands dirty, but the last thing the change agent wants is to make change more difficult than it already is. And there is nothing more likely to heighten resistance than offended dignity or feelings of betrayal. Thus we never see David confronting, or bad-mouthing, or playing upon the glaring inadequacies of King Saul.

He is not overheard in hallways throwing mocking barbs. Far from it; instead, he continued to render personal service to the soul-wracked king, thereby making a highly visible declaration of his loyalty.

David's fidelity, always one of his most pleasing characteristics, shines through brightly at this stage in his career. It's hard to take the abuse of a troubled leader and not get offended. Saul's behavior to Davis is typical of so many fearful executives who, feeling their hands slipping off the wheel of control, lash out arbitrarily, much as the king hurled his spear at the young hero. David chose the route of humility, dodging the shafts and managing the king as best he could. His honorable conduct made the king's behavior especially shameful, and no doubt won David more sympathy and support than a thousand complaints ever could have.

But what can you do, as a champion of change, when confronted by seniors who refuse to see what is so evident to you, who place their personal perks above the morale and commitment of the organization, whose thoughtless behavior forces you back one step for every two forward? You can do what David did, you can *lead by example*.

In the end, Saul's intentions to place David in harm's way greatly advanced the change agent's cause. For there is no worse place for an innovator and transformer than on the chief's staff. The staff of an executive like Saul is always politicized to the core, riddled by paranoia, and motivated by a desire to avoid failure of any kind. It is bound to be a place of frustration and impotence for the change agent. Lacking the authority to execute plans on his own, the staff manager must seek the approval of uninspired superiors who, more likely than not, are quite content with the status quo. It means expending energy tending the wounds and placating the fears of the king and his status-conscious courtiers. Still, we may think, the staff manager is uniquely placed to influence and persuade key players. But lacking the means to initiate change, the staff change master is more likely to be diverted or co-opted into the prevailing framework. In most organizations, the best way to persuade is to produce the numbers, and in some it is the only way. Therefore, to productively challenge an organization and point the way to new possibilities, the change agent must generally avoid staff positions and seek out a genuine opportunity to prove his point for right or for wrong.

So it was a blessing for David to be sent out to the field in command of troops. David's presence gnawed at the king, for it reminded him of what he no longer had, and what he had never really been. We are told the following as a summary of David's performance:

> Whatever Saul sent him to do, David did it so successfully that
> Saul gave him a high rank in the army. This pleased all the
> people, and Saul's officers as well.
>
> (1 Samuel 18:5)

Before long, David was in command of a thousand troops, whom he led into battle. Not understanding the source of David's success, Saul hoped for a disaster and actually resented the mounting victories of his own forces. David was indeed on the spot, and this is a place every change agent needs to become comfortable with. The new way of leading and the agenda for change had better be right, and David staked his own life and success on it. And as he continued to produce results so strikingly different from what had been the norm, each battle won more adherents than a thousand slide presentations ever could:

> In everything he did he had great success, because the Lord was
> with him. When Saul saw how successful he was, he was afraid
> of him. But all Israel and Judah loved David, because he led
> them in their campaigns.
>
> (1 Samuel 18:14–16)

So David *proved his point out in the field*. What, then, was the next challenge to come his way? The most dangerous of all, the not-so-subtle temptation to sell out for personal rewards. As we saw earlier, this was a slippery surface for David to negotiate, as Saul dangled not only his daughter but the status of son-in-law to the king. It was certainly the quick way to power, but at the enormous cost of independence and his chance to make a difference. In the end, all change leaders must temper the need to acquire positions of influence with a watchful eye for this kind of bait.

Clearly, though, David *was* interested in acquiring some levers of influence. Thwarting Saul's jealousy through loyal service, skirting the touchy issue of a royal marriage, and trying to keep his head on his shoulders in his vulnerable situation, it remains clear that he nonetheless proactively *accepted personal advancement as a route to corporate change.* This too the change agent must set out to achieve. Despite noble intentions and a self-sacrificing spirit, the fact remains that the flock demands a shepherd. When no one seems able to see the way through a time of change and apprehension, then the agent of change must seek to become change's leader.

We see this all too clearly when David accepted Saul's younger daughter in marriage. What was different this time, compared to Saul's earlier offer of the maiden's hand? It was this: In the demand for the booty of a hundred enemy foreskins, Saul had granted David the chance to accept on his own terms. Saul had said to himself, "I will not raise a hand against him. Let the Philistines do that!" Yet, when David returned with not one hundred, but two hundred Philistine trophies, he entered into his new status with his leadership and reputation not only intact but quite enhanced by the affair.

David the change agent placed little hope in his ability to persuade a man like King Saul to honestly and openly face the situation before him and to embrace a vision and a style of leadership that mocked all that he was. Of course, Saul at this point was an exceptionally malignant chief execu-

Four things David did as change agent: He avoided confronting the leaders themselves, *He* led by example. *He* proved his point out in the field, *and He* accepted personal advancement as a route to corporate change.

tive. But, although Saul is an extreme example, his resistance to change is typical of many senior executives. He was entrenched and isolated from reality. His thinking was reinforced by the status quo. At the end of his career, he most valued approval for the very principles the change agent now challenged. Therefore, David's balanced response to this situation provides a relevant model for today's visionaries and transformers who must work from within and below such a superior. He both respected and challenged, all the while he put his vision to the test, and himself with it.

As long as Saul sat on the throne, David would find neither approval nor safety, but he still planted the seeds of purpose and progress. In tending and defending those shoots of growth, David determined to win a prize greater than any Saul had even aspired to. *That is what it means to be a change agent: to plant and to sow new possibilities, and to tend them with passion and conviction.* Those who risk everything and still survive, as David did, emerge as the true leaders of a new generation.

SONGS OF
DELIVERANCE

MAN ON THE RUN

אדם־הרצ

You have had this dream. Something happens at work, maybe a sudden downsizing or a catastrophic failure, for which you receive the blame, perhaps an incident that turns your boss against you. With little warning you are out on the street, fired. Suddenly your savings are being depleted, your house goes on the market at a buyer's price, your Lexus is traded in for a Corolla. The smell of panic fills your nostrils as your pulse races upward. We all have such dreams at times, representing the fears we dare not face in the light of day.

David, pushing hard in his role as change agent and skirting the edges of disaster, had to have such dreams troubling his own nights. Continuing to hope that Saul and the government might change, he went on with his duties, and his attempts to both prod and support the king. Finally, it was Saul's son Jonathan who confronted David with the reality that he was himself avoiding: "My father Saul is looking for a chance to kill you" (1 Samuel 19:2), he revealed. And so the morning came when David didn't show up for work, while Jonathan attempted to talk his father out of his murderous rage.

"Let not the king do wrong to his servant David; he has not
wronged you, and what he has done has benefited you greatly.
He took his life in his hands when he killed the Philistine
[Goliath]. The Lord won a great victory for all Israel, and you
saw it and were glad. Why then would you do wrong to an
innocent man like David by killing him for no reason?"

(1 Samuel 19:4, 5)

Saul, a man deeply divided within himself, was placated by these
words for a time. But remember the reasons for his antipathy toward
David. It wasn't that David gave any sign of disloyalty, though he stub-
bornly refused to be bought. It wasn't that his accomplishments did not
further Israel's position, for they represented significant advancements.
The problem was not in who or what David was, but in the fact that he
exposed the truth about Saul. Every virtue of the young hero, every brave
act, every selfless sacrifice, was a ray of light exposing Saul's darkness.
And the people had taken notice. Saul hated David precisely because he
confronted him with his own failings and made him fearful of his status
among the people. David's actions were purposely designed to recall the
nation to its abandoned heritage, and because his leadership drew so
much energy and attention to himself, David was inevitably a marked
man in a kingdom ruled by Saul.

I would like to say that this is an unusual situation for the rising star
who leads by virtue and purpose. But the temptation for the declining executive to resent the challenge to his own legacy, to love his own past more
than his company's future, is a strong one. Jonathan succeeded in turning
Saul from his course, but only briefly, for in the quiet of the night and the
darkness of his heart, Saul burned with resentment. David went back to the
court and resumed his service to the king, but before long the poison of
Saul's heart vented itself in another uncoordinated attack on David's life.

This time, it was David's wife, Saul's daughter Michal, who confronted him with the danger of his situation. Evidently she had been
keeping tabs on events in the court, using her position as princess to
eavesdrop, and she learned of an imminent attempt on David's life. Helping him escape out a window of their apartment, even as the trap was
about to be sprung, she watched as he escaped for good into the night.

It was a pretty ugly situation in Saul's court. Loyalties were being divided, as his own son and daughter lent support to the man Saul had declared an enemy, both of them giving clear evidence of reluctance in their actions. Imagine the paralysis of such a headquarters, the frayed nerves and the darting eyes of the frightened and suspicious. Yet these are precisely what we can expect when senior executives care more about their own image than the future of the organization and cherish their own position instead of the purpose for which it was given to them.

What would you do in David's shoes? He has lost his position, his source of income, and his sense of protection. Without money and hunted by those who should be helping him, he was not yet without resources completely. For David, like so many faithful change agents betrayed like this, still possessed the clarity of sight and passionate heart that so many longed to see guiding the orga-

> *Divided loyalties, paralysis, frayed nerves, darting eyes of the frightened and suspicious. . . . These are precisely what we can expect when senior executives care more about their own image than the future of the organization.*

nization. This is the story of many of the great innovators of our own time. As their ideas are rejected by an insulated hierarchy, their challenges interpreted as disloyalty, their popularity taken as a threat, they find themselves cut off from support, sometimes, like David, even threatened and maligned by those they had tried to serve. Like David, their present situation seems extremely grim, and yet should they survive the storm, they might live to see brighter days ahead. So many of these innovators look back on the day of their betrayal as their own independence day, and the day their executive swaddling clothes were stripped off so that the true champion might emerge.

But what would you do, that first morning after a betrayal? Probably the very thing David did. He ran, desperately, and sought refuge. And it should come as no surprise that he turned to Samuel.

Interestingly, this is the first time since David's anointing that we see these two natural allies together. David, it seems, had not cultivated a mentor relationship with the aged prophet, just as he had done little to capitalize on his ties with Jonathan. Intent on winning over King Saul and buttressing the regime, David showed not only a certain innocence but a bit of overconfidence. Aggressive change agents do well to not only practice loyalty to the boss but also to cultivate leveraged sources of influence in order to mitigate the chances of a meltdown of the kind David now faced. Finally, now, he draws upon the wisdom and faith of the ancient man of God, Samuel, though too late to help him see the way through the labyrinths of Saul's court. Now David surely spent hours profiting from this accomplished executive's insight into leadership and governance. Together they traveled to Naioth at Ramah, which was a sort of monastery for the prophets of Israel, praying, talking, and reflecting on events past and events to come.

Saul's hand had now been played. Instead of making erratic, hot-headed attacks, he turned his hounds loose on David. And now he received word of David's refuge among the prophets, and of his open alliance with the old meddler Samuel, who had caused him so much trouble in the past. We can imagine his explosion at receiving this news: "Hah! Didn't I tell you they were plotting against me! It is mutiny!" Any resistance in the remnants of his heart was now broken; Saul would throw his full weight at the rebels.

David may have been a hero, but he was not immune to the trials of life. He was weak, and he knew it. He was desperate, and there is no doubt that he felt his confidence draining away. We know this because of the record he left in the Psalms, one of which bears a heading relating it to just this period of his life.

Psalm 59, which is a prayer to God, begins exactly the way our prayers would begin in such a situation:

> Deliver me from my enemies, O God;
>   protect me from those who rise against me.
> Deliver me from evildoers
>   and save me from bloodthirsty men.

Psalm 59:1–2

What a far cry this is from his bold, self-confident posturing before the face of giant Goliath! Was Saul not more offensive to God than Goliath was? Isn't the present situation at least *less* desperate than that earlier one? It is one thing, however, to sell your life cheaply to a clear and visible enemy, with your countrymen watching in wonder and praying for your success. It is quite another to find the hounds of your own household tracking you through the night, every neighbor and former friend a potential assailant!

We see how shaken David's confidence was as he continues his prayer, now seeking to persuade a seemingly absent God:

> See how they lie in wait for me!
>   Fierce men conspire against me
>   for no offense or sin of mine, O Lord.
> I have done no wrong, yet they are ready to attack me.
>   Arise to help me; look on my plight!
>
> **Psalm 59:3–4**

I wonder how many executives, rising stars or setting suns, really think that God is concerned with what they do and what happens to them? Does it ever occur to us, when a difficult decision looms, to get onto our knees and ask for wisdom? As we plot our ways through difficult days, perhaps like David trying to balance danger and difficulty while still attempting to make a difference, do we ask God for help? Are we so impressed with the strength of our own hands that we seek no aid from Him? How easy it is for us, particularly when, like David, we have early on achieved success, to forget the Author of our talents and abilities. As the apostle Paul remarks in the New Testament, "For who makes you different from anyone else? What do you have that you did not receive?" (1 Corinthians 4:7).

It is noteworthy that in the Bible's account of David's actions from the time of his entry to Saul's court to his precipitous flight, we see no words of prayer. So just as he had not sought out Samuel, a man known to bear the word of the Lord, neither had David sought the face of God. No wonder, then, that he felt the need to remind God of his situation, as though He were the negligent one; for though He watches over sparrows and nurtures even the lilies of the field, the prayerless man inevitably perceives God as far off and unconcerned.

Does it occur to us, when a difficult decision looms, to get on our knees and ask for wisdom? As we try to balance danger and difficulty while still attempting to make a difference, do we ask God for help? Are we so impressed with the strength of our own hands?

Perhaps David felt a little guilty for offering up his prayer only now that his need was so dire; this would explain the tentative nature of the prayer. Is it all right to call upon God in times of trouble, when we have forgotten Him in triumph? Can we, in repentance, hope for mercy? What we see in this psalm tells us we can, just as we can expect prayer to change the attitude that led to prayerlessness in the first place.

We see just this in the progression of David's plea. Halfway through his psalm, as David is trying to muster confidence that God is indeed paying attention, he writes, "O my Strength, I watch for you." He is looking, desperately seeking for the One who is Strength. And even as he prays, his own heart is lifted up, his own countenance lightened, so that by prayer's end we find him writing,

> O my Strength, I sing praise to you;
>   you, O God, are my fortress, my loving God.
>
> **Psalm 59:17**

David goes from anxiously watching for God to singing His praises, illustrating one of the ways in which prayer can make a difference for us. And to sing praises amid fear and danger is to have received strength for the heart. As Charles Spurgeon wrote, "Any fool can sing in the day. When the cup is full, man draws inspiration from it . . . [But] it is not natural to sing when in trouble, 'Bless the Lord, O my soul,' for that is a daylight song . . . Songs in the night come only from God; they are not in the power of men."[1]

---

1. *Charles Haddon Spurgeon:* Spurgeon's Sermons, *vol. 2, Grand Rapids: Baker Books, p. 169.*

The first thing we need in a desperate time is strength for a faltering heart, sustenance for a starving hope. And this is offered to men and women through prayer, even for desperate people like David, who had forgotten their God under sunnier skies.

One reason to pray before, during, and after the difficulties of our lives, is that prayer gives us a divine perspective on our situation. And, seeing our trial through the eyes of a loving God, we receive wisdom and strength. But David was looking for not just these, but for an intervention from God, and that is another reason for his prayer.

Do you believe that God involves Himself in the events of your life, your company, your country? It is striking to observe how many figures in history have dramatically challenged their times, have dared to stake out boldly on a path of purpose, and have done so believing in God's providence. Providence is God's intervention for the good of those who trust him. The letters of George Washington during the American Revolution are peppered with references to God's providence, as are the writings of Abraham Lincoln, and indeed those of most of this nation's early leaders. One of the noblest Americans ever, Robert E. Lee, wrote this regarding his own travails: "I know in whose powerful hands I am, and on Him I rely, and feel that in all our life we are upheld and sustained by Divine Providence."[2] The best days of our country have therefore been days of prayer, when humble men and women cried out for God to take part in the affairs of human beings.

David received a major lesson in the providence of God, for it was blatant divine intervention that saved him from the jealous hand of King Saul. When Saul got wind of David's union with Samuel, he sent men to Naioth to capture him and drag him back to face the music. As these rogues approached they found Samuel leading the prophets and David in worship. What an easy target! But here is the Bible's own account of what happened:

> The Spirit of God came upon Saul's men and they also
> prophesied. Saul was told about it, and he sent more men, and
> they prophesied too. Saul sent men a third time, and they also

---

2. C.f. John Woodbridge, More Than Conquerors, *Chicago: Moody Press, 1992, p. 27.*

prophesied. Finally, he himself left for Ramah . . . But the Spirit
of God came even upon him, and he walked along prophesying
until he came to Naioth. He stripped off his robes and also
prophesied in Samuel's presence.

(1 Samuel 19:20–24)

And so David escaped, having relearned a lesson about self-reliance
and prayer. David, like us, was slow to learn this lesson and quick to forget
it. But years later he would write another great psalm celebrating God's
presence in his trials, Psalm 139:

Where can I go from your Spirit?
　Where can I flee from your presence?
If I go up to the heavens, you are there;
　if I make my bed in the depths, you are there.
If I rise on the wings of the dawn,
　if I settle on the far side of the sea,
even there your hand will guide me,
　your right hand will hold me fast.

Psalm 139:7–10

Do we have a right to rely on God, turning our faces to Him in times
of trouble? We can when we trust that He is purposely working toward
the good of our organizations and fellow men. In ways both small and
large, the woman or man seeking to serve and seeking difficult change
can and should ask God for His help. Then, we should seek guidance
from the Word He has given us, the Bible, while keeping our eyes open
for His aid. In David's own words:

For the Lord watches over the way of the righteous,
　but the way of the wicked will perish . . .
Blessed are all who take refuge in him.

Psalms 1:6, 2:12

THE LIGHT OF LIFE

באור־החיים

The events of this period mark a major transition in the life of David. Up until the point where Saul's actions made his malicious intent crystal clear, David had been the assertive subordinate. Though challenging the prevailing order, his strategy involved winning the king's confidence in order to change Saul's regime. From this point forward, however, David was the leader of a distinct opposition movement, serving as both its symbolic focal point and the key to its success.

A difficult path lay before David as he scrambled to keep his dream of change alive. He must have thought back many times to the strange and wonderful day when Samuel the prophet came and poured the oil of anointing over his shaggy head, proclaiming him a king. He had been chosen, God revealed, not for what was seen on the outside but for what was on the inside. "Man looks at the outward appearance, but the Lord looks at the heart." As far as externals went, David was now about as low as you could get. Evidently, then, the time had come for his heart to be tested, so that all could see just what the young maverick was made of.

In the time elapsed between David's escape at the monastery of Naioth until Saul's death in battle, David began to build the makings of a new organization. Indeed, what David was starting, as he struggled to put the pieces of this new beginning together, was a new kingdom, a new dynasty, and even a new covenant for the people of Israel. Consciously or not, as David scraped from month to month, desperately seeking to survive, he was also fanning a spark until it burst forth in flames and spread throughout the land. Ironically, Saul's betrayal was ultimately for David's good, forcing him to plan and build without compromise.

David did build, with the raw material of hope, conviction, and purpose. David begins this stage of his career with a small band of a few unnamed supporters. It didn't take him long, though, to gather roughly four hundred armed compatriots and then settle them in a refuge where a new force could be exerted in the land. In addition to the family, friends, and colleagues who joined him, various strangers who had also suffered under Saul's pernicious rule began to look to him for the leadership:

> All those who were in distress or in debt or discontented gathered
> around him, and he became their leader.
> **(1 Samuel 22:2)**

David's opposition was to Saul, not to Israel, so he set about claiming the hearts of the people to his cause. His was a start-up government and army, erected by necessity in opposition to the present regime. The gauntlet had been thrown down once more and there, again, stood David outmanned and outgunned. If Saul had learned anything from experiences with David, he was the one who should have been most worried.

David's first priority was simply to survive. To this end he traveled south of Saul's home in Gibeah down to the town of Nob, near Jerusalem, where the high priest of Israel dwelt with the tabernacle of the Lord.

David's motive in going to Nob is not completely clear, but it seems that he intended to go into exile. The best explanation for his behavior is that he was seeking direct guidance from the Lord. Having already visited the prophets he has now come to the priests, who served before the Ark of the Covenant and had the authority to directly petition the Lord. It was a serious thing for David to leave the land of his fathers and seek refuge among the enemy nations; we should not be surprised that David would first visit the priests to gain confirmation of such a move. Perhaps, also, he simply wanted to pay his respects before going into exile for an unknown length of time.

However accurate these speculations may be, David clearly needed food for his growing force and hoped to acquire provisions from the priests. But at his approach he found less than a warmhearted welcome:

> David went to Nob, to Ahimelech the priest. Ahimelech
> trembled when he met him, and asked, "Why are you alone?
> Why is no one with you?"
> David answered Ahimelech the priest, "The king charged me
> with a certain matter and said to me, 'No one is to know anything
> about your mission and your instructions.' As for my men, I have
> told them to meet me at a certain place. Now then, what do you
> have on hand? Give me five loaves of bread, or whatever
> you can find."
> (1 Samuel 21:1–3)

Now this is a strange exchange! Evidently the high priest had at least some knowledge of David's position with regard to Saul. Because the king was growing less and less disposed toward rival sources of power, such as that of the religious authorities, Ahimelech had much to lose if he were to aid the fugitives. Therefore, David quickly perceived this man as a shaky source of support. So, in one of those split-second judgment calls we often come to regret, David lied. To explain why he was alone, David claimed to be on a special mission from the king, thereby employing the threat of Saul's name for his own benefit.

The somewhat grudging priest complied with David's request, taking the ceremonial bread from within the Lord's tabernacle, bread that by law was only to be eaten by the priests. The fact that David asked only for five loaves of bread indicates how scant his following was at this point. Receiving the food, David next inquired if the priests had any weapons he could take, claiming that the urgency of the king's mission required him to leave without his own. David knew very well that at least one weapon of note had been deposited there, and he was far too savvy to leave this powerful symbol behind. So it is that we read Ahimelech's reply,

> "The sword of Goliath the Philistine, whom you killed in the
> Valley of Elah, is here; it is wrapped in a cloth behind the ephod.
> If you want it, take it; there is no sword here but that one."
>
> (1 Samuel 21:9)

So off went David with the provisions, wearing a symbol of his earlier great victory. Indeed, David didn't stay around for any pleasantries at all, for among the visitors to the priests, he spied one of Saul's personal servants, a man who would recognize the outlaw and possibly turn him over to the king.

The next place we find David is outside the boundaries of Israel, in the realm of the Philistines to the west. And it was not just any Philistine town David went to, it was Gath. As in "Goliath *of Gath.*" Now imagine the townspeople setting their eyes on the very man who had single-handedly overthrown the Philistines' cherished hopes of victory over Israel, the man who had remarkably slain their great hope, Goliath. Adding insult to injury, he had the audacity to come bearing the very sword of the hometown hero he had slain!

It was not unusual in those days for an out-of-favor champion to seek refuge with his former enemies, provided he joined the ranks of his new sponsor. It is hard to believe, though, that this was really David's intention, particularly if he hoped to maintain the support of his own people. Most likely, he simply had nowhere else to go. In any case, the reception he encountered called for a change of whatever plans he may have had:

> But the servants of Achish said to him, "Isn't this David, the king
> of the land? Isn't he the one they sing about in their dances:
> 'Saul has slain his thousands,
> and David his tens of thousands?' "
>
> (1 Samuel 21:11)

Hearing this, David made yet another of those split-second decisions, this time turning to another ancient custom of the time:

> So he pretended to be insane in their presence; and while he
> was in their hands he acted like a madman, making marks on
> the doors of the gate and letting saliva run down his beard.
>
> (1 Samuel 21:13)

A common superstition of the time was that lunatics were touched by the gods and therefore were to be left alone; this is what David was counting on. He was just hanging on, compromising his dignity and, yes, his integrity, in the process. If nothing else, this is a testimony to the honesty of the Bible. It would be tempting to derive some hidden significance from these events, but it seems that David was simply trying to survive, using (and here, losing) his wits as best he could.

It is noteworthy that of the handful of psalms which are tied to specific events in David's life, three come from this very period, and they show clearly what was on David's mind. Psalm 34 is one of them, written about his time as a lunatic in Gath:

> *I sought the Lord, and he answered me;*
> *   he delivered me from all my fears . . .*
> *The Lord is close to the brokenhearted*
> *   and saves those who are crushed in spirit.*
> *A righteous man may have many troubles,*
> *   but the Lord delivers him from them all;*
> *he protects all his bones,*
> *   not one of them will be broken.*
>
> **Psalm 34:4, 18–20**

David was more than happy to gain his life at the mere expense of his dignity. Indeed, he took it as a sign of divine favor that in such a situation he had come out alive at all. Furthermore, he was learning real lessons in humility and dependence on God. Look, for instance, at his own emotional state: David's fall has left him brokenhearted and crushed in spirit. In Psalm 52, written in response to his escape from Saul's agents at Nob, we find him dwelling on the wickedness of his pursuers, while exhibiting real thanksgiving that yet God has protected him:

> *Why do you boast of evil, you mighty man?*
>   *Why do you boast all day long,*
>   *you who are a disgrace in the eyes of God . . .*
>
> *I trust in God's unfailing love*
>   *for ever and ever.*
> *I will praise you forever for what*
>   *you have done;*
>   *in your name I will hope, for your name is good.*
>
> Psalm 52:1, 8, 9

Sometimes all you can do is hold on, and at this point in his life David has nothing to hold on to but his trust in God. These episodes are perhaps given to us as highlights from this time of flight, or perhaps we should say lowlights, considering just how grim the situation was. Yet still David held on, avoiding the pursuit of a now thoroughly depraved Saul and dealing with various crises as they came along. He didn't survive without compromising his self-esteem and his integrity, however, and he would come to regret this. But he did hold on, despite his questionable decisions and imperfect faith.

Ultimately, David found safe haven back in Israel, in the cave region of Adullam southwest of Bethlehem. So far he had not accomplished much for himself, and yet his perseverance paid off handsomely. Little by little, many others who were suffering under Saul's rule, as well as those who were too closely aligned with David to be safe elsewhere, found their way to his refuge. Indeed, it is striking that David's whereabouts were well-enough known that four hundred rebels made their way to him! This suggests that resistance to Saul's rule was becoming more widespread, for it is clear that many possessed knowledge of David's whereabouts without Saul and his henchmen finding out.

There is an old adage among soldiers that says, "If you can't think of anything useful to do, at least give your enemy a chance to make mistakes." And this is what David had done by holding on. We can well imagine that many Israelites had struggled within themselves about the fate of their former valiant leader. They needed time to wrestle with the issues and gain the courage to stake their all on principle. Perhaps they would need to make arrangements for their families before setting out to support David. He had bought himself time—time in which Saul's maliciousness would argue eloquently for David's cause, time for the faint of heart to make decisions—and the time paid off handsomely. There, in the mountain refuge of Adullam, he made his beginning.

The first mandate for anyone starting over is to simply persevere. After achieving this, David now turned to the next stage in his strategy, which was to *challenge those on the sidelines*.

There are always many people on the sidelines, and often most people can be found loitering in the margins. They can respond to inspired leadership, they can complain about injustice and incompetence, but left to themselves they are more than willing to *not* take a solid stand. Leaders often make the mistake, perhaps from a compassionate spirit, of not confronting such people. The shepherd has a bent for protecting those who are weaker, for taking all the burden on himself or herself. But in reality this is no help to the fence-sitter; though he may survive by avoiding all confrontation, this survival comes at a fearsome cost to the soul.

What is it that fence-sitters be challenged to do? To live up to the spirit of the offices they hold. To fulfill their own particular calling, and to uphold all the principles and values this involves. To make something of themselves, to make a stand, to back up the words they dare only to whisper in hallways, and to take up the mantle of true integrity.

David recognized the importance of calling people off the sidelines. First, of course, there was Jonathan, Saul's virtuous son. David had visited him, the man who had sworn undying loyalty, on his way to the priests at Nob. Jonathan's position was a difficult one indeed, yet David called upon him to make good on his promise of friendship. He wanted one last confirmation that reconciliation with the king was impossible and, at great risk to himself, Jonathan sought this out, ultimately warning David to flee for his life. Obligated to his father, he remained with Saul, and yet he did so with his sympathies for David and his cause well known. During this episode the two friends renewed their bond of friendship, as is so often needed in turbulent and threatening times:

> So Jonathan made a covenant with the house of David, saying, "May the Lord call David's enemies to account." And Jonathan had David reaffirm his oath out of love for him, because he loved him as he loved himself.
> (1 Samuel 20:16, 17)

David's wife was another who was forced to choose sides, and she had done so in assisting David's earlier escape. But, when later confronted by Saul, she reconsidered her options and falsely accused David of threatening her life.

Just by turning to the priests at Nob, David had forced these sworn men of God to place themselves in harm's way. Here they had the choice between the *formal rules* of tradition, for the bread they had given David was lawfully meant for only the priests, and the *spirit* of that heritage, for those very loaves which rested within the tabernacle symbolized the merciful providence of a loving and just God. Centuries later, Jesus would cite just this episode as a right application of law: The form of regulations must not be allowed to override the intent with which they were given. Jesus observed that to commend the priest's violation of the letter in order to fulfill the spirit is also to understand these words from God: "I desire mercy, not sacrifice" (Matthew 12:7).

In times of crisis, when the future hangs in the balance of the present, a leader challenges stale institutions, knowingly places people at risk, instead of allowing slow death. He initiates action on the part of others, simply on the merits of his own conviction.

This is what the leader must do in times of crisis, when the future hangs precariously in the balance of the present. He must challenge stale institutions to view themselves in light of their true meaning and purpose. When necessary, she knowingly places people at risk, instead of allowing slow death. By his very actions, the leader forces those less hearty to commit themselves, to look deeply into the mirror and take charge of their self-definition. He initiates action on the part of others, simply on the merits of his own conviction. To do otherwise is no mercy. In David's case, his knowledge of God's will, acquired through his interaction with Samuel and his own prayer, gave him particularly clear convictions and powerful words of exhortation.

There is another reason why leaders, and particularly those seeking to initiate change, must challenge those on the sidelines. The calling must find expression or else it dies. There comes a time when the upstarts can no longer just talk about what they would do if given a chance; *there must be action.*

Two things happened that forced David's hand. The first was Saul's retribution on the priests at Nob. Doeg the Edomite, the servant who had seen David with the priests, brought word to the king of his visit. Here was the situation, which gives added insight into Saul's rapid moral decline:

> And Saul, spear in hand, was seated under the tamarisk tree on the hill at Gibeah, with all his officials standing around him. Saul said to them, "Listen, men of Benjamin! Will the son of Jesse give all of you fields and vineyards? Will he make all of you commanders of thousands and commanders of hundreds? . . . No one tells me when my son makes a covenant with the son of Jesse. None of you is concerned about me or tells me that my son has incited my servant to lie in wait for me, as he does today."
>
> (1 Samuel 22:6–8)

Here we see the position Jonathan's loyalty had placed him in, as well as the rabid paranoia with which Saul viewed David. At this time, Doeg, another of the soulless courtiers who always surround such leaders, viewed this as an ideal chance to share his useful information:

> "I saw the son of Jesse come to Ahimelech son of Ahitub at Nob. Ahimelech inquired of the Lord for him; he also gave him provisions and the sword of Goliath the Philistine."
>
> (1 Samuel 22:10)

So Saul summoned Ahimelech to his court at Gibeah, together with the whole company of priests, to stand before a charge of treason. The

High Priest defended himself by stating that David was, after all, captain of Saul's bodyguard and had come to Nob on royal business many times before. Besides, he went on, he knew nothing of any affair involving treachery from David. But Saul, blinded by rage and unwilling to listen, turned to his guards and ordered all the priests slaughtered. When the soldiers stood still in shock, for it was beyond infamy to strike down the priests of the Lord, Saul had Doeg himself do the dirty deed.

Saul had passed into absolute tyranny, and he followed this crime by wiping out the town of Nob, including the families of the priests. It would be like the President of the United States ordering the leaders of all the religious denominations to the White House, then striking them down one by one. The shame of Saul's act surely stunned the nation and mobilized support for the rebel David.

One of Ahimelech's sons managed to escape this carnage and bring the news to David. His words struck as sword blows up David's heart. Now David sorrowed over his lie, for his duplicity had not protected the priests by letting them continue to straddle the fence, but instead kept them from acting in their own defense. It was with humility, then, that he comforted the youth, taking the responsibility for what had happened upon himself:

> "That day, when Doeg the Edomite was there, I knew he would
> be sure to tell Saul. I am responsible for the death of your father's
> whole family. Stay with me; don't be afraid; the man who is
> seeking your life is seeking mine also. You will be safe with me."
> (1 Samuel 22:22, 23)

David was discovering that the man who would be king must act the part even when he is not wearing the crown. So when the next important news reached David, he was prepared to respond differently. The Philistines had attacked again and seized the Israelite town of Keilah. David, asking Ahimelech's son to inquire of God, then decided he would act as the defender of that nominally important town. When his refugee band hesitated at the thought of leaving their mountain stronghold, David, now seeing firsthand the need for positive action, prevailed upon them, and the ragtag army went forth on behalf of the nation.

There comes a time when survival must translate into achievement, when activity must bring life to the organization. This is what David was doing, with conscious intent. Remember that David's vision, for which he was risking all, was of a nation with its twelve tribes united, completing the work of their fathers in securing a homeland, and serving as God's beacon for the nations. What an ideal chance this was to strike a blow for unity! David therefore decided to turn from his weak defensive posture and take action for the security of his vulnerable countrymen.

We have seen that Saul's regime, originally based on support from all twelve of Israel's tribes, had devolved into little more than a dictatorship presided over by his own tribe of Benjamin. Now David would support weak and isolated Keilah, a village with nothing to give him in return. What an opportunity to make a statement! The time of survival was past and from now on David must build his future on the strength of action and the merit of his cause.

David did save Keilah, and in so doing won legitimacy for his ragtag army, even though coming out into the open exposed him to dangers from Saul's forces. He had survived, and as every passing day brought with it evidence of Saul's moral deterioration, more and more Israelites responded to David's action. What we are seeing is a pattern for others in situations like David's: The change agent having been cast aside, the innovator denied access to implementation, the herald whose warning voice is snuffed out. All these must pass through similarly rough waters if they are to land on safer and greener shores. Some, like David, are blessed with a forceful break from a leadership that would only snuff out the spark, while others remain tempted by ambiguous, yet false hopes. But in all such cases, the leader must aim himself or herself to seize the vital chance for action, for there only may be one golden chance.

> *The man who would be king must act the part, even without the crown . . . The time of survival was past; from now on David must build his future on the strength of action and the merit of his cause.*

Let David's experience be an encouragement, then, and an example of how a powerful idea can overcome brutal force. For what was at stake, after all, was these two opposing approaches to leadership, not merely the fortunes of two rival leaders. Saul had naked might, and with this alone he sought to control and dominate. There are modern applications, more or less subtle, of this very theme. It was against such might that David set forth the power of a dream, a vision with vigor and moral urgency. History bears record that in the short run leaders like Saul can and often do prevail. But the cork can only be held in the bottle's neck for so long; in the long haul the idea always wins. Our own generation, witnessing the fall of totalitarianism behind the Iron Curtain, has been blessed with a demonstration of precisely this truth. For tyranny is a beast that devours itself, whether in nations or in corporations. And history is a tale that is always written on the living hearts of human beings, a drama played out in a world ruled by a just God. So dreams remain alive along after the tyrants are gone.

> *Naked might versus the power of a dream . . . In the short run leaders like Saul can and often do prevail. But history is a tale that is written on the living hearts of human beings, a drama played out in a world ruled by a just God. So dreams remain alive long after the tyrants are gone.*

It was knowing that his cause would indeed prevail that gave life to the anxious heart of David, and it was therefore in the shadow of death that he found inspiration to write these words in song, from Psalm 56:

> When I am afraid,
>   I will trust in you.
> In God, whose word I praise,
>   in God I trust; I will not be afraid.
> What can mortal man do to me?
>
> For you have delivered me from death
>   and my feet from stumbling,
> that I may walk before God
>   in the light of life.
>
> **Psalm 56:3, 4, 13**

THE CRUCIBLE OF CHARACTER

מצרף־לבים

When do we learn what kind of person someone really is? One way is to see him in a crisis situation, with all his normal supports removed. This is the situation in which we have been viewing David. On the run from King Saul, David revealed who he really was, including some cracks in his developing character. Fear's hand has gripped David's heart, as his memoirs in the Psalms make clear. But his reaction to fear and danger has also shown another side to him, a tenacity that values results above personal pride. David is willing to grovel in the dirt like a lunatic if this will buy him one more chance to turn the tide. And over time, through his sheer persistence, David's faith is asserted and proved anew. Indeed, David emerged from the crisis stronger than when he went into it; as so many have discovered while passing through the flames, his heart was refined by the heat of the fire like precious metal.

On the one hand, then, we have seen that through his perseverance, David has held fast to God. But there is another side to this story, and one that is most relevant for us. *David has held fast to God, yes, but God also held fast to David.* He was there to listen and to speak when David finally called. When David challenged those on the sidelines to join the fight, God moved within them to respond. This is God's promise to those who trust in Him, as He spoke through the prophet Isaiah: "When you pass through the waters, / I will be with you; / and when you pass through the rivers, / they will not sweep over you. / When you walk through the fire, you will not be burned; / the flames will not set you ablaze" (Isaiah 43:2).

There is something else, however, that has ruined more good men and women than failure and trial ever have. It is success, the dangling opportunity for security and advancement. For so many of us, this is the crucible where the fire burns hottest, and it is when faced with the prospect of personal triumph that our character is most tried and tested. So it was for David; indeed, it was when fortune smiled and providence opened a door that his faithfulness was most truly revealed.

David's moment of truth occurred in the cave where his band had found refuge once more in the Judean hills of Adullam. The foray to rescue Keilah had proved successful but dangerous. When Saul learned that his enemy had come out into the open, he quickly pounced, chasing David and his men within an inch of their lives. It was then that Jonathan, who was commanding a force in his father's army, came once again to David's aid:

> And Saul's son Jonathan went to David at Horesh and helped
> him find strength in God. "Don't be afraid," he said. "My father
> Saul will not lay a hand on you. You will be king over Israel, and
> I will be second to you. Even my father Saul knows this." The
> two of them made a covenant before the Lord. Then Jonathan
> went home, but David remained at Horesh.
> (1 Samuel 23:16–18)

The Hebrew text literally says that Jonathan "strengthened his hand in God." This is the kind of friend we need in times of trouble, the one who will grasp our shaking hand and set it on a solid support. "Don't be afraid," he told the fugitive hero. "My father Saul will not lay a hand on you." Now on what basis does Jonathan say this? Indeed, at that very moment Saul was bearing down on David's hideout. But Jonathan surely recalled two factors, God's past promise to make David king, and his own knowledge of the state of Saul's heart.

Standing in the line of fire is always difficult, but to stand alone is more than most of us can bear. Even someone as courageous as David must surely tremble in fear. At such times, Jonathan is the kind of ally we most require, the kind who steps out beside us to face the attack, giving strength and steadiness to shaking hands. "Look, David," he was saying, "do not fail to put your trust in God. Remember the Lord's promise that you *will* be king. But in case you are doubting, let me tell you something. Even my father Saul knows that this is how it will end up." The Jonathans of this world are few and far between; they are the hero's hero, and the friends of God.

What comforting news this was for David, particularly the information regarding King Saul. How he must have imagined his foe, sure and steady as he closed in for the kill! How easy it is for us to overrate our adversary when our lives or careers are threatened. In fact, David now learned, it was Saul who was living in fear, Saul who was acting out of desperation.

There is an important lesson here for us, when calamity seems hovering over our shoulders, and it is found in Jonathan's very first words: "Don't be afraid." This is what we must hear when our competition has us on the run and defeat is nipping at our heels. "Do not fear," for fear is the enemy within our own walls, more devastating than the siege weapons outside. Fear causes us to abandon our best weapons, to deviate from our plans and principles, the very guides to lead us out of despair. Fear makes a Goliath out of merely mortal enemies; and if you should face a true Goliath,

> *"Do not fear" . . . For fear is the enemy within our own walls, more devastating than any siege weapons outside. Fear causes us to abandon our strongest weapons, to deviate from our plans and principles.*

fear steals the courage you so badly need. Faith, however, can inspire you to overcome the odds.

The first time David was rescued was when Jonathan appeared at just the critical moment to strengthen David's resolve. The second rescue came from the hand of God Himself:

> Saul was going along one side of the mountain, and David and
> his men were on the other side, hurrying to get away from Saul.
> As Saul and his forces were closing in on David and his men to
> capture them, a messenger came to Saul, saying, "Come
> quickly! The Philistines are raiding the land." Then Saul broke
> off his pursuit of David and went to meet the Philistines.
>
> (1 Samuel 23:26–28)

So David survived again, this time by God's manipulation of events so as to pull Saul off his trail. Now given the opportunity to escape, David and his band headed back into Israel to his old hideout in the cave of Adullam. No wonder, in light of God's faithful presence, he was able to write this in Psalm 31:

> *But I trust in you, O Lord,*
> *I say, "You are my God."*
> *My times are in your hands;*
> *deliver me from my enemies*
> *and from those who pursue me!*
>
> Psalm 31:14, 15

When Saul had managed to chase off the Philistines, he quickly learned of David's whereabouts and renewed his pursuit. Taking three thousand choice soldiers, he began the methodical work of searching out the crags and caves where he was sure he would corner his prey. Here a remarkable turn of events occurred that would offer the most dramatic overthrow of Saul's plans, and here too came the great challenge to the true mettle of David's heart:

> He came to the sheep pens along the way; a cave was there, and
> Saul went in to relieve himself. David and his men were far
> back, in the cave. The men said, "This is the day the Lord spoke

of when he said to you, 'I will give your enemy into your hands
for you to deal with as you wish.'"

(1 Samuel 24:3, 4)

There David and his men were, like little mice, huddled back in a
cave and shrinking in fear, no doubt completely aware of Saul's warriors
camped right below them. How confident Saul must have been in his
strength and security, but even the great king must answer the call of
nature, and, according to the commands of the Hebrew law, he was for-
bidden to relieve himself within the confines of the camp.[1] So the king
moved off alone to a harmless-looking crevice, there to do his business.

"God opposes the proud but gives grace to the humble," says the
Bible (James 4:6) — but we didn't expect God to show such a sense of
humor! What a sight for David and his men when, into their pathetic
little hideout strode the unsuspecting king, dropping his drawers and
squatting beside a boulder. We can hear the shocked delight in the voices
of David's men — "Can you believe it! This is your chance, David! Can
there be any doubt that this is from God? Go get him!"

But let's think about this for a while. This is every persecuted man's
dream. Isn't this what you fantasize about the guy whose petty politics
killed your last project, the boss who unfairly gave you a bad appraisal,
the fading executive whose lack of vision forced you out? Wouldn't you
just love to have the tables turned? Isn't the mere presence of an opportunity proof of divine sanction to strike? Or, from a different angle, is there
any doubt that Saul would not have hesitated to seize the kind of opportunity David now had? *"Go get him, David, this is the chance you've
dreamed of!"* David's men didn't have to be so insistent; the voice inside
his head would have been plenty loud enough.

So up crawled David, quietly and unnoticed, until he was within
striking range of the unsuspecting Saul. And then he hesitated. *"Don't
hesitate, David!"* his supporters must have silently gasped. *"Finish him
off!"* But David did hesitate, before finally reaching forward to act. But it
was not Saul himself for which he reached, it was only his royal robe
lying upon the ground.

---

1. *Deuteronomy 23:12 provides for the sanitary conditions of an Israelite camp, giving detailed
instructions on the placement of latrines, etc.*

Here is the understated report of the biblical narrator:

> Then David crept up unnoticed and cut off a
> corner of Saul's robe.
> (1 Samuel 24:4)

Imagine the outrage of those who had thrown their lot in with David, as they watched Saul about to finish up his business, slip on his garments, and then quietly depart from the cave. In the blink of an eye the golden opportunity was gone. Back came David, his face ashen but calm, even as the look on their faces showed utter frustration for his apparent failure of nerve. But it was not nervelessness that stayed David's hand; indeed as he returned to his hiding place David was conscience-stricken for even the small gesture of vindictiveness he had gone through with:

> He said to his men, "The Lord forbid that I should do such a
> thing to my master, the Lord's anointed, or lift my hand against
> him; for he is the anointed of the Lord." With these words David
> rebuked his men and did not allow them to attack Saul. And
> Saul left the cave and went his way.
> (1 Samuel 24:6, 7)

Is this an overworked sense of honor? Or just some abnormal religious sense of duty? Far from it. Rather, it is a window on the true nature of executive leadership. There upon the defenseless back of Saul, David had seen his own future, and his task as the leader of that future. This was a chance, a precious and rare chance, to define the character of his future organization.

What if David takes the opportunity afforded him, relieving himself from danger by the very weapon that had been pointed at him. What if he ascends to the leadership of Israel by striking down his predecessor? What difference does it make? He would be the new ruler anyway. It makes all the difference in the world if your ambition is for something more than simply personal elevation. *How* you succeed makes all the difference in the world if you are leading others not just to success but to a meaningful purpose.

Surely these were the thoughts racing through David's mind as he fingered his blade and drew near to the vulnerable king. What seemed like an obvious course of action to the onlookers became more complicated with every step he took toward Saul. As he set out from his hiding place, David's thoughts were likely on his own rights, the wrongs that had been done to him, his chance for an end to this long nightmare. But as he came closer to Saul his thoughts moved forward to his followers, and to the principles of justice and mercy he had tried to inculcate. With the next step came thoughts of the nation, and its great need for an example. And then, finally, to the God he claimed to trust, the God who had shown such mercy for the fugitive David, and the leadership that God had anointed him to provide. This is the thought process of the true leader; thoughts of self give way to thoughts of those who follow, to thoughts of the dream they treasure, to thoughts of the purpose with which the executive has been entrusted, finally to thoughts of the great trust for which he is accountable.

David respected the fact that Saul had once been anointed by God. "The Lord forbid that I should do such a thing to my master, the Lord's anointed," David concluded. To have been anointed by God is to have been set apart by Him, for His service. If God has anointed the king, and Saul was anointed by God's command at the reluctant hands of the prophet Samuel, then the king is God's to deal with. And if David expects his own anointing to be respected, then he must also respect the anointing of the wicked King Saul.

There are moments of truth that define every leader, critical choices that reveal the true character of his heart. Once these crossroads are passed there is no going back. It is these that communicate in the clearest terms, that define the reputation,

> *This was a chance, a precious and rare chance, to define the character of his future organization . . . How you succeed makes all the difference if you are leading others not just to success but to a meaningful purpose.*

that make or break the man or woman as leader. And as David drew near to Saul it became clear to him that this was one of those critical moments. *"In what way am I different from Saul? Does it make a difference that given the chance Saul would have struck without mercy?"* How clear such a decision is in retrospect, but in the heat of the moment it is a very crucible where the fires of temptation test the character of a leader.

David did stay his hand, he did walk away, after venting his rage in the symbolic gesture of cutting a corner off Saul's robe. And in that moment, when he turned from shedding blood, his leader's heart was not only revealed but also refined.

There are moments of truth that define every leader, critical choices that reveal the true character of the heart, and there is no going back.

Once he got his bearings, David's mind moved quickly. Quickly rebuking his followers' bloodlust, David himself came forth from the mouth of the cave, exposing himself to the view of his enemies below.

> Then David went out of the cave and called out to Saul, "My lord the king!" When Saul looked behind him, David bowed down and prostrated himself with his face to the ground. He said to Saul, "Why do you listen when men say, 'David is bent on harming you'? This day you have seen with your own eyes how the Lord delivered you into my hands in the cave. Some urged me to kill you, but I spared you; I said, 'I will not lift my hand against my master, because he is the Lord's anointed.' See, my father, look at this piece of your robe in my hand! I cut off the corner of your robe but did not kill you. Now understand and recognize that I am not guilty of wrongdoing or rebellion. I have not wronged you, but you are hunting me down to take my life. May the Lord judge between you and me. And may the Lord avenge the wrongs you have done to me, but my hand will not touch you. As the old saying goes, 'From evildoers come evil deeds,' so my hand will not touch you."
>
> (1 Samuel 24:8–13)

The drama speaks for itself, and like all highly symbolic action it speaks loudly. Here is what God provided for David, not a chance at vengeance but rather the precious opportunity to reach the hearts of those who watched. An opportunity to define the issues with a clarity words alone can never attain. The piece of robe in his hand and the living Saul were irrefutable evidence not only of David's innocence but of the virtue of his cause. At the threshold of temptation David refused to seize mere *formal* authority and thus he gained the more precious *moral* authority, which is always and only earned amid the flames. And in the light of David's mercy, how dark was the sight of King Saul.

What were the principles that led David to set aside personal privilege and vengeance? The first is this: Evil need not be given into. "Two wrongs don't make a right," we say, but there also is something more profound at work here. Just as Saul's maliciousness cannot withstand David's virtue, brutality withers in the face of real mercy and righteousness. Injustice and malice always carry within them the seed of their own destruction. Evil will destroy itself, and will be put away by God in His own time, so that the just need not follow its precepts.

This is the point of David's parable, "From evildoers come evil deeds." To overcome evil with evil is to become evil yourself. The high road is the path of mercy, of faithfulness, of righteousness. How important this is today, for we *are* confronted with injustice in our working lives, with vindictiveness and with petty greed. How is the leader to respond to this corruption? The apostle Paul writes in the New Testament,

> Do not repay anyone evil for evil. Be careful to do what is right in the eyes of everybody. If it is possible, as far as it depends on you, live at peace with everyone. Do not take revenge, my friends, but leave room for God's wrath, for it is written: "It is mine to avenge; I will repay," says the Lord. On the contrary:

> *"If your enemy is hungry, feed him;*
>   *if he is thirsty, give him something to drink.*
> *In doing this, you will heap burning coals on his head."*

> Do not be overcome by evil, but overcome evil with good.
> **(Romans 12:17–21)**

In these words we find not only the path of the faithful but the path of the leader as well.

Evil need not be given into. Evil will destroy itself, and will be put away by God in His own time, so that the just need not follow its ways . . . "Do not be overcome by evil, but overcome evil with good."

That leads to the second statement being made by David. To him, Saul is not first and foremost an enemy, not a piece in a great power game. Saul is a man, and David will treat him as a fellow human being. This too is what David saw as he crept up behind the defenseless enemy in the cave. He saw that Saul was, in reality, nothing but a weak and vulnerable man. The way to approach those who dehumanize others is to treat them with humanity, honor, and kindness. Not with the kind of ingratiating manipulation Saul was used to from the courtiers, but with truth spoken through the medium of grace.

Lastly, David is making clear to the broader audience, to his own soldiers and Saul's, and to all of Israel, which will learn of this day's events, that the true leader is the one who submits before he demands. The things David will, as king, demand of others, he does himself first. The executive who demands faithfulness must first be faithful, he who calls others to purposefulness must first be purposeful, and he who will demand service must first take the place of the servant, even at great sacrifice and risk to himself. David will not condemn Saul's faithlessness without first being faithful himself; in submission before Saul he entrusted himself not to the king's hands but to the hands of God.

Even Saul was not so hard-hearted as to reject such an example as this. Imagine, then, the effect it had on others! Turning to look on the prostrate David, and seeing the piece of cloth that might well have been his life, Saul responded:

> "Is that your voice, David my son?" And he wept aloud. "You are more righteous than I," he said. "You have treated me well, but I have treated you badly . . . the Lord delivered me into your hands, but you did not kill me. When a man finds his enemy,

does he let him get away unharmed? May the Lord reward you
well for the way you treated me today."

(1 Samuel 24:16–19)

What a remarkable statement! For even if the Sauls of this world
cannot be trusted, they are still flesh and blood men and women. Tyranny
is a great evil in ours and every age, and yet the tyrant is the first to be
captured by his power. So David disarmed the weapons of Saul in a way
that murder never could have done. With his own words Saul is undone
forever. In the presence of a mercy he has never known, Saul finds himself unable to avoid the truth. And so he goes on, saying,

"I know that you will surely be king and that the kingdom of
Israel will be established in your hands. Now swear to me by the
Lord that you will not cut off my descendants or wipe out my
name from my father's family."

(1 Samuel 24:20, 21)

What remarkable words they are from this king, words that confirm
what Saul's son Jonathan had stated, that the king has known all along
that he is playing out a predetermined drama. David honored this request
by giving his oath to Saul that he would not revenge himself on Saul's
family, and years later he would have opportunities to honor this word.

How remarkable, after all this, that David does not press the matter
and demand the crown. It was God
who anointed both Saul and David;
David is content to leave matters for
God to resolve. David is ambitious,
yes, but he is not grasping, and there
is quite a difference. David is also,
however, no fool, and he refuses to
place himself at Saul's mercy. Saul has
changed his heart before, though not
in so dramatic a fashion as this, and

> *The executive who will
> demand faithfulness must
> first be faithful, he who calls
> others to purposefulness
> must first be purposeful, and
> he who will demand service
> must first take the place of
> the servant.*

his capacity for malice was not to be underestimated. And so the enemies
went their ways.

David's actions here at the cave of Adullam are remarkable in the eyes of anyone who has ever felt the heat of hatred and vengeance. Indeed, the standard he sets is so high, the quality of his virtue so imposing, that we are tempted to despair of ever reaching such heights ourselves. Such virtue cannot be faked, *but it can be cultivated.* And the journey down the path to virtue is always walked by faith, through trust in a God who vindicates His own, and by the passion for a purpose that transcends even petty human motivations.

But before passing from this scene, however, let's not fail to take note of David's continued growth as an executive leader. From the triumph over Goliath, through the time of danger in Saul's court, and all through the fugitive journeys, David has been the heroic champion. He was the one the Israelites could trust, who could be counted on to lead the people to victory. To follow David was to observe his brilliance shine forth, to watch in wonder as his magic unfolded.

Inspiring as such leadership is, it is always short-lived unless it molds the organization in its own image. Here, then, is the next stage in David's journey as an executive leader, to hold up before the organization the mirror of principle and of truth, to demand faithfulness and integrity not only in himself but in his followers as well. He must dramatically shape the values that will govern by invisible power, and sow the seeds of purpose for tomorrow through the principles and values displayed today.

> *Heroic leadership is always short-lived unless it molds the organization in its own image. Here, then, is the next stage: to demand faithfulness and integrity, and dramatically shape the values that will govern by invisible power.*

No leader, no executive, can win all the battles. As he crept forward in the cave, in the heat of the refining fire of opportunity, David became more than just a hero, he became a true leader. For the greatest leadership is that which creates something new *in the followers* out of the raw materials already there, and which wins not only today's battle but also gives birth to principles and values for tomorrow. This is the champion's challenge, to provide an example that is not merely symbolic but which offers a genuine and irrefutable challenge to the very identity of those who follow, and which cannot be denied even by the enemy himself.

Chapter 5

A Servant's Reward

A WALK IN THE DARK

הלך יחשך

After the events at Adullam David is now fully prepared to assume the mantle of chief executive. He possesses a vision for the nation, the twelve tribes united in the land of promise, fulfilling their divine mandate as God's witness to the surrounding pagan nations. David has shown the willingness to make personal sacrifices for that purpose, and to demand and inspire the same from others. Therefore, when David ascends to the throne it will not be the crowning of a career but rather the beginning of his dream's realization.

When David and Saul parted company at Adullam, the end of their conflict was decided in the minds of all Israel. Now came a time of impatient waiting; Saul's demise was eagerly anticipated by everyone, perhaps even himself, yet annoyingly slow in coming. Despite Saul's repentant words, neither he nor David expected him to change his course. Unwilling to strike Saul down and with nothing further to gain from direct confrontation, David is therefore left to stew. For a man like David, waiting is the hardest chore possible. But wait he must, for news that was as inevitable as it was predetermined in the counsel of God, news that the crown had finally passed from Saul to him.

———

Initially, it seems David expected a quick demise for Saul; in the ancient Orient, a discredited sovereign could usually count on being dispatched by his own courtiers, or even his children. However, perhaps due to the influence of Jonathan, no action was taken against the lame-duck king of Israel. Time passed and David's force whiled away the time in their wilderness fortress, before long finding it more and more difficult to procure provisions and probably harder still to keep from going stir-crazy.

David was now in one of the most excruciating of all situations, waiting for the chance to take charge. You know the feeling. The boss has promised that a golden opportunity is just around the corner. "Your name has been floated around," you are told. Everyone, you are sure, knows that you are the one most qualified for that big position waiting to be filled. "Are they really going to make me go through all the steps in the progression," you ask yourself, "and let less qualified people move on up?" You know where this kind of thinking is leading, if you've even been in such a position. Self-pity. Resentment. Touchiness.

Wait a minute! Weren't we just praising David as the icon of true leadership? The one ready and perfectly suited to be king? We certainly were. Yet what happens in the aftermath of the triumph at Adullam, as David is forced to stew while Saul takes his good time to vacate the throne, leaves us with the conclusion that delay and inactivity were grating on our hero's nerves.

We are going to be seeing a trend with David, that he can rise to astonishing heights of moral and physical courage, but also that his triumphs often lead him to an arrogance and self-righteousness that are less than admirable.

Furthermore, something happened to bring a whole new set of pressures on David:

> Now Samuel died, and all Israel assembled and mourned for
> him; and they buried him at his home in Ramah.
>
> (1 Samuel 25:1)

We have noted that David never really had a mentor, but Samuel was as close to one as he had. Furthermore, we have well documented the huge moral center of gravity that gathered around the ancient prophet and judge. With this influence, this counterweight to Saul's ethos of opportunism, removed from the scene, what would this mean to the balance of forces in Israel? Had God removed Samuel to clear the way for David as His champion? Or, with this symbol of the past no longer around to remind the people of their heritage, would David get swamped in a deluge of greed and divisiveness?

Apparently, questions like these were bearing down on David, for he immediately fled from the center of action and went out into the desert once more. And there, the strain of events began to take its toll upon him.

The first indication of this occurs as a result of David's need for provisions in the desert. There he and his stalwart band were, the heroic champions of Israel's future, and there was Saul back in Israel with all the provisions they could want. Around him, too, were the fat and lazy civilians, unconcerned and uncommitted, even though their very future rested upon David's sacrifices. Soldiers never like to hear about others having it easy, particularly those who profit from their sacrifice of sweat, hardship, and blood.

What really set David off was news of a rich sheep herder named Nabal, who was using the security provided by David's presence to shear his sheep, and yet refused to offer provisions from his overflowing stores. David's initial action was to send a party up to Nabal to respectfully ask if he might spare some of these sheep to feed his hungry men.

Nabal's response was typical of those whose single-minded pursuit of wealth leaves them unconcerned with matters of politics, war, or the well-being of their fellow human beings:

> "Who is this David? Who is this son of Jesse? Many servants are
> breaking away from their masters these days. Why should I take
> my bread and water, and the meat I have slaughtered for my
> shearers, and give it to men coming from who knows where?"
>
> (1 Samuel 25:10, 11)

Talk about poor judgment! Nabal's response was a classic in the art of self-destruction. David, the anointed of the Lord, was outraged at this insult to his dignity and his cause. Was he not the centerpiece of God's plan for the future and the champion of all virtue!

David's material response to Nabal's snub was to send four hundred armed men to advance on Nabal's estate. Nabal, for sure, had shown both arrogance and callous disregard for both David and God. And yet it is impossible to justify the self-righteous and ruthless sequence David set in motion. Here are David's own words as he vented his frustrated rage:

> "It's been useless—all my watching over this fellow's property in
> the desert so that nothing of his was missing. He has paid me
> back evil for good. May God deal with David, be it ever so
> severely, if by morning I leave alive one male of all who
> belong to him!"
> (1 Samuel 25:21, 22)

Not the sort of vow one should make lightly. A far cry this is from the self-controlled and purposeful example David had set just a short while earlier when he spared Saul's life.

As is so often the case with wealthy but idiotic men, Nabal's hide was saved by his subordinates, in this case a conspiracy involving his servants and his wife. Learning of what was about to transpire, one of the house-boys ran to Abigail, Nabal's wife, and informed her of the dire situation. Racing to avert the disaster, Abigail loaded up provisions and raced off to intercept the advancing marauders. Encountering David along the way, she threw herself at his feet, both acknowledging the wrong her husband had done and offering the needed provisions. Sizing up the situation well, she directed her appeal both to David's inflated sense of importance and his sense of duty:

> "Please forgive your servant's offense, for the Lord will certainly
> make a lasting dynasty for my master, because he fights the
> Lord's battles. Let no wrongdoing be found in you as long as you
> live . . . When the Lord has done for my master every good thing
> he promised concerning him and has apointed him leader over
> Israel, my master will not have on his conscience the staggering
> burden of needless bloodshed or of having avenged himself.
> And when the Lord has brought my master success,
> remember your servant."
> (1 Samuel 25:28–31)

A wise woman, indeed! Apparently both the Lord and David came to this very conclusion. When the next morning Abigail informed her husband of what had happened he fell over half-dead, and a few days later God struck him dead for his greedy insolence. David proceeded, wisely, to take Abigail as his own wife, in the place of Saul's turncoat daughter, Michal.

Every executive, particularly a fast-rising one, needs an Abigail to come at critical times to effectively confront the kind of behavior David was exhibiting. As the proverb says, "Like an earring of gold or an ornament of fine gold is a wise man's rebuke to a listening ear" (Proverbs 25:12). With both grace and compelling clarity, Abigail cooled off David's wrath and effectively reproved him for his attitude. What a difference between her conduct and that of Saul's courtiers!

David, suffering from the absence of Samuel's influence, had been richly blessed by her well-placed and courageous words:

David said to Abigail, "Praise be to the Lord, the God of Israel, who has sent you today to meet me. May you be blessed for your good judgment and for keeping me from bloodshed this day and from avenging myself with my own hands."
(1 Samuel 25:32, 33)

Though David was behaving erratically, he was at least willing to listen to earnest and thoughtful advice. And lest we think his behavior in this affair was either far-fetched or unusual, let us look into our own hearts. How easy it is for even the most self-sacrificing among us to think ourselves essential to the greater good. What an affront to us, especially when we are embarked on a cause of purpose and value, when others stand in the way or deride our efforts. It is only a small step from the commitment of yourself to a cause, to the commitment of the cause to yourself. First you point others to the great purpose, and in response the others point to you. If you are not extremely careful, you become the first to confuse the two. Even if your sense of self-importance is essentially accurate, it is a force too powerful to be toyed with. Consider Saul as the prime piece of evidence; and if we are honest, we see a Saul lurking within the heart of even David. Especially in a time of protracted strain and sacrifice, all of us are susceptible to the kind of thinking he has shown here. As Matthew Henry observes, "Long trials are in danger of tiring the faith and patience even of very good men."[1]

> *It is only a small step from the commitment of yourself to a cause, to the commitment of the cause to yourself.*

Our next picture of David comes with yet another run-in with Saul. The king, it seems, had returned to his lack of sense with the passing of only a little time, so when some informants gave him the location of David's new desert hideout, down he went with another large force. David's men, by now, had gained a close familiarity with the land, so it wasn't very long before the prey was stalking the hunter. Sneaking up on Saul's now completely dispirited and undisciplined force, David and his companions found the entire force asleep and Saul completely unguarded. Aparently the sight of Saul served as a tonic to remind David of who he was and what he stood for, for again he refused a golden chance to take vengeance into his own hands. This time instead of a piece of Saul's robe David made off with his spear and canteen:

> "As surely as the Lord lives," he said, "the Lord himself will
> strike him; either his time will come and he will die, or he will
> go into battle and perish. But the Lord forbid that I should lay a
> hand on the Lord's anointed."
>
> (1 Samuel 26:10, 11)

Again, David uses this opportunity to bring public attention to his righteousness and Saul's malicious and unfair persecution, this time waking up the whole army to plead his case; once again Saul responds to David with tears of repentance and assurances that David will ultimately triumph. Here we see the king at rock bottom, no longer fit for the most basic executive tasks and clearly an emotional wreck. David made his way off again, more disgusted than ever with the state of events:

> But David thought to himself, "One of these days I will be
> destroyed by the hand of Saul. The best thing I can do is to

---

1. *Matthew Henry:* Commentary on the Whole Bible, *vol. 2, p. 333.*

> escape to the land of the Philistines. Then Saul will give up
> searching for me anywhere in Israel, and I will slip
> out of his hand."
>
> (1 Samuel 27:1)

Let's not be too hard on David, this kind of life would get old for any of us. But what is he thinking? Or, rather, which David is doing the thinking now? Is it the champion of faith who slew Goliath? The espouser of purpose and principle who twice spared his enemy's life? Or is it the pretended lunatic, dribbling spit down his chin in the Philistine capital? This is not a hard one to figure out, because the next thing we learn is that once again David is headed off to exile in Gath, capital of the Philistine leader and once the hometown of Goliath.

Does David have a dual personality? No, of course not, but clearly the stress of his situation is chipping some cracks in his emotional state and his judgment. It is striking to see how little awareness David shows of this decline, and yet all the marks are there. Earlier we noted that David tended to follow up success with self-reliance and neglecting the God who had stood by him. His sudden rise after Goliath's defeat was accompanied by a notable absence of prayer and psalm-writing. Sure enough, the same is found in this case. There are no psalms ascribed to this period after David's victory of principles at Adullam, and during this stretch of activity there is not one record of him entering into prayer. Thus, not consulting either the Lord or the priests who accompany him, a fed-up David follows his impulse and joins his band with the perennial and quintessential enemy of his people, the Philistines.

> So David and the six hundred men with him left and went over
> to Achish son of Maoch king of Gath. David and his men settled
> in Gath with Achish. Each man had his family with him, and
> David had his two wives: Ahinoam of Jezreel and Abigail of
> Carmel, the widow of Nabal. When Saul was told that David
> had fled to Gath, he no longer searched for him.
>
> (1 Samuel 27:2–4)

Let's see if we can figure out what David is trying to pull off. The Scripture shows him chatting pleasantly with the Philistine king, winning his favor and receiving the town of Ziklag to be his base of operations in Philistia. What was David's selling point? He is the rival of Saul, the enemy of the Philistines. So what if David's defeat of Goliath thwarted their earlier attempt to capture Israel? What's a little compromise between two men of the world like David and Achish?

David's army, we are told, stayed in Ziklag for almost a year and a half, serving as mercenary raiders on behalf of the Philistine king. What, we might ask, was the point of refusing to save his skin by killing Saul, if David then went on to save himself by selling out to the enemy? If the whole point of David's rebellion against Saul is a vision of national purpose and unity, how is this served by playing the part of the consummate free agent?

It is hard to avoid the conclusion that David here is plotting a course that if unchecked will shatter his cause upon the shoals. This time it is not a case of perseverance under desperate circumstances, for Saul's utter inability to destroy David has been well established. Saul is on the ropes and David, unwilling to throw the knockout punch himself, has decided to kill time by consorting with his enemies. If he is not careful, he too will be unfit to reign as champ.

In David's defense, it must be noted that though he spent this time raiding the neighbors of Achish, king of the Philistines, he did not do his marauding against the Israelites (although he carefully misled Achish into believing he did). David was careful to not directly undermine Israel during this period, no matter how badly he was undermining his own reputation. It seems, in fact, that David was using his Philistine refuge to raid several minor enemies of Israel, the Geshurites, the Girzites, and the Amalekites, plundering and utterly slaughtering the enemies he overcame. The picture is not a pretty one. While David was engaged in bloodthirsty slaughter—ostensibly, it seems, in accordance with God's dictates of holy war, but actually to ensure that no survivors were left to inform Achish of his activities—the Philistine king exulted in the seemingly irreparable breech he thought was forming between David and his Israelite countrymen.

> And such was his practice as long as he lived in Philistine territory. Achish trusted David and said to himself, "He has

become so odious to his people, the Israelites, that he will
be my servant forever."

(1 Samuel 27:11, 12)

Fine bedfellows these two have become, each seeking to use and
ensnare the other. It is not to David's credit that he seemed to gain the
upper hand on Achish, nor was it ultimately to his advantage. Surely he
must have realized that it was only a matter of time until his loyalty was
put to the ultimate test by a Philistine attack against his homeland. Evidently David was banking on Saul's demise occurring before this could
happen. As it turned out, God was not compliant with David's scheme.
Before long the orders came: David was to marshal his force to join a
Philistine invasion against Saul's Israel.

David was in quite a fix now, and remarkably, he seems not to have
anticipated this turn of events. Improvising at high speed, however, he
made such a profession of loyalty to Achish that he persuaded the king to
designate this force as his personal bodyguard, thus allowing David's men
to march at the rear of the Philistine army to protect the king. David was
showing himself to be clever all right, so much so that the other Philistine
commanders began to suspect this peculiar arrangement. Together,
Achish's generals demanded to know why the Israelite augmentees were
lurking in the rear, and despite the king's naive defense, they prevailed
upon him to dismiss David and his men:

But the Philistine commanders were angry with him [Achish]
and said, "Send the man back, that he may return to the place
you assigned him. He must not go with us into battle, or he will
turn against us during the fighting. How better could he regain
his master's favor than by taking the heads of our own men? Isn't
this the David they sang about in their dances:

'Saul has slain his thousands,
and David his tens of thousands?' "

(1 Samuel 29:4, 5)

Were the Philistine generals on to David's real plan? It would not be
a surprise to find that it was indeed David's intention to turn against the

Philistines at the last minute; if so it was s clever expedient that might well have worked. But aren't expediency and opportunism Saul's motif as a leader? How misguided of David to place his trust in such a deceptive ruse to bring about a new day for his people. Yes, it might have worked, and in so doing would have established him as a true successor to Saul.

Earlier in this story I noted that the free agent mentality is foreign to the mind of the shepherd-leader. Here we see how odious the opportunist is even to his allies. David the free agent is not even welcome among the ranks of the Philistines, a people consistently presented as lowlifes throughout the Bible. For the executive who is able to change sides and change faces at the drop of a hat is also one nobody can trust when the stakes are high. What an embarrassment this David is to the God who is setting him forward as the model of effective and virtuous leadership! Yet we are seeing a point we would do well to remember: *even David is flesh and blood.* There is no magical persona, no special immunity. David will accomplish something worthwhile if, and only if, he will commit himself to a path of courage and clarity of sight and purpose. And if he will not, then he too will go the way of the Sauls of the world. There is no exemption from the demands of leadership and of life. All this is easy for us to see, and yet the veil had not lifted from David's own self-consumed frame of mind.

> *There is no magic persona, no special immunity. David will amount to something if, and only if, he will commit himself to a path of courage and clarity of sight and purpose. And if not, he too will go the way of the Sauls of this world.*

So David and his band returned to Ziklag, his Philistine base of operations. So far, he must have thought, circumstance and God had let him off the hook. Maybe he was even pleased with himself for avoiding the disaster of fighting against his own people. But as he neared the base where his supplies were kept, the home-way-from-home for his soldiers' families and David's own wives, he saw smoke lingering over the plain. In his absence Ziklag had been raided and, as he soon learned, the supplies were gone. So were the women and children. Now, finally, it all unraveled on poor David.

> When David and his men came to Ziklag, they found it
> destroyed by fire and their wives and sons and daughters taken
> captive. So David and his men wept aloud until they had no
> strength left to weep. David's two wives had been
> captured—Ahinoam of Jezreel and Abigail, the widow of Nabal
> of Carmel. David was greatly distressed because the men were
> talking of stoning him; each one was bitter in spirit because of
> his sons and daughters.
>
> (1 Samuel 30:3–6)

It happens so fast. One moment you are the captain in command, everyone seems to follow, and your cunning is shaping events like a potter shaping a wet jar. The next, they are talking about stoning you to death. Except this is not really something that comes out suddenly. It takes form over time, as followers see you betray the principles you have espoused, as they have watched you mock the vision they have trusted, as they have tried to reassure themselves that you can be trusted, that you know what you're doing, that this is just some minor aberration. The trust and confidence of followers are precious, precious commodities, and it often takes much to wear them away, especially for a leader like David. But it can happen. It does happen when, filled with self-concern and self-pity, the executive ceases to lead and begins only to manipulate. And though it boils slowly beneath the surface, how quickly it rages when the lid has been blown off.

Now, finally, David is a broken man, broken in awareness not only of his circumstance but of the plight of his own heart. And there in the reality of a broken spirit David found himself again:

> David was greatly distressed because the men were talking of
> stoning him; each one was bitter in spirit because of his sons and
> daughters. But David found strength in the Lord his God.
>
> (1 Samuel 30:6)

Perhaps there was a slight change in his expression, a shift to the look of his eyes. We are not told of any great, saving speech that David made in this desperate hour, and this too is evidence that a change really has taken place. David has wept to exhaustion with his men, and now their rage is turned on him. He had just a moment, and it would determine his fate. David filled that moment with quiet but purposeful action.

> Then David said to Abiathar the priest, the son of Ahimelech,
> "Bring me the ephod." Abiathar brought it to him, and David
> inquired of the Lord, "Shall I pursue this raiding party?
> Will I overtake them?"
> "Pursue them," he answered. "You will certainly overtake them
> and succeed in the rescue."
>
> (1 Samuel 30:7, 8)

David regained the leadership he was about to lose by simply leading. It had been a while since those men had seen genuine leadership in him, but they recognized it when they saw it now. In the successful action that followed, the recapture of the families and the supplies, David also regained his hold on himself. He regained himself through principled, purposeful action.

The lessons for us here are a bit harder to pin down, but they are as important as any others. In the words of a certain well-known psalmist,

> *Save me from all my transgressions;*
> *do not make me the scorn of fools . . .*
> *You rebuke and discipline men for their sin;*
> *you consume their wealth like a moth—*
> *each man is but a breath.*
>
> **Psalm 39:8–11**

In the eyes of his followers, in the ruin of his base at Ziklag, David understood the path he had been following. He tasted the bitterness of his own self-pity and conceit, and in the humility of repentance he regained his footing.

We all need to read our own speeches. We all need to check ourselves, check our actions against the values and beliefs we have espoused.

We all need to be held accountable and to monitor our steps, lest we too go the way of Saul, lest we go the way of David walking in the dark.

Yet how often it is that God makes alive our hearts by first breaking them. He makes us wise by exposing the extent of our propensity to folly. David would be a better man and a better leader because of this journey into the darkness of his own heart. It would be nice if there were another way, but if David is any indicator there doesn't seem to be one. And yet there was a price to be paid, the damage to his reputation and the losses from Ziklag's destruction, and this was a potentially fatal loss for both David and his cause.

> *We all need to read our own speeches. We all need to be held accountable and to monitor our steps . . . Yet how often it is that God makes alive our hearts by first breaking them. He makes us wise by exposing the extent of our propensity to folly.*

David's first steps down this path of darkness were those of pride, insulation, and self-reliance. How much better for us to bear our hardships openly, to honestly share our heartaches with each other and with God. How important it is, in the light of David's walk in the dark, to cultivate friendships and accountabilities that will check our progress down such a path. And above all, if we are wise, we will check our heart against the heart of God, which, unlike our own, does not change or give way to the pressures of the day.

> The Lord is close to the brokenhearted
>   and saves those who are crushed in spirit . . .
> The Lord redeems his servants;
>   no one will be condemned who takes refuge in him.
> **Psalm 34:18, 22**

FALL OF THE EAGLES

נפלו הנשרים

Y ou waited, it seemed, forever, imagining how it would feel, what you would do. The first speech you would make, the first decision, the first action you would take. On a mundane level it was something like starting in your first football game or taking on your first debate. Then you antici- pated that first position as a leader of men and women. You could taste it, you were sure. But when the call came, the feeling was somehow different, for anticipation and the actual calling are two different things altogether. No matter how well you plan your response, when the tap falls upon your shoulder it is different than what you expected. The time of preparation is over and from now on, the score will be kept and posted.

The fall of King Saul is so long in coming we are almost surprised when it happens. David, parting from his Philistine patrons as they bore down on the demoralized host of Israel, seems not to have given it a thought. Perhaps he was so accustomed to victory that it did not occur to him that deep storm clouds were rolling west from Ashkelon and over his homeland. Or, equally as likely, David was so consumed with his own predicament that he lost sight of any larger frame of reference.

The end, so long in coming, crashed in upon Saul suddenly. It was obvious, after the episodes chasing David in the desert, that his was no longer an effective military force. Now, abandoned by a God he has himself alienated, bereft of the heroes he has persecuted, unfortified by virtues he himself has neglected, Saul is at the mercy of the onrushing Philistine army. The biblical report is as brief as was the suspense:

> Now the Philistines fought against Israel; the Israelites fled
> before them, and many fell slain on Mount Gilboa. The
> Philistines pressed hard after Saul and his sons, and they killed
> his sons Jonathan, Abinadab and Malki-Shua. The fighting grew
> fierce around Saul, and when the archers overtook him, they
> wounded him critically.
> Saul said to his armor-bearer, "Draw your sword and run me
> through, or these uncircumcised fellows will come and run me
> through and abuse me."
> But his armor-bearer was terrified and would not do it; so Saul
> took his own sword and fell on it. When the armor-bearer saw
> that Saul was dead, he too fell on his sword and died with him.
> So Saul and his three sons and his armor-bearer and all the men
> died together that same day.
> (1 Samuel 31:1–6)

Thus ended a memorable career which has instructed us greatly. I have always found it true that those who fail in the task of leadership are among its best teachers; for in their glaring mistakes and distorted values we at least see what we must avoid, with a clarity often harder to discern in those more successful. Saul, as a paradigm for all that is wrong with executive leadership now and in any age, has met the only end possible for him and for his imitators.

Here is the conclusion to the story begun that forlorn day when God commanded Samuel to give the people what they wanted. " 'We want a king over us. Then we will be like all the other nations, with a king to lead us and go out before us and fight our battles' . . . And the Lord said to Samuel, 'Listen to them and give them a king' " (1 Samuel 8:19–22). Saul had fit the bill perfectly; a king like that of the idolatrous nations, he had been self-serving and arrogant, uninspiring and cruel. The people only had to follow behind him into battle, there to be stripped of their very identity, to be used like the pawns they had so longed to be, and ultimately to be cut down by the enemies they so longed to mimic.

Saul's defeat was a disaster of huge proportions for the people of Israel, as are the failures of executive leadership in our own day. Israel lost the core of its army, and in the aftermath it forfeited much of its territory and many of its homes as well. There on the hills of Gilboah Israel lost many of its best men, Jonathan not the least among them. It is a bitter pill to see such a great man as Jonathan pay the price for the transgressions of another, but the reality is always that failed leaders drag down many with them. And yet we suspect that in Jonathan's case, for all his contempt for the ways of his father, he would not have been anywhere else but at his side on that dark day.

> When the Israelites along the valley and those across the Jordan
> saw that the Israelite army had fled and that Saul and his sons
> had died, they abandoned their towns and fled. And the
> Philistines came and occupied them.
> (1 Samuel 31:7)

The Sauls must always fail, that is the lesson being driven home by this story. They fail their country either during their rule or during the dark days following their demise. The Sauls of this world will rarely end their executive lives dying peaceably in their beds. Even at the height of their splendor they represent only what they have taken from the nation, from the company, from the family. In their days of glory they share the stage with no one, but in their fall many are gathered to their side. That is where the image, where the facade, and where the opportunistic vigor ultimately lead. In their passing such leaders leave behind an organization in shambles, as Saul did for the people of Israel. Perhaps the most wrenching thought is that it need not have been this way.

> *In their days of glory the Sauls share the stage with no one, but in their fall many are gathered to their side.*

David was one of the last to hear the news. We saw earlier how despair turned his heart from the path of ruin, near failure brought him back to the source of his strength. And it is striking to see how full a recovery he makes.

This point is well illustrated by the radical change in behavior David exhibits during his pursuit of the Amalekite raiders who made off with the provisions and families of his little army. Shortly after the chase began it became apparent that about a third of his force could not continue to keep the pace, no doubt wearied by the continual trials to which they had been subjected. David briefly stopped to address this problem, leaving them behind in good defensive terrain to defend the few provisions left. Banking on a strategy of speed and surprise, he then rushed forward with his remaining troops.

As is so often the case, David's audacity generated its own good fortune, for as he bore down upon his inattentive prey, he encountered an Amalekite slave who, showing sign of illness, had been abandoned by his master. Having received assurances of safety from David, this slave led the pursuers to the place where the raiders had drawn up to enjoy the fruits of their plunder.

> He led David down, and there they were, scattered over the
> countryside, eating, drinking and reveling because of the great
> amount of plunder they had taken from the land of the
> Philistines and from Judah. David fought them from dusk until
> the evening of the next day, and none of them got away, except
> four hundred young men who rode off on camels and fled.
> (1 Samuel 30:16, 17)

David's victory recovered all that was lost at Ziklag: supplies, families, and the confidence of his soldiers. As an expression of their gratitude for the recovery of their wives and children, the men brought all the wealth and placed it before him. Here we see just how completely David's heart has recovered. Not only did he refuse to enrich himself, but he insisted on giving a share of the riches to those soldiers left behind. When confronted by those who had gone forward and fought, who demanded that they alone receive the spoils of the enemy, David was adamant:

> David replied, "No, my brothers, you must not do that with what
> the Lord has given us. He has protected us and handed over to
> us the forces that came against us . . . The share of the man who
> stayed with the supplies is to be the same as that of him who
> went down to the battle. All will share alike."
>
> (1 Samuel 30:23, 24)

Here, again, much to our relief, is David as true leader, thinking and acting out of deliberate intention, consciously crafting his actions to build and to draw together, to lift others up to a common cause. All who had played a part in the success would benefit together; indeed David even paid a dividend to those towns in Judah that had supported him during the years of his long flight from Saul. *All who shared his risks would share his gain.*

It is clear that David has passed through the waters of trial and come out all the stronger for it. As gold is tried by fire, refined so that the dross is removed from the precious substance, so too are true leaders made strong by the tribulations they pass through. And like gold, David now shone as he gathered his seasoned troops and prepared for further action. What now was his intention now? The Bible gives no direct indication, but there can be little doubt that David's mind turned to the threat facing his people. Shaken from his moral malaise and infused with renewed purpose, we can be sure that David was preparing to enter the fray on the side of his homeland against his recent allies, the Philistines.

He was still regrouping in Ziklag, however, when a messenger appeared. His clothes were torn and his face was matted with dirt, and he raced to David and threw himself before him.

> "Where have you come from?" David asked him.
> He answered, "I have escaped from the Israelite camp . . .
> "The men fled from the battle. Many of them fell and died. And
> Saul and his son Jonathan are dead."
>
> (2 Samuel 1:3, 4)

Imagine what must have raced through David's mind. *"Finally, it is over! Saul has gotten what he deserved and I can return . . . Indeed, now I will be king!"* Surely these thoughts did come to him, and we see him grabbing up the man, demanding:

> "How do you know that Saul and his son Janathan are dead?"
> "I happened to be on Mount Gilboa," the young man said, "and
> there was Saul, leaning on his spear, with the chariots and riders
> almost upon him. When he turned around and saw me, he
> called out to me, and I said, 'What can I do?' . . .
> Then he said to me, 'Stand over me and kill me! I am in the
> throes of death, but I'm still alive.'
> So I stood over him and killed him, because I knew that after he
> had fallen he could not survive. And I took the crown that was
> on his head and the band on his arm and have brought them
> here to my lord."
> (2 Samuel 1:5–10)

Just like that, and there were the symbols of kingship rolled out before David's feet. The objects for which, one way or another, he had been striving all these hard, heartbreaking years. At the sight, tears filled David's eyes, but not tears of joy. Tearing his clothes, David wept at the news and fasted in mourning for the deaths of Saul and Jonathan.

> They mourned and wept and fasted till evening for Saul and his
> son Jonathan, and for the army of the Lord and the house of
> Israel, because they had fallen by the sword.
> (2 Samuel 1:12)

This was not, we imagined, the kind of reception the opportunistic fugitive had hoped for when he sought out David's camp. And things would rapidly go downhill from here. For when the weeping was done, David brought this messenger forth and demanded:

> "Where are you from?"
> "I am the son of an alien, an Amalekite," he answered.

David asked him, "Why were you not afraid to lift your hand to
destroy the Lord's anointed?"
Then David called one of his men and said, "Go, strike him
down! . . ." For David had said to him, "Your blood be on your
own head. Your own mouth testified against you when you said,
'I killed the Lord's anointed.' "
(2 Samuel 1:13–16)

How ruthless! But David was ruthless, passionately committed, when
acting on principle. Was it wrong to execute this man who at the least
was seeking to ingratiate himself to the new strongman, at the expense of
the fallen eagle? To David, the issue was straightforward: Saul was God's
anointed, the inviolate king of Israel. This is why David himself refused
to raise a hand against his enemy and persecutor. And this, as one also
anointed of the Lord, he would expect from all others. What he demanded for himself, he demanded of others and the Amalekite king-
slayer must therefore die. Saul's fate was God's prerogative, and this is
something David would consistently defend with a holy zeal.

So ends this major chapter in the life of David. Indeed, with Saul's
death we reach the major turning point in his life. No more is he the
rising champion, the change agent and persecuted visionary. With the
opening of this door to opportunity and responsibility, out of David's heart
floods a torrent of impassioned words. While others might issue memo-
randa or make speeches, David sings an eloquent song. And the first
thought to emerge from his heart is that of mourning and lament for what
was and what might have been:

Your glory, O Israel, lies slain on your heights.
  How the mighty have fallen! . . .
O mountains of Gilboa,
  may you have neither dew nor rain . . .
For there the shield of the mighty was defiled,
  the shield of Saul—no longer rubbed with oil.
2 Samuel 1:19, 21

It makes quite an impact to see David remember his old nemisis, a man who wronged him without cause, so generously and so tenderly. David looks on Saul in death as a man, as a hope his people once cherished; he chooses to mourn over the best that was in him and the promise that went unfulfilled. David the executive is always David the man first and foremost, and his magnanimity draws us to him.

> *Saul and Jonathan—*
> > *in life they were loved and gracious,*
> > *and in death they were not parted.*
> *They were swifter than eagles,*
> > *they were stronger than lions.*
>
> 2 Samuel 1:23

Of course, Jonathan receives special attention. The loss of this friendship, so essential during these years of trial, would never be replaced.

> *How the mighty have fallen in battle! Jonathan lies slain on*
> > *your heights.*
> *I grieve for you, Jonathan my brother;*
> *You were very dear to me . . .*
> *How the mighty have fallen! The weapons of war have perished!*
>
> 2 Samuel 1:25–27

Even after Saul's death, David stands out in contrast to him. He chooses to love when there is no obvious reason to do so, just as Saul chose to hate for no good reason. He chooses to see the best, he longs to find virtue in even his enemies, while Saul trod a different path all through his reign. David is not made insecure, he is not threatened, to have the praises of another sung; indeed, he composes and raises his voice in this song of praise! All across the board, he is driven by a different set of motives: love versus lust, selfless purpose versus selfish ambition, faith and hope versus fear and despondency. Let us not forget this contrast, nor fail to make our own choices wisely.

So the faithful servant has had his reward. The crown lies cast to the ground before David's feet. Yet it is not the glitter that catches his attention, but the principles embodied there, the mandate to serve and live out God's calling. This is what David has looked for in Saul and will demand of himself. When God anoints a man to be king, he does not intend this as an invitation to selfishness and excess, but to sacrifice and purpose.

All this is to say that the heart is where leadership takes place; it is born there and there it dies as well. On the heights of Gilboah Saul found a death many will think he did not deserve, a memorable death, and a noble one. And yet we must say that for all the grace that permitted this ending to so sordid a tale, the Philistine arrows were but the last stroke to a death begun long ago.

It is after a storm, however, that the rays of light burn brightest. In Saul's sad death, and sadder still in Jonathan's, the flames of David's heart were rekindled, the vision receiving fresh clarity. Out of that death David came forth with a living heart once more, a heart that could lend life to a nation and to a people. This, not a crown of gold, was the servant's true reward.

> *The heart is where leadership takes place; it is born there and there it dies as well . . .*

DAVID, CEO

"Bless You,
for What
You Have Done"

ברכים אתם כי עשיתם הדבר הזה

One thing the Bible shows us is that much wisdom regarding leadership is found in stories. We do not tell enough stories in our working life; we do not share them or listen to them. We do not recall the great day when the right decision was made for the right reasons. We do not tell the history of the rising star who went wrong or of the time when principle stood up against a tide of fear. And so by forgetting the past, we face it again unknowing, as if we have not been down these roads before.

In stories we find our bearings for the future; vision is discovered in what has been lived. There we recall what it is that our hearts sing for, what brought us down the road we now travel. Vision is found in what we love and in what we hate, in our joys and in our sorrows, and these are uncovered in the stories of our lives.

David's life provides, of course, an excellent example of how important stories are for today's leader. And yet here we are encountering a story that is more than just a story. David's is a story told by the Bible, told by the God of the Bible. So here is a story not only providentially *told* but also providentially *orchestrated* as it unfolds; this story develops before our eyes as a message from the Author of both the life and the story.

We have seen this most clearly at certain key points along the way. First of all, we recall that it was God who directed Samuel to seek and anoint Saul in the first place. The people had come and demanded a king, not one after God's heart but one who would follow the ways of the surrounding nations. Though God mourned over this choice, there was a method to what would seem to be madness. God was shaping events, readying hard hearts for the man after His own heart, the leader who would reflect His leadership. As it was for Israel, so also for us. While reading about the faithlessness of Saul's executive reign we are asked, indeed required, to gaze into our own hearts, and then to gaze upon the heart of David. God's message here is about both character and competence, about the heart which guides the hands, and of the faith and love which always guide the heart.

At his best, it is this integrity that David exemplifies. Psalm 78, written by a man named Asaph, summarizes God's gracious action in giving David to Israel, a gift of mercy after the hard winter of preparation under Saul:

> He chose David his servant
>   and took him from the sheep pens;
> from tending the sheep he brought him
>   to be the shepherd of his people Jacob,
>   of Israel his inheritance.
> And David shepherded them with integrity of heart;
>   with skillful hands he led them.
>
> **Psalm 78:70–72**

Integrity of heart guiding skillful hands; that is the pattern revealed in the leadership of David.

So Saul is dead. After his period of mourning, David remained at Ziklag for some time, ultimately turning to the Lord for direction. "Go *up to Hebron,"* said the Lord, and so David and his band returned to the center of their homeland. There the men of Judah had gathered to meet him, and there they anointed David and acknowledged him as their king. So it was done: finally David was king. It is true that many did not as yet concede this, for David was now king only over the one tribe of Judah. But from now on, he will not be merely the renegade champion, but the chief executive wielding the reigns of power. From now on David will lead from the top, as the CEO of a large, complex organization.

If there is one thing we know and emphasize today about executive leadership, it is that the first priority of the new executive is to communicate a *vision*. How used and overused is this poor word in our day. In fact, it is positively abused by the lip-service paid to it. But it is a good word. *Vision*. We may not know how to find it, we may have difficulty recognizing it when it is there, but we always know what things look like when it is absent. So, yes, the first task we will see David setting out to do as CEO is that of articulating an inspiring ideal for the company. Not just getting a vision, or having a vision, that is what repels so many of us from the word, but rather David set about the task of gathering the people together around a shared sense of purpose and identity: binding their hearts around a shared aspiration for the future, and challenging the organization and himself with clear and compelling values. That is what vision is meant for, and it is to this task that David first turned his attention.

Upon rising to executive office in Israel, David was faced with a situation most new chief executives will encounter. There before him was a badly divided organization, a company fragmented and warring against itself from within. Is this not exactly the situation many leaders face today? This was David's problem and it is our problem: not the absence of just vision, but the lack of cohesion and unified effort toward a common goal. Vision is not a remedy for mere sightlessness, because the problem in our organizations, as in David's Israel, is not a shortage of visions for the future. The problem is rather that there is no *shared* vision, no shared *purpose* for which our hearts and minds are united as we face the challenges of the days ahead. And, therefore, the solution is not the procurement of something entitled "Vision" on a slide presentation, but rather the kind of leadership that unifies a fragmented organization around a common purpose for tomorrow.

> *The problem is not the absence of just vision, but the lack of cohesion and unified effort. The problem is that there is no shared vision, no shared purpose for which our hearts and minds are united.*

In these early scenes from David's reign as king we will see him masterfully bind together those who were torn by strife and division. For him, vision was not an end but a means for healing that which was sick and drawing together those who could only achieve their destiny together. For *visionary leadership does not produce vision.* It produces inspired men and women, committing themselves and their labors to a shared dream, toward shared values and to principles that will mark out a path before them.

The event in David's story that triggers these reflections is not a first-day leader's speech nor an off-site workshop attended by his staff. Instead, it was a sacrificial act of kindness performed on Saul's behalf, and David's official response to it as king of Judah.

> *Visionary leadership does not produce vision. It produces inspired men and women, committing themselves and their labors to a shared dream, to shared values and principles.*

The ancient world was a bloodier, gorier place than most of us are accustomed to. And such a world was not kind to those who have fallen. Saul's case, however, is not just a typical one, but it is a particularly brutal example as well. His death was a big deal to the Philistines, and not without reason. So to share the good news with the folks back home, they cut off Saul's head and dismantled his royal armor. Messengers were then sent throughout Philistia bearing the joyous tidings to be proclaimed in the temples of their pagan idols. Not only was Saul's armor put on display, but his body was fastened to the wall of one of the major shrines, along with the bodies of his sons, to be picked apart as carrion and abused by his enemies.

News of this spread far and wide, as was intended, and it ultimately reached the simple people of a town called Jabesh Gilead. Where have we heard this name before? *Jabesh Gilead.* It was the site of the young King Saul's first triumph, the town he had raced to rescue, the battle he had forcibly thrust upon all the twelve tribes of Israel. The men of Jabesh Gilead were the ones whose eyes were to be gouged out by Nahash the Ammonite, unless young King Saul could find a way to save them. Save them he did, and they remembered.

So when the news spread of wicked Saul's death in battle, and of the humiliation of his remains in the temples of the godless, there were none moved to action, none except the men of Jabesh Gilead. Here is what the biblical record informs us:

> When the people of Jabesh Gilead heard of what the Philistines
> had done to Saul, all their valiant men journeyed through the
> night to Beth Shan [where Saul's body was fastened to a wall].
> They took down the bodies of Saul and his sons from the well of
> Beth Shan and went to Jabesh, where they burned them. Then
> they took their bones and buried them under a tamarisk tree at
> Jabesh, and they fasted seven days.
>
> (1 Samuel 31:11–13)

This is the last word on the reign of Saul. Yes, he had become twisted in his later years, and yes, he had failed miserably in the end, bringing down scores of Israelites with him. But even after his horrible downfall, the memory of his earlier heroism, by which real men and real women were saved, lived on. The men and women of Jabesh Gilead loved Saul for what he had done, and with the news of his humiliation that love took wings. They traveled a great distance and into great danger, from one end of Israel to the other, from beyond the Jordan to the coast of the sea, to pay homage to a man they loved and to whom they owed a debt of gratitude. They came not to create a scene, not to call attention to themselves or to fallen Saul, but to do what was right.

It was shortly after being anointed king of Judah that David learned of this action. And it was in his response to this gracious action that David as CEO began the process of articulating vision and building cohesion.

When David was told that it was the men of Jabesh Gilead who
had buried Saul, he sent messengers to the men of Jabesh Gilead
to say to them, "The Lord bless you for showing this kindness to
Saul your master by burying him. May the Lord now show you
kindness and faithfulness, and I too will show you the same favor
because you have done this. Now then, be strong and brave,
for Saul your master is dead, and the house of Judah has
anointed me king over them."

(2 Samuel 2:4–7)

How do you articulate vision? By action. David simply took the time
to write a note expressing his thanks to these noble citizens. Big deal?
When was the last time you wrote such a note? When was the last time
you crept out of your skyline hideaway, walked downstairs, sat down next
to one of the front-line employees, and said, "I really wanted you to know
that what you did for that customer was tremendous. It's that kind of thing
that this company is all about." When did you last take time out of your
action-packed executive schedule and write a simple note, saying, "I want
you to know that I observed the effort your team put into this project and
was really inspired. You have reminded me that we are indeed joined
together for something meaningful. Thanks a lot."

It was just a note, a personal letter from David son of Jesse expressing
gratitude to the people of Jabesh Gilead. An official letter from the king
of Judah and the anointed of all Israel, to the good people of Jabesh
Gilead, commending their wonderful action. But it was worth forty stump
speeches, because it showed that David noticed and took the time to show
his appreciation. David was putting his true heart on display and not
performing some procedurally driven drill, and that is what makes him a
true leader.

Was David acting on simple impulse or was this a savvy act of leadership? Clearly it was both, as is so often the case with real leaders. He knew
what he was looking for and when he saw it he responded *deliberately* and
impulsively. He was speaking to all the organization—this note was public
enough to make it into the Bible—and saying, "This is what we are going
to be about!" And that is vision.

Looking at this short note, we are observing a masterpiece of communication. First, David communicated, "I heard about and noticed what you did. Bless you." How do leaders communicate vision, the values and principles and purpose that will define a team, except through what they bless? "The Lord bless you for showing this kindness to Saul your master by burying him." The minds of men and women are not captured by the bullet-pointed items on our formal vision statement, as our near universal inability to remember these daily recounts. Rather, vision is seen in the actions that bring the leader's infectious praise and excitement. It is what causes the slap on the back, the shaking of the hand, the gazing intently into the eyes as the leader exults, "Yes! That's it! Thanks!" Vision is revealed in the passion and emotional release between the leader and his followers, fellow-laborers looking backward and forward together.

Of course, you have to think things like this are important. You have to believe that acts of faithfulness and love, risks taken and challenges embraced, are what transcend the numbers. You have to believe that the organization is not just a set of numbers, not merely a collection of input-output systems, but the people who inhabit it.

> *How do you articulate a vision? By action. Not the bullet-pointed items from our vision statement but the actions that bring the leader's infectious praise and excitement. Vision is revealed in the passion and emotional release between the leader and his followers.*

And that means that the organization exists in their thoughts, their fears, their passions, like the memory that lived on in Jabesh Gilead.

Notice then what David says: "May the Lord now show you kindness and faithfulness, and I too will show you the same favor because you have done this." What is he saying but "You want to know what will get you ahead in my outfit? You want to know what I will reach out and embrace and love and reward? It was just lived out in front of you by the men and women of Jabesh Gilead." But how often it is in our organizations that promotion decisions, opportunities for new challenges, recognition, and rewards are totally divorced from our espoused vision. We say we want teamwork and we reward individual numbers. We say we want collaboration but the last thing leaders keep track of is the sharing of ideas. We have opted for a neutral "fairness" based on measurements that are either wholly at odds with or irrelevant to our declared strategy. Then we wonder why neither leader nor led gets the message. *Visionary leadership is not neutral, nor even objective.* It is passionately committed to *particular* principles and actions that themselves embody the vision. And it offers them up to the light of day, both deliberately and instinctively. "May the Lord bless you for this — and I'll bless you too!"

What is most fascinating about David's actions is that Jabesh Gilead wasn't even in his jurisdiction. Yes, David had been anointed by God as king over all twelve tribes of Israel, but as of yet only Judah had hailed him. These people weren't even in his department, and he is going out of his way to praise them, to hold them up as an example for all. But who they were didn't matter to David. What they did was real and it was right and so it got his immediate response. But, then, he knew what he was looking for.

> *Visionary leadership is not neutral, nor even objective. It is passionately committed to particular principles and actions that themselves embody the vision.*

David concludes his message with a call to join him in the kind of work begun by their faithful actions to dead King Saul. "Now then, be strong and brave, for Saul your master is dead, and the house of Judah has anointed me king over them." What is he saying but, "I really need you." Of course the strength and bravery of such followers is the thing every leader does need, and yet how seldom this is said.

We have not seen here the whole of the task of leadership, nor even the many ways a leader can inspire a sense of purpose around a shared vision. But this kind of action is a great start. What would happen in your organization if simple actions like this became the norm for you and for others? It is a start, and more.

Standing in
the Gap

עמד בתרך

David's attitude upon coming to power is clearly seen in his honorable treatment of Saul's memory, as well as in his impassioned praise for the people of Jabesh Gilead. David is a man driven by ideals, and he will now seek to bind his people together on the basis of these ideals.

Yet, telling as David's actions have been, I would not suggest for a moment that effective leadership boils down to simply writing notes and giving praise. These gestures have shown how David set out to gain a grip on the hearts of the people and of the intention that drove his actions. Yet the difficult situation he would soon be faced with would require quite a bit more skill, principle, and good judgment than perhaps he had ever needed before.

Anyone who has ever risen to the top will tell you that there are always factions within the organization to deal with, some of them resentful or even openly hostile. In David's case it was the latter, for while Saul was now dead there were still many in positions of power whose wagons had been hitched to his star. Such people were not likely to quickly submit to David's rule and would surely have been more than a little afraid of being punished for their own past misdeeds.

Foremost among these former enemies was Abner, Saul's chief general, who had managed to escape the disaster at Gilboah. In fact, while David was singing his laments over the dead king, Abner was busy installing one of Saul's surviving sons as king over the northern territories of Israel. This son's name was Ish-Bosheth, and when David gained control over Judea and the south, this puppet king gathered the old Saulite forces in opposition.

Abner's behavior is hardly surprising, for those who have clung to power instinctively scramble for positions of influence in times of turmoil. And yet we have had clear indications that Abner, like nearly everyone else, knew that David was destined to be king; Abner himself had heard as much from Saul's own mouth. So while Ish-Bosheth's reign was doomed from the start, the circumstances surrounding this opposition served as a stage upon which David exhibited some of the most striking leadership of his career.

Saul's old army was not only decrepit but had been virtually wiped out in battle with the Philistines. David's war band was relatively small, but it was well equipped (by the Philistines) and fresh from a long record of victories. Before long the two forces were locked in battle and the outcome was hardly in doubt. Abner began the action by advancing south on David's position, and David's general, Joab, quickly demolished this force in a day of heavy fighting. This was the worst sort of battle, countryman against countryman, cousin versus cousin. For David, the danger was not defeat but the stirring of hatreds that were already very near the surface, as civil wars always do whether they are national or corporate.

From David's perspective, this sort of contest presented singular dangers. Even if he triumphed over Abner's puppet, King Ish-Bosheth, as he surely would, the cost to his plans could be very high. His vision was of a united Israel, with its twelve subsidiaries, that is tribes, advancing as one toward their God-directed destiny. David saw an age-old promise, a promise made when Moses had led the nation out from the bondage of Egypt and Joshua had captained a victorious Israel into the Promised Land. It was that ancient vision, never yet realized, that David now saw dangling before him. The long centuries of chaos and division had distracted the people from any sense of purpose, and instead they had accepted the occasional and temporary periods of peace as achievement enough. Under King Saul national unity had devolved into a privilege-seeking corruption, as his own tribe of Benjamin rose to prominence and wealth. This is not what Moses had looked forward to as he gazed across the Jordan River just before his death. It was a united nation that he saw, a people living as one under the Law and serving as an example for the heathen nations around them.

So, from this perspective, the sight of Israelite striking down Israelite was not one that warmed David's heart. What was at stake for him was not the security of his own position, but the advancement of his dream. Surely this explains why David did not go up himself to lead his army in this battle. Taking a defensive stance and keeping his own hands clean of the blood of his countrymen, David at least acted to minimize the animosity of those who would lose sons and brothers and husbands in this fight.

Defeat and petty intrigue naturally brought the regime of Abner and Ish-Bosheth to its demise. So it was not long before the politically nimble Abner approached David about the possibilities of defecting to his side. Imagine what must have raced through David's mind. Here was Abner, the general who had eagerly supported Saul in all his tyrannical deeds, and in the long persecution of David himself. Surely his stomach turned at the sight of this man now coming with palms open, when just a short while before he would have gladly have stuck his sword in David's back. The last person David would want in his camp was a man like Abner, and yet, to the surprise of many, David eagerly accepted the proposal. All he demanded was that the general return Michal, Saul's daughter, who though married to David had since been given by Saul to another man. If she was returned, Abner would be allowed to surrender his forces in peace. The significance of this is clear: with David acknowledged again as Saul's son-in-law, it would be that much easier for the rebel faction to recognize him as king. On these terms, Abner departed to make the necessary arrangements.

It was not long before an outcry reached David from his own ranks, led by his own commander, Joab, who had recently won the costly victory over Abner's force:

> So Joab went to the king and said, "What have you done? Look,
> Abner came to you. Why did you let him go? Now he is gone!
> You know Abner son of Ner; he came to deceive you and observe
> your movements and find out everything you are doing."
>
> (2 Samuel 3:24, 25)

Had David forgotten his principles or become naive? Did he so lightly value the loyalty of his faithful supporters? Oh, but he was acting on principle, a clear and self-sacrificing principle. And, yes, he did value the loyalty of his followers, enough to point them to something greater than raw triumph over enemies, than revenge for its own sake. The principle David espoused was that of reconciliation among countrymen, a reconciliation that sooner or later would be essential to his ambitions. Yes, Abner was a lowlife and yes, he was guilty of crimes against David and his men. But Abner was an Israelite and he represented factions and stakeholders who would be essential to the life of a united organization. Compassion and faithfulness and courage, these were the ideals on David's mind. And if his followers, both present and future, were unwilling to live up to so high a standard, David was ready to set aside his own personal revenge and his own malice and anger, thus setting an example for others to follow.

Reconciling factions means reconciling people. It means setting an example of mercy and conciliation for followers. Reconciliation means sacrificing past grudges, so as to preserve a strategy and to advance a higher purpose than mere vengeance. It means that those who would develop a culture of trust and openness must take the lead by trusting others, including many who have not merited it, and of being personally trustworthy as well. David set out to establish a win-win principle among a people who instinctively measured their own success in terms of the loss of others.

How essential this is to executive leadership today, when success demands not merely the absence of conflict but genuine trust and collaboration. In so many of our organizations, interoffice scheming and finger-pointing has prevailed for so long that there is no hope of true unity unless a dramatic intervention is made by the executive leader. Possessing the means to subject or destroy this rebellious faction, David instead seized the opportunity to establish a new mode of relating and to instruct in the way of peace.

David's action bore fruit in two directions. The first was an almost immediate end to the rebellion against him in the north. Abner, it seems, had been testing the waters. And isn't this just what we should expect of those willing to lay down their arms and yet who are still fearful of retribution? Yes, Abner's motives were more than mixed and he surely intended to somehow profit from this turn of events. But through a willingness to reconcile, David gained an influence over this enemy which otherwise would have been impossible. As it turned out Abner went so far as to appear before the elders of the rebellious northern tribes, appealing to them on David's behalf:

> "For some time you have wanted to make David your king. Now
> do it! For the Lord promised David, 'By my servant David I will
> rescue my people Israel from the hand of the Philistines and
> from the hand of all their enemies.'"
>
> (2 Samuel 3:17, 18).

They had known all along what the right thing to do was! They had understood the inevitable outcome. They had been scanning the horizon for evidence that David would not take revenge against those who had stood by Saul during his persecutions of the man who now was king. They had been hoping all along that a win for David did not require a major loss for themselves. But until there was a credible reason to hope for reconciliation they were willing to go on tearing the nation in two, just as the fearful faction leaders do in corporations today. In just this way, it is the task of leadership to seek ways for old enemies to join together in one coalition.

Of course, the tribal chiefs accepted Abner's approval, and probably with a sigh. Abner then departed to make a special plea to Saul's own tribe of Benjamin, ultimately bringing all the rebel tribes to recognize and embrace David's authority. How many of our own organizations could profit from such a venture in trust-building and reconciliation as David undertook, however risky and unpalatable it may seem to those who have long been divided in opposition to one another.

Reconciling factions means reconciling people . . . Those who would develop a culture of trust and openness must take the lead by trusting others. David set out to establish a win-win principle among a people who instinctively measured their own success in terms of the loss of others.

The second result of David's act of mercy was less pleasant, and less supportive of his designs. The problem was that David's most loyal supporters, Joab and his men, simply could not reconcile themselves to the idea of peace with their northern cousins. Remember, these were men who had joined David's cause because of the injustice visited upon themselves by that old regime Abner now represented. They too had been chased and persecuted within an inch of their lives, had lived in caves and deserts for long years. Joab, David's own nephew, would surely have felt the sting of Saul's hatred from the earliest days of David's flight. And just recently, Joab's own brother had been struck down in battle by the hand of Abner himself. Apparently that was the straw that broke the camel's back. Regardless of David's commands Joab would not accept peace, and instead he used the present truce as an opportunity for revenge.

Joab's plan was simple. Tracking his old nemesis, who thought himself under the protection of the king's truce, Joab finally caught up with Abner. Drawing him aside in seemingly harmless conversation, Joab brutally thrust his sword into Abner's stomach. Now here is a stratagem that has been repeated over the ages! What a price we pay even today for such conflict, born of mistrust and past misdeeds, that ends in just this kind of assassination, albeit in more subtle and modern forms!

David was beside himself when the news reached him, and he lashed out with curses upon Joab and his cohorts.

"I and my kingdom are forever innocent before the Lord
concerning the blood of Abner son of Ner. May his blood fall
upon the head of Joab and upon all his father's house!"
(2 Samuel 3:28, 29)

David commanded Joab and his men to tear their clothes in sorrow
for Abner, and to walk in mourning before his body in the funeral proces-
sion. Behind the casket walked the king himself, as he laid his old enemy
to rest with honors there in Hebron. And there King David wept over the
body of this wicked man, whom he must have hated in life and yet genuinely sorrowed for in his death.

It can take a long time and a great deal of effort to get across a message. Joab simply hadn't gotten it, blinded as he was by personal malice
and partisan sentiments. How much he would have resented David's di-
rectives! Here was the old and wretched enemy who got what he deserved, what he had given to others, receiving funeral honors while the
loyal supporter walked in humiliation!

What was it Joab couldn't get? That David was not advancing a faction but a set of principles and a vision for the entire nation. That David
was aimig higher than his own personal redemption. That the sacrifices
of the past were not made just so David and Joab could behave with the
same kind of hypocrisy that Saul and Abner did. That the kind of leadership which draws together an organization is self-sacrificing leadership,
forgiving leadership, and believing leadership.

Here too we see David weaving together the fabrics of a vision for his
reign. Consider the fortitude his actions required! Yes, Ish-Bosheth's reign
was unwinding and no longer posed a real military threat. But consider
the threat to the peace so tentatively woven, and the threat to David in
the midst of this blood-soaked malice. Here he stands alone in the kind
of defining moment that most true leaders can recognize. The captains
of the north, learning of the murder, might well take up arms again. But
now David steps out from the ranks of his own army, out from beside his
captins of the south. He stands alone in the place of reconciliation, which
may well become the place of his undoing. He stands there because his
vision is there. Here we see the executive thrusting his own personality,

his own body, right into the gap between two bloodlusting factions, drawing attention and, perhaps, hostility to himself in the process. It is what we call leadership. And it is such put-it-on-the-line leadership that wins

> *David himself steps into the gap, alone. It is such put-it-on-the-line leadership that wins hearts to a vision, for there is no separating the leader's vision from the leader himself.*

hearts to a vision, for there is no separating the leader's vision from the leader himself.

Is this a foolish path of self-destruction, however noble? Is this the way to enjoy a brilliant, commendable, but brief reign at the helm? No, it is not. And the reason is that people do watch when a leader puts it on the line. They do understand, most of them anyway. They do seize upon the opportunity to believe in a chance for something better, at least many of them do. David was staking it all on his vision for the future, and this is exactly what every true leader is often forced to do. And people began to notice:

> All the people took note and were pleased; indeed, everything the king did pleased them. So on that day all the people and all Israel knew that the king had no part in the murder of Abner son of Ner.
> (2 Samuel 3:36, 37)

Leadership often entails dramatic, decisive action. Not every day, but when it counts it has to be there. Here, again, is leadership from the heart, leadership that cannot be faked, and people do take notice. David

> *People do watch when a leader puts it on the line. They do understand many seize the opportunity to believe.*

was confrontational in setting forth his mandate for the future, the ideals that must mark his rule. He confronted the praiseworthy with his applause, the faithless with a chance to win back trust, and the divisive with the blazing heat of his wrath. Not all were as yet drawing together under his reign, but he was steadily gathering many, and soon most, to the particular mandate he set forth in person. And the people took note and were pleased, for the heart of an executive had stepped forth in Israel.

Through these actions, actions both highly symbolic and very real, David had accomplished much. In fact, he had accomplished enough to be acclaimed king over all the tribes of Israel in a dramatic ceremony reminiscent of Saul's earlier coronation:

> All the tribes of Israel came to David at Hebron and said, "We are your own flesh and blood. In the past, while Saul was king over us, you were the one who led Israel on their military campaigns. And the Lord said to you, 'You will shepherd my people Israel, and you will become their ruler.'"
>
> When all the elders of Israel had come to King David at Hebron, the king made a compact with them at Hebron before the Lord, and they anointed David king over Israel.
>
> (2 Samuel 5:1–3)

Though the narrative is brief, we are struck by the contrast between this coronation and that of Saul. The words are few, but a transition has taken place for which God Himself had long been working. David is not acclaimed for his height, for his appearance, for his résumé. He is received and acclaimed because of his heart. "Man looks at the outward appearance, but the Lord looks at the heart." David was acclaimed because he had shown himself to be God's shepherd over His flock, Israel.

Notice too that while the first king had proceeded directly from coronation to feast table, this second king moved his followers over to a table where the war maps lay spread out. "The king made a compact with them at Hebron before the Lord." What was this compact? We will not be long in doubt, for immediately afterward we read of action. The army of a united Israel, ragtag though it may be, would advance on Jerusalem with David at its head.

We have now seen David systematically embark on a path of leadership that is intent on drawing together former enemies into a united nation. Now, with this accomplished, he sets before them a clear and compelling goal. It was their hearts he was seeking: it is always the heart that the true leader seeks, the trust and the passion and the drive. David was drawing them around himself and trying to personally embody the very principles he was urging his people to follow. And yet there was much still to do, many scars and bruises to be nursed, questions still to be asked and bonds yet to be forged. So David wasted no more time on words, instead directing his kingdom, like an arrow shot out of a bow, on a direct course toward a true challenge, toward a goal that was meaningful to all of them, the fortress city of Jerusalem.

Earlier we noted that Jerusalem had long been on David's mind. It was not only a prominent and strategically vital location right in the heart of Israel but its ability to hold out against the Israelites was a centuries-old symbol of their failure, faithlessness, and mediocrity. Other brave men had tried to take Jerusalem, brave warriors who had marched in Joshua's conquering host, and they had ultimately shrunk back from the task. Jerusalem was the ideal defensive position, snug atop Mount Moriah, the very mount that had witnessed the crowning act of Abraham, the father of Israel, when he had obeyed God by his willingness to offer up his son Isaac. So to take Jerusalem would be more than a coup, it would be the kind of success around which a new identity is forged. For Israel, a future in Jerusalem meant the fulfillment of its past and the promises such fulfillment held for tomorrow. It was vital to David's plans, therefore, that Jerusalem must no longer be a symbol of failure and a source of pagan corruption, but must be seized as the capital of a new and vibrant nation.

The story here is short and sweet. As David's host aproached the walled city, the Jebusite inhabitants who had so long fended off all assaults, called out with jeers. *"You will not get in here; even the blind and the lame could ward you off!"* But while his forces outside distracted their attention, David moved with a smaller force to a water shaft that led up behind the city walls. At the mouth of this tunnel, he turned to address his troops:

> "Whoever leads the attack on the Jebusites will become
> commander-in-chief."
>
> **(1 Chronicles 11:6)**

And who should answer the call, but Joab, the former commander now disgraced. How is it that he was so well positioned for this opportunity? We are growing suspicious of this David, ever the reconciler. Indeed, it is not hard to imagine the new king looking in the eyes of his nephew and longtime associate as he spoke, a man he surely understood and yet a man he had needed to confront. "Whoever leads the attack . . . will become commander-in-chief." And Joab stepped forward, leading the troops up the shaft, and securing the way for the overthrow of this ancient rival.

Did David know about this way of entry in advance? Was it this knowledge that put the look of confidence on his face as he led his uncertain column toward this invincible fortress? Or had he just happened to stumble upon this previously unknown way of entry? Was it God who placed this opening before him? The Bible leaves all this unanswered, but again we are more than a little suspicious.

I think there is another answer, and what a piece of work it shows David to be! Here, he teaches us a valuable lesson: if you have a card up your sleeve, if you have a choice stratagem waiting to be used, then know when to play it and make it count! Remember that David had come to Jerusalem before, when he planted Goliath's head outside its gates. It was probably then, or from subsequent inquiries, that he learned of the secret entryway into the city. But if he knew all along, why had he not taken Jerusalem before? Because the timing was not yet right. Because a victory for Judah alone, a triumph for his own tribe to shame all the other tribes, would detract from his larger designs. But if he could just get the tribes together, even though they doubted themselves and mistrusted each other, that would be the time to play the card.

And so David's Israel had its victory and gained a crowning symbol of achievement. Not merely a Judean capital, this city would bear the name it still carries to this day: *the City of David.* And working together, the people of Israel tasted a victory previously thought impossible, a victory worth singing out. All courtesy of David, their king and CEO. Indeed, he'll even write the song of triumph himself:

> As smoke is blown away by the wind,
>   may you blow them away;

as wax melts before the fire,
  may the wicked perish before God.
  But may the righteous be glad
    and rejoice before God;
    may they be happy and joyful.

Psalm 68:2, 3

It is in the experience of achievement that purpose is cemented in our hearts. David was able, with God's help, to manufacture a big triumph, but the taste of even small victories will often serve to stoke the flames. There is no tonic like success for bringing men and women together, for erasing old grudges and turning doubt into confident belief. It is the role of the executive to define such victories and lead his followers to them. David's masterpiece at Jerusalem was not just that he produced such a success, but that he produced the *right* success. It was a success achieved through the right principles, through unity and faithfulness to a noble calling. In the minds of his followers, the victory was not just for David, but for what David had so forcefully set before them. And in the city on the hill, fabled Jerusalem, all this was symbolized for the people to behold. In this way, not just a reign, not just a kingdom, but *a nation was reborn.*

> *It is in the experience of achievement that purpose is cemented in our hearts . . . The taste of even small victories will serve to stoke the flames, erase old grudges, and turn doubt into confident belief.*

In these scenes we see David the executive standing in the gap, personally staking his own fortune on the vision and the principles that were the sum of his leadership. His aim was for something much greater than personal acclaim or personal glory. Rather, David was pursuing an identity for his organization. To that end he held up a standard for his people, and that standard was himself. It was not about David; it was about Israel. And yet it was David's personal credibility, David's personal perseverance, his own risk-taking, and his own resourcefulness that paved the way. But when he led his people into Jerusalem, we can be sure it was to them that he pointed, and to the city on the hill that now was theirs, together.

To Build a City

In the ancient world, the city and the king were one. The strength of the walls and the strength of the throne were indistinguishable, so also the city's wealth and glory and honor. The city was not where the king dwelt, it *was* the king. So the great king always had a great city: for the Egyptian Pharaoh it was Memphis, for the kings of Mesopotamia it was Ashur or Babylon, and for David of Israel it was Jerusalem, also known as "the City of David."

The city gave substance to a king's labors. It was the city which the followers together shared and were nourished by, where those who bled in the armies and strained in the mines and labored in the fields looked to for much of their identity. To be without a city was to be without security, to be without an enduring identity, without a stable home in which to build and plant and grow, and one day to lay your bones to rest in peace.

In all these respects, the ancient city is analogous to what the corporation will need to be in the years ahead of us. "It's more than a job" is not just a slogan, but a mandate from an age that requires sustained capability and constant growth. But the corollary is this: "It's not just a business, either." The mandate for today's organization is to be a place where relationships are formed and commitments are made and sustained, wherein we are both challenged by and shielded from the storms of chaos and uncertainty. It is a place where membership is gained through participation in something great, where opportunities to contribute are seized and combined with those of others until the walls rise and the towers shine. That is what executives must build, or rather, lead others to build: a shining city where individuals contribute to and share in a larger identity without surrendering their own. And it was precisely this that David set out to build in Jerusalem.

Of course this city analogy is imperfect, for we cannot be so immovable today, nor will we likely find such rigidity of structure appropriate or helpful. It is, rather, the heart of the city that is appealing to us, the human entity with empowering and nurturing institutions, with clarity of purpose and shared challenges, and most of all with a real sense of community and participation and purpose. For a city is defined not so much by the height of its walls or the width of its streets but by the character of its inhabitants. Think about New York or Chicago or Paris, for instance.

> *The ancient city is analogous to what the corporation will need to be in the years ahead of us. "It's more than a job" is not just a slogan, and its corollary is this: "It's not just a business, either."*

One cannot admire the achievements of these cities without first admiring the character of their inhabitants.

We are in our time emerging from an era that thought quite differently. It was a time of nomads, of people who formed only temporary liaisons. A time when the free agent was the ideal, the man was loyal only to his own résumé, the woman who's chief collaborator was the corporate recruiter. You've heard the talk and felt the attitude: "The company man is a loser." "The company as family cannot compete." But you have also felt, more and more of you every passing year, that there is something more than moving higher and higher up the skyscraper. There is something worth more than earning boasting rights at the class reunion. We live in a time that is longing to turn in the nomad's tent for a place in a city, there to build and grow and to leave something behind us that others will know. Yes, we rightly seek challenges for growth and opportunities for advancement, yet we find that *self-actualization* has become a golden calf to which we have foolishly sacrificed the possibility of meaningful work and community.

Looking at the story of the Bible from a macro-perspective, from Genesis to Revelation, we see that it too is a journey from wilderness to city. Early in the Book of Genesis, Adam and Eve were expelled from the garden paradise because of their disobedience to God, to wander in the wastes as pilgrims without a home. Over time, God began to reveal His remedy, launching a new beginning in the life of Abraham, who was called to wander as a pilgrim in a land God promised to give to his descendants. The Lord made two great promises to Abraham. The first had to do with an abundance of descendants: "Look up at the heavens and count the stars—if indeed you can count them . . . So shall your offspring be" (Genesis 15:5); the second pertained to a land to call home: "To your descendants I give this land, from the river of Egypt to the great river, the Euphrates" (Genesis 15:18).

That longing for a land, an enduring and peaceful home, has been at the heart of Israel throughout its millennia of existence, most of which has been spent as pilgrims in a land not their own. Indeed, this longing for a land, a resting place, is central to the Bible's portrait of the life of faith. Solomon explained this longing for a higher meaning, stating that God "has set eternity in the hearts of men" (Ecclesiastes 3:11). Finally, this longing for a home, this sojourn from wilderness to city, is shown in fulfillment in the last book of the New Testament, the Book of Revelation, as the Bible's story reaches its culmination:

> I saw the Holy City, the new Jerusalem, coming down out of
> heaven from God, prepared as a bride beautifully dressed for her
> husband . . . It shone with the glory of God, and its brilliance was
> like that of a very precious jewel, like a jasper, clear as crystal.
> **(Revelation 21:2, 11)**

The new Jerusalem, that is what awaits those who look in faith to the Lord. It was the first Jerusalem that David set out to build, a prototype of heaven itself. It was not personal glory that drove him, but the longing of his people for a home, a place to belong, a unifying center for their corporate existence.

This drive rests in the heart of the true executive, in the breast of the leader: to build a city. To stand among and before the builders, to watch as the joy of achievement fills the faces of those who raise high the towers. To leave something behind us when our bones have been laid to rest within the walls, and so to know that we will be remembered. The city is not heaven itself, and we are wrong to think it is, but it is something of heaven on earth. It is a home for our labors and for ourselves. And in building his city, Jerusalem, David reached the pinnacle of his career.

In many ways, David was ill-suited for city building. Or, more accurately, David was well suited for establishing the foundations of his city, and yet lacked the qualities needed to finish the job. It is true of most of us, if not all, that we alone are not capable of providing the full range of leadership needed for such a monumental project. From this point forward David's success would not be measured in terms of the leadership he displayed but in the leadership he developed. In other words, he was now a CEO, responsible for a complex range of tasks well beyond the capacity of any one man or woman.

It is this transition that confounds many who excel as lieutenants yet flounder at the top. The position of faction-leader, which David had held most of his career, is much like that of corporate department head. We have seen that David possessed leadership abilities of a profound nature, and yet this leadership had been poured into one functional area. He was a military captain, a soldier, just as many CEO's or general managers come to that job as well-honed marketers or financiers or production managers. In David's case, his broader experience was limited due to the fact that his staff time in Saul's court had been, shall we say, cut short. Here was a warrior king, now setting out to be a city builder.

As it turned out circumstances conspired to keep David focused on his habitual function of military chief. Actually, it was not circumstances but his old friends the Philistines:

> When the Philistines heard that David had been anointed king
> over Israel, they went up in full force to search for him, but
> David heard about it and went down to the stronghold.
>
> (2 Samuel 5:17)

The stakes here were extremely high for David and for Israel, and it must have been that his force was ill equipped to meet the full strength of the Philistines. This probably explains why David returned with his war band to the old hideout-fortress at Adullam, the "stronghold" spoken of here. This strategem had much to commend it. The Philistines were looking for the king himself, knowing little about the activities taking place at Jerusalem and unaccustomed to the idea of a real Israelite capital. It was David they were after, for with the David they knew at the helm of their rival Israel, trouble would surely be in store for them. If David could be removed, the long-awaited day of Philistine retribution might well be realized. Understanding this, David therefore drew away from his new city and brought this formidable enemy onto territory more than familiar to his own forces.

The details of David's victories in this new phase of combat are few, but a familiar pattern clearly emerges. David takes his counsel from the Lord and is rewarded with much needed wisdom and information. Constantly aware of his enemies movements, his own troops gain a decisive advantage by fighting on terrain that is difficult for their enemies but familiar to them. In short order, then, David defeated the Philistines in a series of hit-and-run actions in which he not only whipped their field army but also rooted out their occupying garrisons.

Yet in this very scene of triumph, a disturbing trend is seen developing. We are given snapshots from these battles, the first of which is as follows:

> At that time David was in the stronghold, and the Philistine
> garrison was at Bethlehem. David longed for water and said,
> "Oh, that someone would get me a drink of water from the well
> near the gate of Bethlehem!" So the three mighty men broke
> through the Philistine lines, drew water from the well near the
> gate of Bethlehem and carried it back to David.
> (2 Samuel 23:14–16)

How a king has to watch what he says! Here is David, facing the enemy garrison occupying his own hometown. He looks out and what does he see? The old well from which he drew water as a boy. The cool waters that refreshed him upon bringing the sheep back home from a long season at pasture. It was like the front porch of his own hometown, and the tears welled up in his eyes at the sight. Letting his royal guard down for a moment, the king turned to his bodyguard and simply sighed, "Oh, what a sight! How precious to me is that well . . . how wonderful to drink from those cool waters once more."

It wasn't a command. It wasn't part of the battle plan. It was just a little overflow from the heart of a man made lonely by the sight of his hometown. So David turned back to the matters before him and when he looked up, what did he see: There went his soldiers, risking their lives to get the king a drink of water. When they returned, David was appalled:

> "Far be it from me, O Lord, to do this!" he said. "Is it not the
> blood of men who went at the risk of their lives?" And David
> would not drink it.
>
> (2 Samuel 23:17)

People act foolishly around a king; they do so out of respect, love, and fear for the royal presence. The king gets a cramp in his leg and every masseuse in the country is standing outside his door. The CEO remarks that blue is a lovely color, and the next day she arrives to find the building repainted and the carpets changed. The general or senator reminiscences about the tree he climbed as a youth, and every landscaper in the county is summoned. It's just proactive subordinates trying to impress the boss, trying to anticipate her requests, trying to get ahead. David wanted a cup of water, and so the whole battle plan was shelved, the element of secrecy was lost, and there were the brave warriors huddled around asking, "Was it cold enough for you, sir? Or should we go looking for ice cubes?"

Not only was David learning to watch his words but he slowly found that the front lines were no longer the place for him now that he was king. And yet this was the place he felt most comfortable. Who could command in battle better than David? But if David allowed himself to focus on the battle going on in front of him, the broader perspective and the broader needs of the kingdom would necessarily be neglected.

Executive leadership at the highest levels is not about peak performance for today. It is not about maximizing the effectiveness of the army, or the marketing arm, or the production line, but of developing and integrating all the functions and systems for sustained performance. It is about developing the whole package of capabilities, about a coherent and sustainable strategy for the organization as a whole.

> *Executive leadership at the highest levels is not about peak performance for today, but developing and integrating all the functions and systems for sustained performance.*

It took David a while to catch on, and he continued to provide personal leadership in numerous fights with the enemy. As the toll upon him grew it was finally his own men who demanded a change:

> Once again there was a battle between the Philistines and Israel.
> David went down with his men to fight against the Philistines,
> and he became exhausted. And Ishbi-Benob, one of the
> descendants of Rapha, whose bronze spearhead weighed three
> hundred shekels . . . said he would kill David. But Abishai son
> of Zeruiah came to David's rescue; he struck the Philistine down
> and killed him. Then David's men swore to him, saying, "Never
> again will you go out with us to battle, so that the lamp of
> Israel will not be extinguished."
> (2 Samuel 21:15–17)

So David dragged his weary body back to Jerusalem, no doubt wishing he had never been anointed king. When he got there he found that laborers had arrived from the king of Tyre, having been sent as a good will gesture to help work on his city. Did they know what David intended for Jerusalem? Had David's officials followed up on this opening for a joint venture with this important and nearby nation? Were sustaining institutions, besides those of the army, rising up and gaining focus? Surely they were not, for the king was playing war-chief with his old pals. So, no doubt muttering under his breath, David handed over his sword and settled into the work of a king.

What is the task of the senior executive? It is that of *integrating*.

David had shown much skill and determination in drawing old rivals together for his new venture in Israel. But now the time had come for him to give direction to their various efforts, to establish goals and put coordinating measures into place. The priesthood would need to replenish the ranks so decimated by Saul's anger, and take up their rightful place in the national life. The builders would need guidance, to be integrated into the overall military strategy. Someone would have to take control over foreign affairs, with a coherent plan for using diplomacy to support the military and economic program. It was so much easier just wielding a sword!

David probably struggled throughout the remainder of his career with the challenge of integrating the various components of his city and kingdom into a single coherent whole. Ultimately it would be left to his son and successor, Solomon, to consolidate what he had gained. But there is one other crucial element of senior leadership of which David was a past master, that of establishing and inspiring an identity for the organization.

As we have seen over and again, David had long committed himself to this task. It was his drive for a higher calling and sense of purpose that had launched him as a change agent in the first place. It was his concern for values to guide his kingdom that determined his behavior in the cave at Adullam and in his dealings with Abner. David was resolved that, if nothing else, his Israel would come to know who it was, and what it was called to be.

Executives who do a good job of shaping the company's identity make it one of their highest priorities. They take pains to keep in touch with the motivations and pressures bearing upon their people. Some engage in continual discussions of the company credo, others are constantly on the road, listening and challenging. For David and his Israel, the identity would forever be linked to Jerusalem, and so to that city he drew the people of God. So it was that David gathered them there on the walls, at the gates, along the narrow streets, in order for them to watch him bringing the Ark of the Covenant, the throne of the Lord Almighty, into Jerusalem. Read the Bible's own account and see if you can fail to sense the electricity:

> David again brought together out of Israel chosen men, thirty
> thousand in all. He and all his men set out from Baalah of Judah
> to bring up from there the ark of God, which is called by the
> Name, the name of the Lord Almighty, who is enthroned
> between the cherubim that are on the Ark . . . David and the
> whole house of Israel were celebrating with all their might
> before the Lord, with songs and with harps, lyres,
> tambourines, sistrums and cymbals.
>
> **(2 Samuel 6:1–5)**

How often our grand ceremonies fail to grasp the heart of our men and women. Flashy million-dollar extravaganzas may generate short-term awe, yet they still fail to inspire precisely because they deal more with appearance than with substance. But not so David's grand statement: *God Himself dwells among us.* This was the idea that had led young David down into the ditch before Goliath. *God Almighty is our Lord.* It was this that had stayed David's hand from striking down Saul. *We are together God's people.* It was this that caused the king to weep before the grave of the would-be enemy Abner.

David was making a significant statement that day, focusing the people's gaze not on his own glory but on that of the Lord. But things would not go just as he planned that day, for he was not the only one to make a statement and Jerusalem was not merely his city, but God's city as well.

Maybe it was due to haste in their preparations and maybe it was the result of sheer ignorance, for the Ark had been absent from the scene during Saul's ruinous reign. Whatever the cause, David's men badly botched the handling of this holy object. It was bad enough that they just plopped it on a ox-cart, when Moses' Law demanded that priests carry it by the attached poles. Worse still, when one of the animals stumbled and the Ark threatened to fall to the ground, one of the attendants, Uzzah, actually reached out and placed his hand upon the Ark of the Covenant of the Lord.

> When they came to the threshing floor of Nacon, Uzzah
> reached out and took hold of the ark of God, because the oxen
> stumbled. The Lord's anger burned against Uzzah because of
> his irreverent act; therefore God struck him down and he died
> there beside the Ark of God.
>
> (2 Samuel 6:6, 7)

What, is God touchy? No, He is holy. Does God not care about human life? That is not the point, but rather that He is pure beyond comprehension while the hand of man is impure and defiling. God had warned them about trifling with His holiness. Moses' writings are full of instructions regarding this and it was because of this that the priesthood had been given to the people, that they might intercede and mediate between holy God and sinful man.

What a crisis this was for David and his long-anticipated festival. His intent had been to dedicate the city in the name of the Lord, and now God stepped in to make sure that this very point was clear to David himself. It was a point God had made the last time Israel gathered on a mount before Him, when Moses brought the people to Mount Sinai. There, amid the smoke and fire and raging thunder, God spoke to them from out of the storm:

> " 'Now if you obey me fully and keep my covenant, then out of
> all nations you will be my treasured possession. Although the   .
> whole earth is mine, you will be for me a kingdom of priests
> and a holy nation.' "
>
> (Exodus 19:5, 6)

Now, at perhaps the most significant gathering of the nation since that very day, God was making the same point again, hammering home the reality of their corporate identity. They were to know themselves as His people, were to follow His ways and revere the Lord as holy. By this they were set apart from the nations with a distinct identity and calling.

David, of course, was beside himself over the needless loss of this man Uzzah and the unintended affront to the Lord. Perhaps too he saw how he had taken center stage beside so august a Host as God and now felt rightly ashamed. He had gathered the people to worship their God, to celebrate their great cause, but it was David who attracted all the attention. Now, he and the priests spent three months researching and arranging the procedures God had established for the handling of the Ark, which were found in the writings of Moses. Then he gathered the people once more to observe as the Ark was brought into Jerusalem. This time it was the Lord, who was Himself the vision and the cause Israel was called to serve, who received the honor of the people, and not David.

It is challenging for the executive to keep his pride in check, to stem her longing for personal glory, to distinguish between the vision and his own ambitions. For your triumph is not itself inspiring to anyone but you. It is the triumph of the cause, of the faith, of the quest and the calling that electrifies the hearts of followers. Whether you are kicking off a new initiative or commemorating a huge success, it is the cause that must get the attention. Wonderful though you may be, it is not you that people want to celebrate, but the achievement itself, the challenge to which they have sacrificed and in which they found their identity. In the case of David's Israel, their identity could only be formed in terms of their relationship to God Himself, the holy God who demands holiness in return.

> *Your triumph is not itself inspiring to anyone but you. It is the triumph of the cause, of the faith, of the quest and the calling that electrifies the hearts of followers.*

Can there be any doubt that when God's throne finally made its way up through Jerusalem the celebration had a different tone than before? Celebration, yes, but celebration mixed with solemnity and awe of God and what He had done in Israel.

> David went down and brought up the ark of God . . . to the City of David with rejoicing. When those who were carrying the ark of the Lord had taken six steps, he sacrificed a bull and a fattened calf. David, wearing a linen ephod, danced before the Lord with all his might, while he and the entire house of Israel brought up the ark of the Lord with shouts and the sound of trumpets . . .
>
> They brought the ark of the Lord and set it in its place inside

the tent that David had pitched for it, and David sacrificed burnt
offerings and fellowship offerings before the Lord. After he had
finished sacrificing the burnt offerings and fellowship offerings,
he blessed the people in the name of the Lord Almighty.

(2 Samuel 6:12–18)

Symbolic acts, like the entry of the Ark of the Covenant into Jerusalem, are vital for an organization. They communicate with great clarity
the identity and the aspirations, the values and the principles that define
the organization. But symbolic leadership is only credible when the
leader himself takes the first place in submitting, when the executive also
stands in awe before a higher accountability, before the shared faith, and
better still, before God. David's actions before the ark were highly symbolic and they made a profound point to all who beheld them. But they
were also more than symbolic, they were genuine acts of faith and worship, by which he made public declaration of his allegiance. David was
at his best not when he was the object of worship, but when he stood
among the ranks of the worshipers, leading others in submitting to a
higher cause.

*Symbolic acts communicate
with great clarity the identity
and the aspirations, the
values and the principles
that define the organization
. . . But they are only credible
when the leader himself
stands in awe before a higher
accountability, before the
shared faith, and better still,
before God.*

The establishment of David's Jerusalem concludes with one of the
most significant passages of the entire
Old Testament, as God Himself gives
His assessment of what David has
done. We have been saying all along
that David's story is not just *a* story
about leadership, but the Bible's portrait of effective and faithful leadership. Therefore we are not surprised
that here again the Scripture slows down to editorialize on what has transpired.

God gave his assessment to David through a prophet named Nathan.
The first item on His agenda had to do with David's bringing up of the
Ark and his intention to build a temple for the Lord in Jerusalem. God
asked him, "Are you the one to build me a house to dwell in?" (2 Samuel

7:5). God had done perfectly well without a house of wooden timbers for thousands of years, and David should be careful not to become presumptuous about his own standing. God wanted to make absolutely clear that far from David having done any great favors for the Lord, far from him having made God's name great by building this city, the opposite was quite the case. So while God fully approved of what David had done,

> "I took you from the pasture and from following the flock to be
> ruler over my people Israel. I have been with you wherever you
> have gone, and I have cut off all your enemies from before you.
> Now I will make your name great, like the names of the greatest
> men of the earth. And I will provide a place for my people
> Israel and will plant them so that they can have a home and
> no longer be disturbed."
> (2 Samuel 7:8–10)

That is the first point we are to reckon with, that all our greatest glories pale before the brighter light of heaven. David needed to hear this, to remember that while in building Jerusalem he had done much for his people, he could have just as easily ended up in obscurity or, worse, dangling on the end of Goliath's sword. There was much that he could look back on with pride, and yet the proper posture for considering his success was upon his knees before the Lord.

Many of us need to consider this as well. Why did we get the opportunities, why did the promotion come our way, why did we achieve such great results? "It was because of my hard work and ability." I do not mean to downgrade such things, but let's not kid ourselves, there were plenty of others with just as much ability and even more effort who did not make it. No, we have no warrant for boasting. How many sacrifices of others went into your success? Who was passed by as you were selected? Whose sore limbs and wearied minds put your plans into effect? We make a serious mistake if we forget them, if we cast our adoring gaze on only, or even mainly, ourselves. And we make an even more serious error if we forget the God who directed our paths, guided our hands, and to whom we are accountable in our privilege and power.

The apostle Paul put it most pointedly in his first letter to the Corinthians:

> "For who makes you different from anyone else? What do you
> have that you did not receive? And if you did receive it, why do
> you boast as though you did not?"
> (1 Corinthians 4:7)

So God, wanted to ensure that David did not go astray on this point. Furthermore, He proclaimed that it was not for David to build the great temple, which would become the focal point and greatest glory of Jerusalem. For David, a man of war, a man of blood, would not build God's house. That would be reserved for the man of peace who would follow him.

Yet with all this business settled, God turned to what was foremost on His mind: His joy at the kind of leadership David had displayed, the leadership that seeks not just a wall of trophies for itself but a city for its people. To show His pleasure, God marked David's leadership as the model of His own, the pattern of the Messiah who was yet to come and who would be the true hope of Israel. To show this, the line of David would be the line of the Savior, who would sit forever upon a throne founded by David's leadership:

> "The Lord declares to you that the Lord himself will establish a
> house for you: When your days are over and you rest with your
> fathers, I will raise up your offspring to succeed you, who will
> come from your own body, and I will establish his kingdom. He
> is the one who will build a house for my Name, and I will
> establish the throne of his kingdom forever. I will be his father,
> and he will be my son . . . Your house and your kingdom
> will endure forever before me; your throne will be
> established forever."
> (2 Samuel 7:11–16)

It would be Solomon, David's son and heir, a man born in a land of peace, who would build God's temple. Yet it is also clear that another one to follow, another Son, is in mind here. For the true representative of David would build God's eternal house, raise up an eternal city, and reign upon an eternal throne, none of which Solomon or any mere man could do. So greatly praised was David's leadership that it was declared by God to foreshadow the very Messiah He would send, with a promise to endure forever.

Neither you nor I are engaged in building God's city; most of us are engaged in affairs much more mundane than David's construction of Jerusalem, with its temple and the special presence of the Lord. Does that, therefore, make our labor as leaders and executives less holy? In one sense, the answer is clearly "Yes," for we should not confuse our efforts with those happening in the biblical story. And yet in another and very real sense what we do as leaders *is no less holy* than what we see in the Bible. For the issue is not really profits or performance goals, real and significant to us as they are, but the legacy we leave as we pursue these things. Are we building something that will endure? Are we embarked on a pursuit analogous to the rising up of a city, be it an organization or department or a season of achievement in which our followers find themselves and discover meaning beyond that of the daily grind? In leading others do we see the imprint of our work on the souls of men and women? If not, we are falling far short of the leader's calling, which like David's is holy work and pleasing to God when issuing forth from faith and love and a longing to see His pleasure in our lives.

Chapter 7

THE SEDUCTION OF SUCCESS

THE LIMITS OF
POWER

גבול־חזקה

In warfare it is called the "victory disease." That was the phrase coined by the commander of the Imperial Japanese Fleet, which went into the Battle of Midway in 1942 undefeated but came out with all four of its aircraft carriers sunk. The victory disease is that misplaced confidence which makes you so convinced of your invincibility that you stop doing the things that made you invincible in the first place. It is a disease that strikes only the triumphant, and it is generally fatal.

In sports it is called the "Sports Illustrated Jinx." That is, the tendency for stars whose picture adorns the cover of this sports magazine to immediately go into a protracted slump. Perhaps the fielding of agents' phone calls and the signing of autographs get in the way of mundane things like batting practice. However mysterious its power, the curse is real enough; while it only afflicts heroes, it often turns them into failures.

Success has a disorienting effect on most of us. Having struggled so long in the upward climb and worn ourselves out, we arrive at our long dreamed-of position at the top only to stop doing the things that got us there in the first place. Having so long denied ourselves, having sacrificed present pleasure in pursuit of future gain, once there it is difficult not to drop everything in order to smell the roses.

We have already seen this tendency in David's life, and so we should not be surprised if his great success opens the door to lapses of various sorts. Yet when we see it happen it is still shocking, particularly in light of how far such a man as David can fall, and how fast. So it is, however, that in the realm of leadership and power, David contributes his own addition to our list—we'll call it the "Bathsheba Syndrome." This, too, only afflicts those at the top, but it possesses the power to drag them all the way down to the bottom.

After bringing up the Ark to Jerusalem before the gathered tribes of Israel, David had united a nation behind his leadership. Capitalizing on this union of strength and purpose, he immediately set about to provide a permanent solution to the nation's age-old military problem. Earlier we noted that Saul's victories were little more than minor tactical gains that left the broader strategic situation basically unaltered. David, however, had something more in mind. Having drawn the tribes together, not just in body but in spirit, and having given them a taste of victory that brought confidence in his leadership, David now set out to permanently carve out a space for Israel's homeland.

The list of enemies David defeated during these early years reads like a roster of Israel's historic opponents. First, of course, came the Philistines to the west. Next he broke the power of the Moabites to the East, nearly annihilating their armed force. Turning north, the Israelites attacked the Arameans of Damascus, seizing this strategic site, establishing an armed garrison there, and placing all of Syria under tribute. The result of these campaigns was a national security unprecedented in Israel's history; indeed, what David had achieved was little short of the fulfillment of Moses' grand design for the Promised Land, a holy endeavor begun by Joshua and left unfinished for so many generations.

How few of us ever see our youthful dreams brought to real fruition. From the very beginning of his career, immediately after his victory over Goliath brought him to prominence, David began pointing to the great unfinished work that was both an obligation and a promise for the people. Through the long struggle and climb to the throne he had kept his gaze fixed on that purpose, and when then the opportunity for realization appeared he wasted no time or effort in bringing about its fulfillment. The Bible sums up this high water mark of his career with justified satisfaction:

> The Lord gave David victory wherever he went.
> David reigned over all Israel, doing what was just and
> right for all his people.
> (2 Samuel 8:14, 15)

From this point forward David's main task would be to consolidate his massive gains and build institutions that would both last and profit Israel. His kingdom was not only large but it had also become rich from the spoils of successful wars. David was rich, powerful, and responsible for a far-flung empire. Therefore, when a new and relatively minor military threat surfaced from the Ammonites in the east, David delegated the task to his commander, Joab, and remained behind to provide broader strategic leadership.

> In the spring, at the time when kings go off to war, David sent
> Joab out with the king's men and the whole Israelite army. They
> destroyed the Ammonites and besieged Rabbah. But
> David remained in Jerusalem.
> (2 Samuel 11:1)

This terse narrative betrays a hint of reproach that David the king did not go out to personally lead the men in battle. As we have noted, however, David was not only general but shepherd for the whole flock of Israel. Perhaps the biblical account would be more generous if he had in fact devoted himself to this broader role, but the fact is that he did not. Whether he was paralyzed by the extent of his own achievement, uncertain of how to engage in the new and unfamiliar roles of the CEO, or maybe just plain tired of serving others all the time, the fact is that David gave himself over to self-indulgence while his servants went off to battle. Thus began a fall from which David would never quite recover. Here is the way the sad tale is told:

> One evening David got up from his bed and walked around on the roof of the palace. From the roof he saw a woman bathing. The woman was very beautiful, and David sent someone to find out about her. The man said, "Isn't this Bathsheba, the daughter of Eliam and the wife of Uriah the Hittite?" Then David sent messengers to get her. She came to him, and he slept with her.
>
> **(2 Samuel 11:2–4)**

Pretty stunning, isn't it? We are struck by David's crude and straight-forward plunge into iniquity. As soon as he took his eye off his duty it rested on a bathing beauty; before a second thought was given he had indulged in a sin he would never put behind him.

What happenened here should serve as a warning to every man or woman of action who has attained a position of power. What we see here is all action, with no deliberation or analysis. In the grips of a lust that is common to all of us, the very propensity for decisive action that has so well served him in the past leads David directly into a freefall. So it is that the executive who allows the hand of power to brush aside all deliberation and critical analysis removes his own best defense against power itself.

> *His propensity for decisive action leads David directly into a freefall . . . The executive who allows the hand of power to brush aside deliberation removes his own best defense against power itself.*

Look at the verbs that mark David's course: he saw, he sent, he slept with her. Each one is a study in the abuse of power. There he was gazing over his glorious city when his eye caught the form of Bathsheba bathing on a roof (not at all an unusual practice for the time). Why can David observe this? Because of the lofty perch that comes with his station in life. Rather than turn away, his eye lingers, his mind soaking up what rests before him. What then? He summons a messenger, one of those assigned to serve him in the exercise of power. Will he send him to warn the lady and advise her of the need for discretion? To the contrary, he bears this message: "The king, David himself, has summoned you, madame . . ." So she comes, one of the lambs David is commissioned by God to protect and nurture. Surely she is confused, awed, and disoriented. So does he set her right, does he orient her upon a path that will benefit her? Not at all. He takes her.

Walter Brueggemann neatly sums up David's incredible descent into the grips of lust and unbounded power: "He can have whatever he wants, no restraint, no second thoughts, no reservations, no justification. He takes simply because he can. He is at the culmination of his enormous power."[1]

What do we see here but the realization that there is a struggle within ourselves, a struggle made both more difficult and more vital as we rise in power and privilege in this world. There is a Saul within each of our breasts, a Saul even within the anti-Saul David. It is not a pretty sight, and it certainly mars our opinion of David. Matthew Henry records our own sentiment well, writing, "We wish we could draw a veil over it, and that it might never be known, might never be said, that David never did such things as are here recorded of him. But it cannot, it must not, be concealed."[2]

Do we remember what Saul had warned when he objected to the people's demand for a king? The king will take from you. He who has much will take more, he will take the best for himself. David, who at last count has six known wives, must now have the one wife of Uriah, because he is king, because he can.

Maybe we're being hard on David. Imagine the stress and the strain, the responsibility and pressure that he alone bears in Jerusalem. Yes, he has let down his guard and has committed an indiscretion. He is, after all, mortal. Is there really any harm done? He can repent, ask God's forgiveness, use his position to gain control of the situation, and move on wiser for the experience, right?

The very next verse of Scripture shatters such delusions; David will not control these events but will be swept along by them. For it was not long before a message came that chilled David's heart, as it has done to countless men both before and after his time. The message was simple and straightforward: "*I am pregnant.*"

That was all she said, but of course there was much more implied,

---

1. *Walter Brueggemann,* First and Second Samuel, *Louisville, Ky.: John Knox Press, 1990, pp. 273, 274.*
2. *Matthew Henry,* Commentary on the Whole Bible, *vol. 2, p. 386.*

such as, "What are you going to do about it, David?" Under Israelite law those convicted of adultery were to be stoned to death. Bathsheba's husband Uriah was off fighting in David's army, so this birth would raise more than a few eyebrows. Bathsheba needed David's protection, and David needed her cooperation. So much for maintaining control.

David is in quite a fix and he knows it. Where will he turn? Will he turn to God? Will we discover poetic lines recounting his search for forgiveness and aid? Sadly, he did not and we will not. Instead David turns to his own power to control, his prerogative to dictate both events and reality. And in this way he flings himself deeper into trouble.

Let is not be said, however, that David lacks cunning. Indeed, in just a short time messengers were sent out with his remedy in tow:

> So David sent this word to Joab: "Send me Uriah the Hittite."
> And Joab sent him to David. When Uriah came to him, David
> asked him how Joab was, how the soldiers were and how the war
> was going. Then David said to Uriah, "Go down to your house
> and wash your feet." So Uriah left the palace, and a gift
> from the king was sent after him.
> (2 Samuel 11:6–8)

Do you see where this is going? It must have been unusual for the king to summon one of the modest rank for such discussions, but David masks his intent with queries regarding the situation at the front. There is biting irony in these lines, for a literal translation of the Hebrew here would have David asking about *the welfare* of Joab and *the welfare* of the soldiers, and *the welfare* of the war. The word repeated here is *Shalom*, normally rendered as "peace" but here as "welfare." And yet *peace* or *welfare* is the last thing on David's mind! As the prophet Jeremiah lamented, "The heart is deceitful above all things/and beyond cure./Who can understand it?" (Jeremiah 17:9). David's turn of heart is indeed bewildering, and yet we are forced to ask ourselves what we would do in his situation.

David's plan is as subtle as it is cunning. Having brought Uriah, probably a mid-level officer, to render a report, he good-naturedly smiles and makes a natural suggestion, soldier-to-soldier. "Thanks, Uriah. Hey, and since you're here in Jerusalem, why don't you take a little furlough? Did you say your wife is staying here? Wonderful! Why don't you stop by and *wash your feet?*" Get it? "Wash your feet . . . make yourself comfortable . . ." And if Uriah does—and who wouldn't?—then when the child is born no one will be the wiser! What a wonderful solution!

Before we feel relief for our hero's escape, let us take not of how far this affair is leading him from his principles, from truth and faithfulness and justice. Oh, it's a great plan, but not a *good* one. And much to David's dismay, the plan doesn't succeed either:

> So Uriah left the palace, and a gift from the king was sent after
> him. But Uriah slept at the entrance to the palace with all his
> master's servants and did not go down to his house.
> When David was told, "Uriah did not go home," he asked him,
> "Haven't you just come from a distance?
> Why didn't you go home?"
> Uriah said to David, "The ark and Israel and Judah are staying
> in tents, and my master Joab and my lord's men are camped in
> the open fields. How could I go to my house to eat and drink
> and lie with my wife? As surely as you live,
> I will not do such a thing!"
> (2 Samuel 11:8 – 11)

Unbelievable! Just what David needed, a principled man! What he needed now were men of expedience and self-interest, men appropriate to what David had allowed himself to become, appropriate to the kind of leadership he now provided. Isn't that one of the great tragedies of execu-tives who, like David, fall from the path of virtue? For now it is his most loyal subordinates, his most committed and faithful followers, his most principled *Now that he has fallen from the path of virtue, it is his most loyal subordinates, his most committed and faithful followers, his most principled men who are the greatest danger to his regime.* men who are the greatest danger to his regime. It happens all the time in our own day, and explains why it is often the best of our men and women, those who have dared to believe our statements of vision and purpose, who have to be the first to go.

What was it that drove Uriah to refuse the respite David offered him? It was his solidarity with fellow soldiers who that very night would be facing hardship and danger. His sense of loyalty to Joab, his general, who would enjoy no such pleasures this day. His gratitude to God Himself, and his respect for the Ark of the Covenant, that holy and divine symbol of God's presence, which was being kept in a simple and humble tent that night. Where did Uriah get such passionate devotion? From David, that's where. From the marvelous words that had pierced his heart and set his soul aflame. From the king's own example of duty and faithfulness and purpose. Uriah, a Hittite by birth, has become the truest Jew in Jerusalem. So he must be dealt with by the king who has betrayed himself, his people, and his God.

Not one to give up easily, David tries again, this time inviting Uriah over to get drunk before sending him off in lovely Bathsheba's direction. But even with his brains addled Uriah will not deviate from his course. Surely frustrated to the ends of his wits, David finds he simply cannot command or control the conscience of so faithful a man. Here is where he finds the limits of power drawn.

What happens next truly send shivers down our spines. The line of reasoning David follows is terrible: "Uriah is a pawn, he has made himself a nuisance, he is a threat to me, and I am the king. Uriah must die." It happens all the time today, as those with competence and principles find themselves being terminated for committing the gross crime of exposing the boss's lack of both.

It would have been easy for David to justify all this to himself. "The king cannot be held to the same standard as the Uriahs of this world" . . . "Yes, it's wrong but as king I am above being held accountable." And by coming up with this scheme he assumed the very garments of Saul he had so carefully refused long ago, and insanely grasped a spear to throw at this admirable man, Uriah, the very image of his youthful self:

> In the morning David wrote a letter to Joab and sent it with
> Uriah. In it he wrote, "Put Uriah in the front line where the

> fighting is fiercest. Then withdraw from him so he will
> be struck down and die."
>
> (2 Samuel 11:14, 15)

Now this is despicable; pride and desperation have truly twisted David's heart. He even has the callousness to have Uriah unwittingly bear his own death sentence. But can David trust Joab to carry out so rotten a scheme? Of course he can. Joab was a hatchet just waiting to be picked up. It was Joab who murdered Abner and Joab whom David had shamed as an example to everyone else. How delighted Joab would be to get David's order. "I always knew you were no better than me," he surely laughed to himself. "Ah, David, suddenly a man like me is a useful thing to have on your side . . ." Joab would do David's evil will, thus to be forever free from any righteous demands this king might place upon him.

Joab obeyed, but due to his carelessness a whole company of brave men died in the successful attempt to remove Uriah. It was not long before Joab's messenger returned to the palace, a messenger who was carefully briefed by his commander on how to handle David's reaction to the loss of so many soldiers:

> Joab sent David a full account of the battle. He instructed the
> messenger: "When you have finished giving the king this
> account of the battle, the king's anger may flare up, and he may
> ask you, 'Why did you get so close to the city to fight? Didn't
> you know they would shoot arrows from the wall?' . . . If he asks
> you this, then say to him, 'Also, your
> servant Uriah the Hittite is dead.' "
>
> (2 Samuel 11:18–21)

David's response indicates that he got the message very well indeed. Framing the whole affair as the necessary if unfortunate by-product of war, he merely replied,

> "Don't let this upset you; the sword devours one as well as
> another. Press the attack against the city and destroy it."
>
> (2 Samuel 11:25)

And so Uriah was out of the way and things could go back to normal. David tied up the loose ends by making Bathsheba his wife after her mourning period was over, after which she bore him a son. The only problem was that things would never really go back to normal again.

Let's reflect on what we have seen. The first thing we must notice is that *personal infidelity always leads to professional infidelity*. Always. That is because there is no separating the man from the officeholder. Who wields the authority? The man or the official, the woman or the executive? It is all the same. In David's case this reality is glaringly evident. As king he was responsible for upholding the laws of Israel, and yet that is the very thing he can no longer do. He certainly cannot allow inquiries into Bathsheba's pregnancy[3] and he cannot protect innocent Uriah from the ravages of injustice. Indeed, he has also effectively lost the ability to discipline Joab and who knows how many others. What a mess, for David and for Israel. The integrity of the organization and that of its leader are always inseparable.

> *Personal infidelity always leads to professional infidelity. For the integrity of the organization and that of its leader are inseparable.*

Thus it is that those who abuse their power to control people and events inevitably lose the power to control. This is what has happened to David. He could command Bathsheba to share his bed but he could not command her womb to be barren. He could command Uriah to return home but he could not compel him to betray his principles. And never again would he exert a positive moral influence on Joab, now his secret accomplice.

That leads to our last observation: The executive who betrays his principles, eventually discovers that his once faithful followers are now his greatest opponents. And that is a loss as tragic as the loss of integrity itself.

What is the value for us of this episode in David's life? For one thing it helps us to see that David is no plaster saint. He will prosper according

---

3. *While Bathsheba's name will never be synonymous with virtue, it is interesting to note that Scripture never accuses her for this affair. Mainly, the Bible regards her as a victim of David's exploitation. Indeed, she will later receive the significant commendation of being the wife who produces his great son and successor, King Solomon, thus attaining a position of power and honor.*

to his deeds, according to the character he cultivates in his heart. Surely David had justified this affair to himself on the pretext that because he was king he was a special case. But there are no special cases. I am not special. You are not special. Do you consider the implications of this terrible scene for us? If such a thing is possible for a heart so great and noble as David's, then what lurks around our unguarded corners? Therefore, let those who long for power understand what they are getting into, let them stand vigilant over their avarice and pride. And let every leader among us pray to God, as Jesus taught us with good reason, "Lead us not into temptation."

It may seem that David's logic was accurate and that he could, in the end, control events. By his great power and cunning he was able to tie up the loose strands, all at the cost of just one more soldier among the many who had died. Yet there is one last comment in the biblical account of this episode, indeed the very last line:

> But the thing David had done displeased the Lord.
> (2 Samuel 11:27)

It was, as these things go, a pretty tidy arrangement. David knew. Bathsheba and Joab knew, but they would be silenced by their complicity. Maybe a few bodyguards or couriers saw into what was going on, but they could be managed. But there is always one other who knows even our most secret deeds. As the New Testament reminds us: "Nothing in all creation is hidden from God's sight. Everything is uncovered and laid bare before the eyes of him to whom we must give account" (Hebrews 4:13). Here was David's ultimate miscalculation, one we should have thought impossible for him. And yet if David found it easy to forget this most crucial truth, then how much more easy would it be for you and me?

In his commentary of this episode, Walter Brueggemann points out the conflict between David's understanding of the moral value of his action, and God's. In the literal reading of the Hebrew text, David had advised his confederate Joab, "Do not let this matter *be evil in your eyes*" (v. 25). "There's really nothing wrong with what we have done, don't you see!" he argued. But God will reject this twisted way of thinking. Brueggemann notes:

The royal seductions of power and security have skewed the moral vision of Israel. The king may act. The king may kill. The king may be self-satisfied. The king, however, is not capable of revising moral reality . . . The king may imagine he is morally autonomous and subject to no one . . . But that does not change the moral reality to which David must answer.[4]

Those who abuse their power to control inevitably lose their power to control . . . The executive who betrays his principles eventually discovers that his once faithful followers are now his greatest opponents.

This remains just as true for those in today's palaces of glass and steel as it was for David in Jerusalem. David will answer for his apparently secret deeds, will be confronted with those nasty loose ends he thinks he has tied. Once David forgets the limits of earthly power, he is committing himself to a path of deceit that will lead him to nowhere but ruin. And so it is for us all.

4. *Brueggemann, p. 279.*

"I HAVE SINNED"

חטאתי

We left our story on an ominous note, and necessarily so. David has fallen from his pedestal and committed a grievous crime. What will become of him now? We think back to Saul's story and we tremble for David. The old king had sinned against God repeatedly and as a result he forfeited God's favor and support. But what will God do in response to David's heinous abuse of power?

We are not left to wonder long, for God acted swiftly. The previous episode concluded, "But the thing David had done was evil in the eyes of the Lord." Immediately, then, we see God taking action: "The Lord sent Nathan to David" (2 Samuel 12:1). God sent the prophet Nathan, who apparently had come to fill Samuel's shoes, to confront David with his sin. What amazing grace this is. God would have been justified had he simply struck David down, as He did in the case of greedy Nabal, Abigail's former husband. If not that, surely we would not protest if God sent Nathan to inform David of his removal from office, as He did in the case of hard-hearted Saul. But instead Nathan is sent to reason with David and show him the wickedness in his heart.

Here we confront one of the greatest myths regarding leadership, that which says, "Everyone must be treated the same." But everyone is not the same, and wise leaders do not treat everyone the same way. The leader must have the same aspiration for everyone, the same willingness to lift everyone up, to serve them and guide them. But it is sheer folly for a leader to treat everyone as if they were not different, and God certainly does not fall into this error. Indeed, God is perfectly able to discriminate between people, for "man looks at the outward appearance, but the Lord looks at the heart" (1 Samuel 16:7). Indeed, the main difficulty most of us have is that we do not know the hearts of our people. We hardly know our people at all, and so we ineffectively deal en masse.

There was a fundamental difference in Saul, Nabal, and David. The former king was hardened in heart against God, while Nabal's corruptness stemmed from raw avarice. Though David had embarked on an incredibly wicked course of action, his heart was not fundamentally hardened against the truth, and so God provided a response suited to his true condition.

One of the greatest myths regarding leadership is that everyone must be treated the same. But everyone is not the same.

It is not, however, as if David somehow deserved better treatment from God than others. What we are seeing here is what the Bible calls *grace*: God's love and mercy to those who deserve the opposite. God's grace is not opposed to His justice; indeed, Scripture informs us that it is God's nature to be both merciful and just. But while His justice instills fear and awe, it is God's grace that produces love for Him in the hearts of men and women, as David himself rejoices in his Psalm 103:

> *The Lord is compassionate and gracious,*
> *   slow to anger, abounding in love.*
> *He will not always accuse,*
> *   nor will he harbor his anger forever;*
> *he does not treat us as our sins deserve*
> *   or repay us according to our iniquities.*
> *For as high as the heavens are above the earth,*
> *   so great is his love for those who fear him;*
> *as far as the east is from the west, so far has he removed*
> *   our transgressions from us.*

As a father has compassion on his children,
   so the Lord has compassion on those who fear him.

                            Psalm 103:8–13

What, then, is the answer for us when, like David, we fall into sin? God's compassion for sinners. God's readiness to forgive and restore those who trust in Him and fear Him. Now, if this is David's own teaching, *then why didn't he do this himself!* The answer must surely be that he was avoiding the hard truth regarding what he had done, and therefore the truth regarding God. David's wise son Solomon would later write, Through the fear of the Lord a man avoids evil . . . Blessed is the man who always fears the Lord, but he who hardens his heart falls into trouble (Proverbs 16:6; 28:14).

The fear of the Lord is not some cringing dread, but a willing recognition that God does rule over us, that His ways are right, and that we must give an account of ourselves to Him. As David had said, the man or woman who thus fears the Lord may come to Him in confession and seek forgiveness, and yet it was David's unwillingness to confront God's justice that kept him from God's compassion. David was left, then, to plunge deeper and deeper into sin, until he was not only an adulterer but a murderer as well.

How much greater, then, is God's grace that in just this situation *He comes to David;* knowing David's true heart and loving him as a son, God initiates the process of restoration Himself. Perhaps it was in later reflection on this that David would pen these words regarding the man or woman who trusts in the Lord:

Though he stumble, he will not fall,
   for the Lord upholds him with his hand.

                            Psalm 37:24

So Nathan the prophet is sent by God to bring David to his senses, to bring him to his knees in repentance for his sin. What follows is a masterpiece in effective communication, from which we may profit in our own attempts to enable colleagues and subordinates to confront the reality of their performance:

When he [Nathan] came to him, he said, "There were two men
in a certain town, one rich and the other poor. The rich man
had a very large number of sheep and cattle, but the poor man
had nothing except one little ewe lamb he had bought. He raised
it, and it grew up with him and his children. It shared his food,
drank from his cup and even slept in his arms. It was
like a daughter to him.
Now a traveler came to the rich man, but the rich man refrained
from taking one of his own sheep or cattle to prepare a meal for
the traveler who had come to him. Instead, he took the ewe lamb
that belonged to the poor man and prepared it for the
one who had come to him.

(2 Samuel 12:1–4)

Why does Nathan tell a story wholly unrelated to what David has
done? Because it is not unrelated at all; he is engaging an otherwise unwilling David with regard to the very issues at stake. Nathan's approach
sought to create dialogue without first bringing up David's defenses. Look
at the core of this story: a man of power *took* from a weaker man because
of his terrible greed, simply because he could.

David's response to this tale was all that Nathan could have desired:

David burned with anger against the man and said to Nathan,
"As surely as the Lord lives, the man who did this deserves to
die! He must pay for that lamb four times over, because he did
such a thing and had no pity."

(2 Samuel 12:5, 6)

How willing David is to evoke the name of the Lord when it is another's sin in view! Not realizing Nathan's God-given insight into his own
behavior, David is all too ready to condemn injustice and greed, and to
respond not as the guilty criminal he was but as a righteous human being.
Nathan was quick to capitalize on his gains, boldly looking into David's
eyes and responding in clear, concise words: *Then Nathan said to David,*
"You are the man!" (2 Samuel 12:7).

What a masterpiece of effective confrontation! It took preparation and thoughtfulness, but Nathan had devised a subtle way to first open the barred gates of David's heart, allowing him to speak with the blunt force that was necessary.

Why did Nathan go to all this trouble? Because he wanted to restore David, to bring about a willingness to face hard facts, and to produce a change in his heart. Our leaders are rarely willing or skillful enough for this. Instead, they discard men and women in whom much has been invested and who can only be replaced at a high cost and effort. How often in performance appraisals, particularly difficult ones like this, the executive acts merely to get the affair over, to simply wash his own hands of the difficult or struggling subordinate. Nathan took another course and produced another result. He was doing God's work of restoration, which begins with facing genuine truth and then repenting of our ways. But, surely, Nathan also valued David as a person, and for this reason alone his labor was well spent.

In his approach to the king, Nathan was truly serving him, putting genuine concern into action. But that doesn't mean he, or God for that matter, would be going light on David once effective communication was established. Far from it:

> *Nathan devised a subtle way to first open the barred gates of David's heart, only then to speak bluntly. He wanted to restore David, to bring about a willingness to face hard facts, and to produce a change in his heart, not just to wash his own hands of the affair.*

Then Nathan said to David, "You are the man! This is what the
   Lord, the God of Israel, says: 'I anointed you king over Israel,
   and I delivered you from the hand of Saul. I gave your master's
   house to you, and your master's wives into your arms. I gave you
   the house of Israel and Judah. And if all this had been too little,
   I would have given you even more. Why did you despise the
   word of the Lord by doing what is evil in his eyes? You struck
   down Uriah the Hittite with the sword and took his wife to be
   your own. You killed him with the sword of the Ammonites.

Now, therefore, the sword will never depart from your house,
because you despised me and took the wife of Uriah the
Hittite to be your own.' "
(2 Samuel 12:7–10)

Now Nathan is not mincing words. "You killed Uriah with the sword."
What would have been the result if Nathan had begun this meeting with
that accusation? Surely, David would have angrily denied the charge. After
all, it was not his sword that struck down the soldier! Didn't Nathan know
that men died in battles? But now that he has worked his way around
David's defenses, behind his rationalizations and self-deluding lies, Nathan can deal with the real situation. In response, David's whole defense,
his entire scheme of rationalization, collapses to the ground:

Then David said to Nathan, "I have sinned against the Lord."
Nathan replied, "The Lord has taken away your sin.
You are not going to die."
(2 Samuel 12:13)

That was all—"I have sinned against the Lord"—and all else was said
with it. A change had taken place in David's heart, though surely more
discernible to the prophet than the mere statement suggests. And it was
this change that enabled Nathan to restore David to fellowship with God
and to usefulness as king.

One of David's best-known psalms records the work taking place here
in his heart. In Psalm 51 we gain a glimpse into genuine repentance and
the effects of sin in breaking the human heart:

Have mercy on me, O God,
  according to your unfailing love;
according to your great compassion
  blot out my transgressions.
Wash away all my iniquity
  and cleanse me from my sin.
For I know my transgressions,
  and my sin is always before me.

Against you, you only, have I sinned
  and done what is evil in your sight,
so that you are proved right when you speak
  and justified when you judge.

Psalm 51:1–4

There is no avoidance of the truth here, only a reliance on God's compassion for forgiveness. David asks forgiveness not because he believes his past deeds merit it, but because of the grace of God alone. Indeed, he confesses the rightness of his guilt and condemnation, having emptied himself of every rationalization and defense for what is indefensible. When David cries, "Against you only have I sinned," he is not denying the real harm he has caused to Bathsheba and Uriah, but rather the enormity of his guilt before the face of God.

What is vital to this cry of repentance is that David wants not just release from guilt, not just to avoid punishment, but cries out in longing for the restoration of his heart, for God's help in bringing about real change in his life:

Cleanse me with hyssop, and I will be clean;
  wash me, and I will be whiter than snow . . .
Create in me a pure heart, O God,
  and renew a right spirit within me.
Do not cast me from your presence
  or take your Holy Spirit from me.
Restore to me the joy of your salvation
  and grant me a willing spirit, to sustain me.

Psalm 51:7, 10–12

Hyssop was the small plant used by the priests as a brush for the ceremonial sprinklings. Having performed the sacrifice of an innocent animal as a substitute for the guilty offender, this brush was dipped in the blood, which was then sprinkled on the altar before God; similarly the hyssop brush was used to sprinkle cleansing water on the repentant one, symbolizing the cleansing of his heart.

The question we have been avoiding, and which is at the heart of the matter, is that which pertains to God. If God is both just and merciful, how can these be reconciled in the face of transgression? How can God be both merciful to the sinner and just with regard to the sin? The answer is at the heart of all true religion: *Because God accepts the sacrifice of another as payment in the place of the sinner.* It was this idea that was at the heart of the Israelite sacrificial system. Forgiveness could be found by trusting God to accept the sacrifice of another in the sinner's place. In David's time, the sacrifice was an animal, a goat, or a lamb, and by trusting in God's receipt of that sacrifice, the transgressor was restored. Not that an animal was sufficient to atone for human sin, but rather because faith in the substitute pointed forward to the great sacrifice of God's own Son on a Cross. It was the death of Christ as David's substitute that atoned for his sin, and so also for ours as well; David's request for cleansing with hyssop was a cry for the cleansing of the Messiah's substitutionary death, still yet to come.

David not only longs for forgiveness but for real restoration and a spirit within his own breast that would do right in the future. This, he knows, can only be the gift of a forgiving, gracious, and restoring God. And it is only because he trusts in such a God that David is able to recommit himself down a path of righteousness.

There is a great lesson for all leaders in God's handling of David, indeed in God's manner of handling all of us wandering sheep. Grace does not mean the denial of truth. Grace does not mean perversion of justice, but it is only the power of grace that can restore the fallen. Only grace can produce a real change of heart, not just a change in behavior to avoid punishment, but real and vital change. While truth alone condemns, truth with grace restores the fallen. David can face the truth, because he sees that God loves him, that God cares for Him, that God is committed to Him even to the point of providing the sacrifice to make right what David has done wrong.

> *Only grace can produce a real change of heart, not just a change in behavior to avoid punishment, but real and vital change. While truth alone condemns, truth with grace restores the fallen.*

Nathan has succeeded in restoring David, because he bears the love and mercy and truth of the Lord, who is, after all, David's boss. Through

Nathan's communication, and God's restoration, David has been re-deemed.

"The Lord has taken away your sin," said Nathan tenderly. "You are not going to die." David was forgiven and would be cleansed, but that does not mean he would suffer no consequences for his evil actions. David would indeed suffer consequences, grave consequences, simply because that is the nature of doing wrong. Therefore, the prophet went on to give this pronouncement from the Lord:

> " 'Now, therefore, the sword will never depart from your house,
> because you despised me and took the wife of Uriah the Hittite
> to be your own . . . Out of your own household I am going to
> bring calamity upon you. Before your very eyes I will take your
> wives and give them to one who is close to you, and he will lie
> with your wives in broad daylight. You did it in secret, but I will
> do this thing in broad daylight before all Israel.' "
>
> (2 Samuel 12:10–12)

What happened to forgiveness, we may ask! David *was* forgiven by the Lord and would suffer no eternal consequences for his sin, but temporal consequences are another matter. David could reclaim his heart but he could not take back what he had done. It is simply impossible for us to avoid the realization that our wrong deeds produce consequences for us in this life. God proclaimed that because of David's rape and murder, these very crimes would surface in his own household. (And how often it is that sins of the parents resurface in the children!) This is not a judgment from God but a simple yet unerring prediction. Indeed, until the day he dies David will never put turmoil in his own family behind him.

Still, we cannot mask the fact that God does promise to Himself bring calamity upon David. David is forgiven but he will receive the discipline that is always the mark of effective parenting. God is the original practitioner of "tough love," and David will be disciplined in a way that exquisitely matches his own offense. This too along with God's love, is a part of the restoration process, just as remediation must always be a part of our restorative efforts.

Thus ends this grim chapter in David's life, a shocking turn of events that came after the main achievements of his career, after he had already been a glorious success as CEO. Because David has abused his power, he will enjoy little of the glory he had brought to himself. Indeed, there will be suffering ahead for David, and suffering for others near him. If we are appalled at this, that innocents will suffer because of the offense of another, let us note that this is embedded in the very fabric of this world, in the very essence of relationships and community. Children always suffer for the sins of mothers and fathers, just as employees bear the brunt of managerial ineptitude and impropriety. But out of these trials, which will absorb our attention in the next chapter, David's heart will emerge once more refined by fire.

For now, however, let us remember the mercy that is there for those who have gone David's way, and the power of grace that alone affords a chance for restoration and restitution. How much we ourselves have need to be forgiven, how much our hearts require restoring, is for each to answer himself. As leaders, let our knowledge of our own failures and weakness help us to readily bear grace for the restoration of others.

Chapter 8

THE ROYAL OFFSPRING

ABSALOM, MY SON

אבשלום בני

We have now reached the last chapter in David's life, during the course of which he will seek to recover his compromised authority and establish a worthy successor. It would be nice, at this point in the story, to be able to show that David has got it all together now, that his brilliant insights into the task of leadership are no longer marred by character flaws. However, as we will see, David wrestled with the great challenge of executive leadership all the way until the end, battling old enemies within himself, learning and relearning every step of the way, just as you and I will find it necessary to do.

When we last saw David he was repenting for the abominable acts he had committed, acts that arose from the intoxication that accompanies power. Nathan's thoughtful intervention had returned him to the path of faithful leadership, and yet he informed David in no uncertain terms that very real consequences were sure to follow.

David was now approaching the twilight of his career, with his main task, uniting and establishing Israel as a nation, largely achieved. Israel was now truly a nation. It had a secure territory where the people could live in peace, a capital city, an identity, and a common sense of purpose. The challenge for David now was to secure this achievement by developing a new crop of leaders who would be both willing and able to lead Israel into the future David envisioned. For unless he could produce successors to carry on his ideals and vision, it would not be long before all his labor became little more than a footnote in history. So it is for all of us; unless we successfully pass the baton, and nurture successors to receive it, we will ultimately have failed as leaders.

In David's case, it was his own sons who would play the crucial role in the future of the nation. We might think this an ideal arrangement, but for David (as for most practitioners of nepotism) it created problems of its own. Paradoxically, it is often the best kings who produce the worst heirs. The sheer time and energy needed to succeed as a leader make many an executive both a poor parent and a poor mentor. We are fortunate today to not be subjected to the rule of the sons and daughters neglected by our corporate kings and queens. We are, however, subject to the reign of executives in whom neither the values nor the aspirations of the past have been instilled.

Three of David's sons will figure prominently in the story of his waning years; two of them, Amnon and Absalom, we will consider now, while the third, David's ultimate successor, Solomon, we will encounter later. The first thing we should note about these sons is that they all had different mothers. There are eight women listed in the Bible by name as David's wives, and most of them were married to him at the same time. We know also that he had other unnamed wives and a whole harem of concubines. Between them all David had twenty sons and numerous daughters.

Now imagine growing up in such a household. The wives undoubtedly vied for position, and the children were forced to compete for their father's scarce attention. This was hardly a good environment for instilling values, but it was a great one for raising young schemers, which is exactly what we see in David's sons. Now throw into that mix David's lapse into the abuse of power, along with the self-indulgence the presence of so many wives indicates, and you have a combustible situation indeed!

Nathan had warned David that part of the punishment for his sin against Bathsheba and Uriah would be this: " 'Now, therefore the sword *will never depart from your house, because you despised me and took the wife of Uriah the Hittite to be your own.'* " God has created a moral universe, and in such a universe sins like David's cannot fail to produce widening circles of calamity. In David's case that calamity struck his own house first and hardest. The first to be influenced by David's behavior was his oldest son and presumed heir, Amnon. Here was the situation:

> In the course of time, Amnon son of David fell in love with
> Tamar, the beautiful sister of Absalom son of David.
> Amnon became frustrated to the point of illness on account of
> his sister Tamar, for she was a virgin, and it seemed impossible
> for him to do anything to her.
> (2 Samuel 13:1, 2)

Like his father before him, Amnon's eyes rested upon a woman he desired and he was consumed by the need to get what he wanted. In this case, however, the woman was David's daughter, Tamar, Amnon's own half-sister. We know little of Amnon before this, but from what follows it is clear that self-control was not a major aspect of his upbringing. He desires Tamar and so there is no other thought in his mind but to have her. Therefore, no doubt inspired by his father's precedent, he devised a clever ruse that would place him alone with the object of his lust, where he could exercise his royal prerogative. Feigning sickness, he arranged for the unsuspecting young woman to bring him his meals, after which he acted with brutal swiftness:

> Then Amnon said to Tamar, "Bring the food here into my
> bedroom so I may eat from your hand." And Tamar took the
> bread she had prepared and brought it to her brother Amnon in
> his bedroom. But when she took it to him to eat, he grabbed her
> and said, "Come to bed with me, my sister."
> "Don't, my brother!" she said to him. "Don't force me. Such a
> thing should not be done in Israel! Don't do this wicked thing.
> What about me? Where could I get rid of my disgrace? And what
> about you? You would be like one of the wicked fools in Israel"

> . . . But he refused to listen to her, and since he was stronger
> than she, he raped her.
>
> (2 Samuel 13:10–14)

In this terrible scene, one repeated countless times by men eager to exercise their power, it is remarkable to see how well this young woman kept her head. Indeed, in her plea to Amnon we see quite a commentary not merely on what he was about to do, but about the culture that now pervaded David's house.

First she cries, "Such a thing should not be done in Israel!" meaning that this house, this nation, was designed to be a place where people could be free from such abuses of power. The prospect that things would be different under David is what drew followers to his cause in the first place. His whole career was devoted to raising up an organization where right would stand before might, where the Lord would be served in righteousness and justice. But here we see that through his own actions, David had discredited his own cherished ideals. Now, in bitter irony, his own daughter will reap the harvest of what he himself had sown.

The Hebrew word translated here as "he raped her" has the literal meaning of "to oppress" or "to humiliate." How foreign such a motive was to David. Even in the case of Bathsheba he had tried to protect her from disgrace, and ultimately he installed her in a place of honor within his own household. But the seed he had planted bore a more twisted fruit in his son. For after violating his innocent half-sister, Amnon demonstrated the cruel arrogance that had taken residence in his heart.

> . . . since he was stronger than she, he raped her.
> Then Amnon hated her with intense hatred. In fact, he hated
> her more than he had loved her. Amnon said to her,
> "Get up and get out!"
> "No!" she said to him. "Sending me away would be a greater
> wrong than what you have already done to me."
> But he refused to listen to her. He called his personal servant
> and said, "Get this woman out of here and bolt the door after
> her." So his servant put her out and bolted the door after her.
> She was wearing a richly ornamented robe, for this was the kind

> of garment the virgin daughters of the king wore. Tamar put
> ashes on her head and tore the ornamented robe she was
> wearing. She put her hand on her head and went away,
> weeping aloud as she went.
>
> (2 Samuel 13:14–19)

One of the great injustices accompanying the crime of rape is that the innocent woman often bears a harsher stigma than the abuser. It is hard for us today to understand the powerlessness of women that was accepted by all in the ancient world, but Tamar understood all too well what the implications were for herself. She was now a tainted woman, no longer to be cherished, nor wanted by anyone. But rather than hide the shame brought upon her, she tore her virgin's garment and publicly mourned her loss, proclaiming to all exactly what had transpired.

David naturally found out what had taken place under his roof, and the Bible tells us his response: "When King David heard all this, he was furious" (2 Samuel 13:21). That's it. Not that he took pains to comfort Tamar, though it becomes clear that she was protected. Not that he called Amnon in as a father and demanded an explanation. Not that he, as the executor of Israel's laws, implemented the very clear reprisals demanded by the law. Just that "he was furious."

May we surmise that David is incapacitated by his own track record? On the one hand, Amnon was the presumed heir and future king, and so it would not be the first time such a person's indiscretions were ignored. But David's entire program for the kingdom is contrary to just such an attitude. The whole purpose of bringing the Ark of the Covenant to Jerusalem was to serve notice that God Himself was Lord over Israel, and that God's Law was Israel's law. David was furious and no doubt frustrated, but we read of no action on his part. Frustrated by Amnon's vile deed, David reveals his moral incapacity by making no official response to this vicious injustice.

It is difficult to understate how important it is for an executive to immediately attend to matters of fairness and ethics with the greatest urgency. Failure to do so always produces two dangerous viruses in an organization. The first is an environment where anything goes, particularly when accompanied by high-pressure performance expectations. Second, it undermines trust in the organization, with a corresponding impact on employee commitment and loyalty. "*What will happen to me if I am ever in her shoes?*" is a question we often ask ourselves when we see a woman in our own organization in a similar position as Tamar.

Immediately, when such a situation comes up, we respond, "But we have clear ethical guidelines." That may be true, but guidelines are completely useless if relegated to a policy book, if they exert no tangible influence on your decisions. An office environment is only ethical when standards are assertively reinforced in the life of the organization. David's regime had a fine intellectual understanding of ethics, but in the aftermath of his own ethical failure the regime did not put this into action.

David surely did not approve of Amnon's crime, but his passive response spoke louder than any words. Interestingly, while the original Hebrew text offers no explanation for David's behavior, a later version adds the following as an explanation for his lack of action: "David would not hurt Amnon because he was his eldest son and he loved him." But it is precisely in such a situation, when those we especially value are involved, that we must enforce ethical standards if we seriously care about justice in the workplace. It is clear, David's guilt over his own behavior incapacitated him as an executive. How unfortunate that he did not profit from Nathan's earlier handling of himself, that he had never learned to confront and correct and, if possible, to restore. In this, he is not alone among senior executives.

Failure to attend to matters of fairness and ethics always produces two dangerous viruses: an environment where anything goes and an undermining of trust, and thus of employee commitment and loyalty as well.

If David was paralyzed by this situation, there were others, however, who were not. Foremost among them was Tamar's full brother, Absalom. It was to him that she ran when she fled Amnon's room, and it was he who took responsibility for her situation. Absalom was himself an important figure in David's household. The third-born son he was nevertheless the second in line for the throne, the second-born having apparently died in his youth. Now, in light of David's inaction, fierce hatred seeped into the relationship of these two half-brothers and rising leaders. And yet nothing

happened immediately. Instead, while outwardly Absalom showed nothing, inwardly he nurtured an intense anger that sooner or later would
have to boil to the surface. For the time being, however, only a chilled
silence existed between the two:

> Absalom never said a word to Amnon, either good or bad; he
> hated Amnon because he had disgraced his sister Tamar.
>
> (2 Samuel 13:22)

Two years passed before Absalom took his revenge. How his hatred
must have festered during that time, watching Amnon go about the palace, exulting in the honor of being firstborn and heir apparent. Absalom's
resentment of David's inaction must also have grown; every day when he
comforted desolate Tamar, who stayed in his house, his thoughts must
have turned to the faithlessness of his king and father.

Finally an opportunity for revenge presented itself. Amnon, lulled
into a false sense of security over time, went with his other brothers to
observe the sheering of Absalom's flocks of sheep. All seemed well, and
perhaps onlookers hoped this might signal a reconciliation between these
vital successors to David. But Absalom had no such intention; after feast-
ing together with Amnon, Absalom calmly ordered his attendants to strike
him down. The deed was quickly done, the rape of Tamar finally
avenged. And yet how far from justice this was. Indeed, here we see Absalom as a son who is making the same mistakes his father made. As David
had done in the murder of Uriah, Absalom orders his subordinates to
murder without thinking about the impact it will have on his leadership.

The apostle Paul writes in the New Testament, *"In your anger do not
sin"* (Ephesians 4:26). I have often found this to be one of the most helpful injunctions in all the Bible, for the temptation to do wrong is greatest
when we are angry or resentful. Absalom hid his malice and anger for
two long years, only bringing it out in the open by murdering his enemy.
It would have been much better if Absalom had confronted the situation
right from the start, if he had gone to David for help immediately after
learning of the crime, perhaps risking disfavor but avoiding the twisting

of his own soul. Therefore Paul adds this command, *"Do not let the sun go down while you are still angry"* (Ephesians 4:26). We are wise to heed his counsel.

Absalom did not wait around to see how David would respond to the crown prince's death, instead going into exile to his grandfather, the king of Geshur. For two years he stayed away, but the crisis in David's regime did not lessen during this time.

> *"In your anger do not sin." How much better if Absalom had confronted the situation right from the start, perhaps risking disfavor but avoiding the twisting of his own soul.*

Let's stand back and assess what has become of David. Two factors seem to conspire to make him passive and ineffective: the sinful acts he committed that undermined him in the eyes of others and the troubles which then brewed up as a result within his inner circle. Amnon and Absalom were not just David's sons, they were the trained successors upon whom the organization's future rested. David's failure to instill values and character in his key subordinates created a poisonous environment which only grew more malignant with time.

Two years passed with Absalom in hiding from a father who had no energy for pursuit. Absalom was gone but the reality of David's regime lingered, like smoke upon a field of battle. It was Joab, finally, who intervened, realizing how this unresolved disgrace sapped the vigor from David's reign. Serving as an intermediary, Joab brokered a deal whereby Absalom would return, but without either restoration or incrimination.

So Absalom returns, not as a repentant son and successor, not as a restored subordinate, but instead as a visible sign of all that had gone wrong with David's leadership in these latter years. He was just there, the prince-in-waiting. David's motivation in allowing his son's return seems to have been more political than personal. Because he was growing old, David thought it would bring stability just to have the eldest son back in the palace. Once again, David's inattentiveness to the values of the organization threatened their very existence.

While Absalom was eager to return to David's court, it is clear that

he neither loved nor respected his father. His resentment surely originated with David's failure to act after Tamar's rape, and his attitude eventually ripened into contempt and rebellion. Indeed, it was not long before
the unemployed prince began to seek out work for himself:

> In the course of time Absalom provided himself with a chariot
> and horses and with fifty men to run ahead of him. He would
> get up early and stand by the side of the road leading to the city
> gate. Whenever anyone came with a complaint to be placed
> before the king for a decision, Absalom would call out to him,
> "What town are you from?" . . . Then Absalom would say to
> him, "Look, your claims are valid and proper, but there is no
> representative of the king to hear you." And Absalom would add,
> "If only I were appointed judge in the land! Then everyone who
> has a complaint or case could come to me and I would
> see that he gets justice."
> (2 Samuel 15:1–4)

Here we see the bitter fruit of David's lack of attention in dealing
with the next generation of leaders in Israel, his very own sons. This is
exactly what always results when a country has rising leaders who really
don't know the aging king, who have not sat at his feet and grown up
within the circle of his attention. Notice too how isolated and unsup-
ported David has become as a result. Once he had Jonathan, the friend
who stayed his shaking hand; now he is left with Absalom his son, who is
intent on magnifying David's flaws and weakening his hold on power. It
is clear that David truly needs a friend during this time, and yet there is
none mentioned. Absalom is the exact opposite of Jonathan. Indeed,
David has raised up in his own house a whole brood of young Sauls, a
comparison the biblical narrator makes in his description of Absalom's
allure to the people:

> In all Israel there was not a man so highly praised for his
> handsome appearance as Absalom. From the top of his head to
> the sole of his foot there was no blemish in him.
> (2 Samuel 14:25)

Are we surprised to see the anti-Saul, David, produce so Saul-like an heir? For when real leadership disappears people will always follow those who simply look the part, regardless of their motives and real qualifications. And that is why our organizations are so full of false executives today.

So Absalom began whittling away at David's support, slowly drawing people to himself and his big promises while David apparently did nothing in response. Notice that it is the administration of justice that Absalom especially picks at. David's glaring failure to do right in his own family was apparently mirrored in his failure to establish an effective system for dealing with grievances among the people. How easy it was, then, for Absalom to draw frustrated claimants to his cause, probably winning over both sides in every case. For four years he kept this up, until finally he judged himself able to strike.

In this way Absalom gained the loyalty of a large number of the tribal chieftains and he gathered a legion of these at Hebron, David's own first capital. It is astonishing that Hebron should be so loyal to this usurper that he could use it as his base of operations. This is the heartland of Judah, David's own tribe, and a place where David would have known many personally. But when this stronghold was established and his cohorts were spread throughout the land, Absalom felt secure enough to lead his coup into the open.

> Then Absalom sent secret messengers throughout the tribes of
> Israel to say, "As soon as you hear the sound of the trumpets,
> then say, 'Absalom is king in Hebron.'" Two hundred men from
> Jerusalem had accompanied Absalom . . . he also sent for
> Ahithophel the Gilonite, David's counselor, to come from
> Giloh, his hometown. And so the conspiracy gained strength,
> and Absalom's following kept on increasing.
> (2 Samuel 15:10–12)

So extensive was this conspiracy that David's own counselor, his chief strategic planner, was in cahoots with Absalom. Here we finally see the extent to which David had fallen asleep at the wheel. He had failed to settle disputes within his own family, he had set an example of compromise and vacillation, and now he was caught unawares by the complete betrayal of the adviser closest to the throne. Was it age? Was it complacency, now that his initial goals were achieved? Was it an inability to grasp the politics of court life? Probably it was a little of all these, though we are not informed of his state of mind. Indeed, David himself figures little in the biblical account of all these events, giving an indication of how far he has slipped into the background. But he is not the last senior executive to settle down in comfort and then confusion, only to be challenged by impatient and ambitious subordinates.

There is one thing we must observe in all this. David did not make the development of the succeeding leaders a priority. He did not engage them in his vision, did not challenge them with the principles that had made him and the nation great. He treated them as children, as perpetual followers, and not as leaders on whom his own legacy would depend, to whom the entire nation would look for guidance and inspiration. The royal offspring learned envy, cunning, and self-serving ambition. Ultimately, this must all be laid at David's feet. Not only was this sorry state of affairs a direct result of his own lapse into sin and abuse of power but it also reveals a vital component of leadership that is missing from his record.

It is probably true that any one man or woman is not up to the whole range of tasks an executive will face during a full career like David's. But here he reminds all of us that at each step of the way we must examine what is required. The skills and strategies that made yesterday such a success may have little or nothing to do with what tomorrow demands. How many careers have been shipwrecked by a failure to assess the new demands made by new positions and new stages in an organization's development.

> *David did not make the development of the succeeding generation of leaders a priority. He treated them as children, as perpetual followers, and not as leaders on whom his own legacy would depend.*

There is much irony in this wholesale betrayal in David's court. After all, it is strange that the one who more than any other stands out as the contrast to Saul-like, self-serving leadership has himself bred a whole nest of little Sauls, all because he let down his own guard and failed to live up to his own inspiring vision. It is stunning to see what came of David's dip into the pools of self-indulgence, with the stream of rationalizations and cover-ups that followed and so changed the man that his own sons never knew the great leader we have come to admire.

The leader is first and foremost responsible for himself, for the character that continually forms in his own heart, and for setting his own feet on straight and level paths. This is always the prerequisite for long-term success and achievement; apart from this all else is in vain. As David's son, Solomon, would wisely counsel:

> *Above all else, guard your heart,*
> *for it is the wellspring of life . . .*
> *Let your eyes look straight ahead,*
> *fix your gaze directly before you.*
> *Make level paths for your feet*
> *and take only ways that are firm.*
>
> Proverbs 4:23, 25, 26

The next priority for the leader, however, is the hearts of those who follow, and especially those followers who soon will lead.

> "Above all else, guard your heart, for it is the wellspring of life" . . . *The leader is first and foremost responsible for himself, then for the hearts of those who follow, and especially those who soon will lead.*

But, as we have seen before, David insists on learning the hard way. Therefore, the spear in once again pointed at his own throat. Thus it is that this era of his career, what should have been his golden days of consolidation and growth, comes to an end the very same way his time in Saul's court had ended, with David on the run as a threatening army bore down upon him. For it was not long before Absalom went on the move, headed for Jerusalem, and the slumbering David was awoken with this report: "The hearts of the men of Israel are with Absalom" (2 Samuel 15:13).

Friends in High Places

רעהים במעלות

David was a man of repeated patterns, and what we are about to see him do, we have seen before. It began with those lonely days and nights when David the shepherd stood between his flock and the hazards of the wild. We saw it in the Valley of Elah, when that shepherd boy stepped forth alone before the hulking menace of Goliath. We saw it in Ziklag, where the smoke hanging over his shattered compound and the look of murder in his own men's eyes brought life back to his veins and courage into his heart.

David's value for today's leaders lies mainly in these patterns, with the contrasts they present. Important as the contrast between David and Saul is to this story, more important still is that contrast between *David and David.* The David of impulse versus David the man of prayer. The brazen champion who will gladly die for principle and purpose versus the king who callously uses and abuses his most loyal followers. The passive and self-reliant sulker versus the visionary who calls people off from the sidelines and into his cause. The contrast is revealed in seemingly small choices and events, magnified as they influence just which David appears on the scene. And it is relatively small events and choices that trigger a change in David, bringing the contrast into sharper focus.

Absalom's advance on Jerusalem triggered such a change in David, flipped the switch needed to bring back the David God and Israel loved. We are not told just what signaled this transformation, though his pattern for coming alive in times of crisis gives us a clue. But one thing is for sure, that everyone who encountered him could see it. The old resolve had come into his eyes, indicating that David's passivity was at an end. The metamorphosis took place as soon as the news of Absalom's rebellion reached him, and David sprang at once into action:

> Then David said to all his officials who were with him in
> Jerusalem, "Come! We must flee, or none of us will escape from
> Absalom. We must leave immediately, or he will move quickly
> to overtake us and bring ruin upon us and put the city
> to the sword."
> The king's officials answered him, "Your servants are ready to do
> whatever our lord the king chooses."
> (2 Samuel 15:14, 15)

We see here that not only did activity return to David but his moral center as well. Now, with everything at risk, David remembers what it has all been for. Why is he ordering a retreat? Because otherwise "He will . . . overtake us and bring ruin upon us and put the city to the sword." It is very likely that David could have mustered enough support to defend Jerusalem's stout walls, but he was willing to risk his own cause so that blood would not flow through this city. Therefore David set out, no doubt recalling his flight from Saul's court so many years before, not knowing who or how many would rally once more to his cause.

There is one other sign that David has returned to his former self, and that is the presence of psalms written during this period of his life. There are no psalms recorded as having come from the preceding years, between the time of his repentance over Bathsheba and Absalom's revolt. But now in this time of danger he returns to the dependence on the God who has been his savior. Psalm 3 bears the heading "When he fled from his son Absalom," and in it we see both a cry of faith and a firm resolve to overcome this threat to his throne.

O Lord, how many are my foes!
   How many rise up against me!
Many are saying of me,
   "God will not deliver him,"
But you are a shield around me, O Lord;
   you bestow glory on me and lift up my head.
To the Lord I cry aloud,
   and he answers me from his holy hill . . .
Arise, O Lord!
   Deliver me, O my God!
Strike all my enemies on the jaw;
   break the teeth of the wicked.

Psalm 3:1–4, 7

Absalom and his cronies had assumed that since David had turned from God, then God had turned from him as well. But David knew what they did not, that God is ready to receive those who turn to Him in faith and repentance, eagerly seeking His grace. This is what distinguished fallen David from fallen Saul, his willingness to face the truth about himself and then to return to God. So it was that with his faith restored, David led his small band into exile once more.

When David walked out from Jerusalem toward the desert hideouts in the east, across the Kidron Valley and up the slopes of the Mount of Olives, one of the most beautiful scenes of his life unfolded. He began the hike with those of his officials who remained loyal, hastily departing without preparations or provisions. But stopping to look behind him he saw six hundred men marching forward, coming fast to his side. These, the first to rally to David's cause, were the men of his Jerusalem bodyguard, men known as the Gittites.

A Gittite is a person who grew up in the Philistine city of Gath, the hometown of Goliath and the sometime residence of the fugitive David. How remarkable that these sons of David's enemies should rally immediately to his cause. Even David was surprised at this unexpected loyalty; stopping a man named Ittai, their commander, he asked:

> "Why should you come along with us? Go back and stay with
> King Absalom. You are a foreigner, an exile from your
> homeland. You came only yesterday. And today shall I make you
> wander about with us, when I do not know where I am going?
> Go back, and take your countrymen. May kindness and
> faithfulness be with you."
> But Ittai replied to the king, "As surely as the Lord lives, and as
> my lord the king lives, wherever my lord the king may be,
> whether it means life or death, there will your servant be."
> (2 Samuel 15:19–21)

David, like many other Oriental monarchs, employed foreign mercenaries to make up his personal bodyguard, men who would be beholden only to the king who paid them. But here were these soldiers, men with no long-term interest in Israel, men who had grown up cursing the name of David, refusing to stay back to receive their pay from the usurper Absalom, and demanding to stay by the side of the now impoverished and fugitive king.

How can we account for this? For starters, we remember that *men and women are looking for more in life than a paycheck.* They are longing for something in which to believe, for something to admire and commit themselves to. Perhaps they were drawn by the David of old, the David who as a boy struck down their own great champion with faith and skill alone, the David who then built a shining city with the bricks of passion and purpose. They had come to him as mercenaries, but like each and every one of us they longed to be something more than hired hands. Now, they saw, was their chance to make a mark in life, and they boldly seized it, heading out into danger and adventure with this aging leader.

Imagine how heartening this must have been to David! Not only did he now possess a small but high-quality fighting force, but as Jonathan had done long before, these foreigners had "strengthened his hand" in time of need. This first group to come to his aid was motivated by personal loyalty, a willingness to stand beside a leader they admired. Let no leader discount the value of such loyalty, or forget the importance of cultivating personal trust and affection, for when needed it is the most precious thing in the world.

So David sent the Gittites and their families before him, heading out across the Kidron Valley toward refuge in the east.

It was not long before the second source of aid appeared, this time at the far side of the valley. Zadok and the priests were there, and with them was

> *Let no leader discount the value of personal loyalty, or forget the importance of cultivating personal trust and affection, for when needed it is the most precious thing in the world.*

the most precious object in all Israel, indeed in all the world, the Ark of the Covenant of the Lord. How vital a statement was the support of these men! Consider the grave danger they accepted in making it. We remember what Saul had done to the priests when they first helped David escape, and imagine what the rebel Absalom would do now. But, of course, the priests also remembered the honor and protection David had extended to their forerunners in their time of need. David had been there for them and now they were here for him.

So just as the people of Jabesh Gilead had remembered Saul's service to their fathers and thus came to rescue his body from disgrace, so now the priests of Israel rallied to the cause of David. But surely there is more than personal loyalty involved. The Ark signified the presence of the Lord Himself, so it may be questionable whether the priests brought the Ark or the Ark brought the priests. Without doubt, in either case, David was seeing the answer to the prayer of his psalm unfold before him.

Zadok was motivated by more than personal loyalty; his action was also one of fidelity to the institution he served. He was a company man and David was the true king, the anointed one of God. He knew, therefore, that the priests and the Ark belonged at David's side. Perhaps his action here reminded David of his own loyalty to Israel and its principles; we are astonished to find that he refused this support and sent back the priests and the Ark to their place of service in Jerusalem:

> "Take the ark of God back into the city. If I find favor in the Lord's eyes, he will bring me back and let me see it and his

dwelling place again. But if he says, 'I am not pleased with you,'
then I am ready; let him do to me whatever seems good to him."

(2 Samuel 15:25, 26)

"This is not about my own personal fortunes," he was saying.
"Thanks for the offer, but the ark is not to be tied to my individual trials,
but to the true king of Israel. Let me set about becoming that again and
if the Lord blesses me, I will return once more. But if I fail, it is the
institution and what it stands for that is more important."

How stunning this humility is coming from David, the king who
once dragged innocent women to his bed and sent loyal followers to unjust deaths. We are not always pleased by what we see in David, but here
is one aspect of his character we do well to emulate: He is willing to learn
again every day, to face the truth, to see what is going on inside his heart
and emerge a new man. Here, again, we see why matters of the heart are primary for the executive leader. It was what they saw in David's heart that brought the Gittites and the priests to David's side when they could easily have abandoned him, and with a re-freshed heart David found hope once more.

> *Here is one aspect of David's character we do well to emulate: He is willing to learn again every day, to face the truth, to see what is going on inside his heart and emerge a new man.*

So David sent the priests and the Ark back to their places in Jerusalem to resume their duties, but also to keep their eyes open for him as he
sought refuge in the wilderness.

David now marched his band up the sides of the Mount of Olives.
We are told that he was weeping, no doubt because he had perhaps seen
the last of the Ark of God and of the city that bore his name. Along his
way up, news reached him that Ahithophel, his chief planner, had deserted his cause. Clearly, he respected and feared this strategist's mind,
and so he stopped his entourage to pray in response to the news, "O Lord,
turn Ahithophel's counsel into foolishness" 2 Samuel 15:31. David's plan

had yet to be worked out, so he began by aksing God to overcome those things he most greatly feared.

When David reached the summit of the Mount of Olives, which overlooked his city upon the hill, another source of help was waiting for him. This time it was Hushai the Arkite, a man who bore the title "Friend of the King." This was a formal position, something like a human resources director. It must have been wonderful for David to see him waiting, his robe torn and ashes upon his head in accordance with the Jewish practice of mourning.

There are many people who find themselves in the position of "friend" but fail to take up the job in earnest. Hushai, who appears in the Bible only in this episode, was a true friend, and he wore his emotions on his sleeve in support of David. Hushai was a civilian, a man of the court, and yet he too showed his willingness to join David in the wild.

David had been thinking, however, even through the tears, as he climbed the slope that Jesus Himself would later ascend in His departure from Jerusalem. David had sent the Ark back to the city; having the reality of God's presence, he did not require the symbol. Hearing of Ahithophel's betrayal he marked this man as the chief threat and thus had prayed for God to confound his planning. But now as he saw this friend, his plan took more solid form, and so he responded to Hushai with these words:

> "If you go with me, you will be a burden to me. But if you return
> to the city and say to Absalom, 'I will be your servant, O king; I
> was your father's servant in the past, but now I will be your
> servant,' then you can help me by frustrating Ahithophel's
> advice. Won't the priests Zadok and Abiathar be there with you?
> Tell them anything you hear in the king's palace. Their two sons,
> Ahimaaz son of Zadok, and Jonathan son of Abiathar, are there
> with them. Send them to me with anything you hear."
>
> (2 Samuel 15:33–36)

What a sacrifice David asks of this man, his friend—to go back into the teeth of suspicion and mortal danger! But kings and executives must be willing to ask for a great deal, so long as they are willing to give as much in return.

David was probably more active as king in this short journey than he had been in several recent years upon his throne. As he advanced he kept on meeting people. With each encounter, his understanding of his situation improved, as did his material position.

Not long after David left the Mount of Olives behind him, Ziba the servant of Mephibosheth approached him. Mephibosheth was a cripple, the son of Jonathan and the grandson of King Saul. We remember that Saul had begged David not to take revenge on his family, when he acknowledged David at the cave of Adullam. David had honored that request gladly, and the memory of his beloved friend Jonathan, by taking Mephibosheth into his own household and seating him at his own table for meals. This eagerness to honor King Saul's descendant is striking; we should expect quite the opposite. Instead we see the bright side that so dominated David's character, and a charity that sought reconciliation and an eagerness to be a blessing to others.

Now Ziba appeared before David, with donkeys laden with bread, fruit, and wine for his men. But he also brought this report, when David asked the whereabouts of his master: *"He is staying in Jerusalem, because he thinks, 'Today the house of Israel will give me back my grandfather's kingdom'"* (2 Samuel 16:3). Receiving the provisions, David no doubt reminded himself that despite the recent examples of faithfulness, Absalom's rebellion would tempt many to abandon David's cause. Later, it turned out, David would learn the inaccuracy of this report; Mephibosheth too, though heir to the house David had supplanted, had held fast to the cause of this king who had shown such mercy.

David finally arrived at a place of safety across the boundary of the Jordan River, the waterway his forefathers had crossed when first entering this land. There, at a place called Mahaniam, he settled down to wait and rebuild. When he arrived he was greeted by three men of the Transjordan, bearing further supplies and offers of help. The first of these was Shobi from Rabah of the Ammonites. It is hard to imagine why he would side with David, since his people had been conquered and his hometown destroyed by David's forces. Perhaps he was motivated by sheer mercy, or by his appreciation of how his people had later prospered under David's rule.

Another of these men was Makir from Lo Debar, who, as we are elsewhere informed, was a close friend of the above-named Mephibosheth, Jonathan's son. Earlier, in fact, it was this man who sheltered Mephibosheth until he learned of David's clemency. No doubt he appreciated David's fidelity to both his promise and to Jonathan. Here again we see earlier acts of mercy and virtue bearing fruit in David's time of need.

So David had escaped Absalom's trap. Caught off-guard and unequipped, he had found the two things he most needed in these dire times, his own strength of character and his faith in God. With clear evidence of God's providential dealings—can we doubt divine initiative in these many offers of aid?—and the harvest of all that his earlier leadership had produced in the hearts of so many, David was back on his feet.

David's example here speaks to all of us who have either lost our way or find ourselves facing a shocking turn of events. On what, we ask, are we to build the future, particularly when we are faced with danger and uncertainty? We build on the things done right in the past. We build on the human relationships, the bonds of affection and trust and inspiration that lie waiting in our memories, in the people we have served and been served by, in the dreams that once filled us with purpose and resolution. David was not returning to the past itself, but from his own past he was able to build possibilities for tomorrow. From that past he remembered who he was and what it meant to be a leader.

> *We build the future on the things done right in the past—human relationships, bonds of affection and trust and inspiration that lie waiting in our memories, in the people we have served, in the dreams that once filled us with purpose and resolution.*

There is something for us too from the perspective of all these who rallied to David's cause: the Gittite mercenaries, the priests, David's friend and chancellor Hushai, and finally these wealthy Transjordan chieftains. They, like most of us, will never reach the status of a David.

They never had whole books devoted to them but found themselves, at best, appearing in passing reference within the greater life. But they weren't nobodies either. They had come to positions of some influence in their time and place, known and relied upon by many. This is the height at which almost all of us will cease climbing, securing our place in the background of something bigger than ourselves.

So the question is this: Will we have the wisdom to recognize our brief moments upon the grand stage? Do we know what it is that will ultimately give meaning to all we have done? For Hushai, the king's friend, it came down to this: When David called him to risk it all, he accepted. He took up the cause and on his small contribution greater fates would rest. What about Ittai the Gittite? We never hear his name again, but his steadfast loyalty at a time when no others had joined the cause brought strength to David, and thus to his entire enterprise. We could cycle through all these examples, but the point is made. To be a somebody you must be willing to display personal loyalty at great cost, to stand up in the face of danger, in defense of what the past has achieved, to step off the sidelines and offer yourself to something greater than yourself. It may mean simply declaring your loyalty. It may mean sharing an emotional burden or giving some small material aid. But the Davids of this world can build upon this, and God can and does magnify such gifts offered in faith. After all, it was one little boy who gave his lunch to Jesus, but with it God fed an entire multitude. He asks us merely to give what we have to offer, and to trust in Him for the harvest.

Consider the names we will never see in this history, names of men and women who had the same opportunity to act with valor but let it pass by, who kept their provisions for themselves instead of taking them out to David in his flight, who stayed on the fence forever. These are the ones who remained nobodies. These small heroes we do see are just a few out of tens of thousands, but they were the few who remembered, who understood, and who gave of themselves when it counted. And so they each became a somebody, and even now we remember them with honor.

> *This is how to be a somebody—to be willing to display personal loyalty at great cost, to step off the sidelines and offer yourself.*

The story describing David's recovery of his throne is a fairly long one, and does not shed much light on our interests here. To tell the story briefly, Absalom proved to be completely dependent on the advice of his counselors and this was the source of his downfall. Hushai the Arkite, David's friend and chancellor, who voluntarily returned to serve in Absalom's court, succeeded in confounding Ahithophel's wise counsel, bringing success to David's desperate plan.

Absalom's vacillation caused him to delay his attack during the crucial hours when David was most vulnerable. As a result, David escaped and remained at large long enough to win supporters back to his cause. When the battle was joined it was on fairly equal terms and the outcome was not in doubt; Absalom's forces were crushed David's army under Joab's veteran command.

David's emotional response to his son's failed venture is the most telling feature of this episode. He had sent Joab and the other commanders out to battle with this instruction: "Be gentle with the young man Absalom for my sake" (2 Samuel 18:5). David knew he would defeat his rebel son, and he knew such a victory was necessary. And yet he also knew that victory would come at a terrible cost to his heart. Joab, however, disgusted by such sentiment, had no intention of obeying the king. Joab wanted to separate David the king from David the man. How many of us try to pull this off, to compartmentalize our lives in this way. The effort was poisonous to David's heart, as it is for all who try it today.

It turned out that Joab was the one who came upon the helpless Absalom after his army had been defeated and scattered. Without a second thought he cut him down, sending a messenger off to the king with news of a complete triumph.

David, meanwhile, was anxiously pacing in his command post when the messengers raced in to inform him of the victory over the rebel army. In rushed the young courier, a man identified only as a Cushite, flush with the honor of bringing news of this triumph:

> "My lord the king, hear the good news! The Lord has delivered
> you today from all who rose up against you."
> The king asked the Cushite, "Is the young man Absalom safe?"

The Cushite replied, "May the enemies of my lord the king and
all who rise up to harm you be like that young man."
(2 Samuel 18:31, 32)

"May all your enemies be like your son." Your enemies, your son.
David understood all too well what this meant. Immediately he broke
down, responding in a way these men who stood so close to him, but so
far from his heart, simply could not comprehend.

"O my son Absalom! My son, my son Absalom! If only I had
died instead of you—O Absalom, my son, my son!"
(2 Samuel 18:33)

The throne was secure for David, but at the cost of something he
valued far more. Many of us will find ourselves making a similar trade.
We will not admit it, we will not acknowledge it along the way, but as
surely as David's kingship had cost him this son, and Amnon as well, so
too do so many of us sacrifice things dear to us in the shortsightedness of
our ambition.

David might have gone on crying for hours, so broken was he by the
news of Absalom's death. It was Joab, again, who came to thrust his words
into the king's heart just as his spear had entered the son's.

Then Joab went into the house to the king and said, "Today you
have humiliated all your men, who have just saved your life and
the lives of your sons and daughters . . . You love those who hate
you and hate those who love you. You have made it clear today
that the commanders and their men mean nothing to you . . .
Now go out and encourage your men. I swear by the Lord that
if you don't go out, not a man will be left with you by nightfall."
(2 Samuel 19:5–7)

Joab's words were cruel and unfeeling, and yet they were true. So
David, like so many captains and kings before and after him, stuffed his
heart back under his uniform, went out and praised his followers for the
destruction of his own son. We cannot but have compassion for David's

awful predicament, but it was of his own making. His throne was secure once more, but there was a large part of his heart that would never live again.

It was David's many friends who stood beside him during his time of need, and at great risk to themselves restored him to his throne. Let us not forget that it is upon the loyalty of men and women, their commitment to the ideals we espouse, that the executive builds and secures his achievement. Let every one of us who wields power ask ourselves, "Who among these would rally to my cause in an hour of such need?" The answer will tell us just what sort of power we truly hold.

> *Let us not forget that it is upon the loyalty of men and women, and their commitment to the ideals we espouse, that the executive builds his achievement. Let every one of us ask, "Who among these would rally to my cause in an hour of such need?*

It is tragic, however, that many of those who stood with David knew him only at a distance. It would have made quite a difference if Joab had looked upon him as something more than a vehicle for power and wealth. Indeed, David's restoration came not at the hands of the great, but mainly by the faithfulness of little men wo became great in the hour of his need. And yet now, at the end of his career, he finally saw how bitter the taste of power was, how tarnished the glory it gave.

As he made his way back to the Jerusalem he built, his heart and his mind were filled with something other than the return of his throne, the vindication of his cause. In their place were pictures of a little boy who once had bounced upon his knee: "O my son Absalom!" And right then he would then have traded all his power, all his glory, if only his sons could have been returned to life, to share a dream that now seemed so much more empty than before.

A New Beginning

$$\text{רֵאשִׁית חָדָשׁ}$$

David slipped into his old age, his achievement long behind him and an uncertain future before the nation. We left him on the battlefield where his son Absalom had fallen, and there is no disguising that his career, which began so full of life and hope, seemed to be grinding to a slow and bitter halt. Is this what David's career finally amounts to, a warning for us of the perils of power and achievement? And if this is not to be David's final epitaph, we must ask, then from where will hope be restored? If we know David well enough by now we have our answer. Hope and restoration will come from David's friends, his loyal companions; indeed, primary among these was David's one Friend above all, who here at the end of his life has remained faithful. As David himself has told us,

> *The Lord is close to the brokenhearted*
> > *and saves those who are crushed in spirit . . .*
> *The Lord redeems his servants;*
> > *no one will be condemned who takes refuge in him.*
> > > **Psalm 34:18, 22**

Reading this, and knowing David as we have come to know him, we will find our final answers in the relationship between him and his God, the relationship and friendship that more than any other determined the state of his heart.

The verdict on David's career, like all others, cannot be written until the issue of succession is determined. Whether or not he successfully passes the torch of his passion and purpose will determine the security of his legacy. David, as king, must pass on his power to a son, but we have seen all too well what has become of these princes. Therefore, it is God who steps in to provide David with a son worthy to be successor, even as He provided David to Israel in the first place. The first indication of this, in fact, came much earlier in the story, before the disasters of Amnon and Absalom, though it seems clear that almost no one noticed at the time.

Indeed, God's act of mercy in providing a true successor to David originated at very depth of David's failure, his ill-gotten affair with Uriah's wife, Bathsheba. We remember Nathan's stinging pronouncement of judgment: The sword would not depart from David's house, and it did not; the child born of that rape would die, and it did; what David did to Uriah's wife in secret would be done to his own in broad daylight, and just this happened, as Absalom spent part of his brief enthronement taking David's own concubines on the very roof of the palace in full view of the people. David had paid dearly for his horrible crime, though God had ultimately forgiven and restored him.

It is precisely when human beings fail, however, that God acts with saving mercy, and this is the time when God is most wondrously known. Here is God's dwelling place among us, where we need Him most and come best to love Him. This grace alone rescues David's life's work; in this gift to David, God shows His own heart, His abounding faithfulness to flawed people like us who nevertheless trust in Him. Thus, it was through Bathsheba, who David had brought into his own household as an honored wife, that Solomon was born to David. Here is the Bible's account, taking place just after Nathan's rebuke and the subsequent death of their first child:

> Then David comforted his wife Bathsheba, and he went to her
> and lay with her. She gave birth to a son, and they named him
> Solomon. The Lord loved him; and because the Lord loved him,
> He sent word through Nathan the prophet to name him Jedidiah.
>
> (2 Samuel 12:24, 25)

"Jedidiah" means "beloved of the Lord," and this name parallels David's own name, which in the Hebrew language also means "beloved." This passage is inserted into the narrative of great events without further comment, as a brief interruption to the weighty events of the day, and without apparently gaining the notice it deserved. Indeed, Solomon's name does not surface again in the Bible's book of 2 Samuel, which provides the primary record of David's reign as king. But, significantly, the last word on David himself will not be found in the books dedicated to him but rather in the book of 1 Kings, the book which gives us the account of Solomon's career. There is something to this, for the truly worthy career does not end with its own story, but in the story of those who follow. This is what Solomon was given for, to give David's life a legacy, a new beginning to carry his name into the future. What a true gift that was, and one we all should truly desire for ourselves.

The truly worthy career does not end with its own story, but in the story of those who follow.

David begins the last act of his drama an old and sick man, no longer even capable of caring for himself.

> When King David was old and well advanced in years, he could
> not keep warm even when they put covers over him. So his
> servants said to him, "Let us look for a young virgin to attend the
> king and take care of him. She can lie beside him so that our
> lord the king may keep warm."
> Then they searched throughout Israel for a beautiful girl and
> found Abishag, a Shunammite, and brought her to the king. The
> girl was very beautiful; she took care of the king and waited on
> him, but the king had no intimate relations with her.
>
> (1 Kings 1:1–4)

Apparently David suffered from some unspecified illness which gave him constant chills; having someone to snuggle up with him was a pretty standard treatment of the day. But there is something else at work here, for this was also a test of the king's capacity to rule. In the ancient world, a man's virility was linked to his capacity to wield power (okay, this is not just an ancient thing). David's manhood was being tested by the presence of the young beauty. She was given not just as a maid but as a concubine, and the elderly king failed the test.

I have couched this last scene in David's life as a new beginning, and that it is, but new beginnings sadly do not completely erase the past, as events here will show. For upon the news of David's failure, yet another vengeful son, this time Absalom's younger brother Adonijah, seized the opportunity David's frailty presented to stake his claim for the throne.

The Bible tells us only two things about this son's character, that he too was very handsome (do we weary of this yet?), and also that "His father had never interfered with him by asking, 'Why do you behave as you do?' " (1 Kings 1:6). We've been down this road a few times before so I will not belabor my criticism of superficial virtue and a father's failure to raise his sons. The long and the short of it is that Adonijah "put himself foward" and with hands grasping for the crown he saw falling from his father's head, he cried out, "I will be king." This, no doubt, contained the whole of his ambition.

Adonijah was not a very inventive rebel, for the plan he proposed was nearly the carbon copy of his brother Absalom's, only compressed in time. Indeed, it was so compressed that he skipped the entire rebellion itself and proceeded directly to celebrating his ascension to power. Now the eldest son, he simply enlisted the support of the army and some of the priests and moved straight to the coronation.

This is just another echo from the past, but there is one thing that takes this to an all new low, and that is the support given to Adonijah by both Joab and Abiathar. Joab, of course, had long been clinging to his position by his bare fingernails, and we can guess that after killing Absalom he had become persona non grata in a big way. Here he is at the end of a career that was sordid but also filled with many accomplishments. Rather than cap his record with a finale rooted in faithful service, Joab instead chose the low road of grasping for power and position even at the expense of the king his name would be forever linked to.

More shocking still is the betrayal of Abiathar, another old colleague of David's. We remember him as the sole survivor from Saul's massacre of the priests way back when David was first fleeing for his life. Abiathar was David's priest all through the anti-Saul resistance, the man who time and again sought the Lord's guidance on David's behalf. In recent years and for unspecified reasons, David had come to favor Zadok (who we met in the last episode) as his high priest, a choice well borne out in those events and these. Abiathar had held fast to David in the old and dire days, but now he cast his lot with the wave of the future against David's wishes and the word of God.

Russell Dilday summed up the tawdry character of these betrayals well:

> Here is a tragic illustration of how a selfish grasping after power can destroy relationships as well as individual personalities. Over the years Joab and Abiathar had developed intimate friendships . . . Their fellowship, which had been made closer because of shared dangers and suffering, now crumbled under the sad pressure of petty personal jealousies. As leaders, these two should have been more concerned for the welfare of the king and the nation than for the protection of their own futures.[1]

These two, then, were the honored guests at Adonijah's coronation celebration, along with David's other sons and various royal officials. However, by the list of those specifically excluded from this feast, we gather that the plotters knew very well who their opposition was: Solomon, Nathan the prophet, Zadok the high priest, and the officers of David's personal bodyguard. Here were David's known loyalists, along with the son now known to be the true heir. Apparently, Adonijah's plan called for these formidable figures to be cowed into submission. But as it turned out, these stout hearts had not the least intention of giving way so easily.

1. *Russell Dilday, 1, 2 Kings, Dallas: Word, 1987, p. 36.*

It is fascinating to see who these loyalists turned to in their bid to save the day. It was Bathsheba, Solomon's mother, who now stepped forth as the most prominent among David's wives and the key support for her husband. To her Nathan came, and instructed her as to how they might turn the tide:

> Then Nathan asked Bathsheba, Solomon's mother, "Have you not heard that Adonijah, the son of Haggith, has become king without our lord David's knowing it? Now then, let me advise you how you can save your own life and the life of your son Solomon. Go in to King David and say to him, 'My lord the king, did you not swear to me your servant: "Surely Solomon your son shall be king after me, and he will sit on my throne?" Why then has Adonijah become king?' While you are still there talking to the king, I will come in and confirm what you have said."
>
> (1 Kings 1:11–14)

Bathsheba carried off her role flawlessly, adding an improvised conclusion to drive home the importance of David's immediate action:

> "My lord the king, the eyes of all Israel are on you, to learn from you who will sit on the throne of my lord the king after him."
>
> (1 Kings 1:20)

Bathsheba is proof positive that there is redemption for the lost. Despite all David's crimes against her and her husband Uriah, the love and care of succeeding years had sealed her heart to his cause. Now, she was just the person to get through to the aged king, bringing forth a surge of the energy he still held in reserve. "I will surely carry out today what I swore to you by the Lord, the God of Israel," he replied. "Solomon your son shall be king after me, and he will sit on my throne in my place" (1 Kings 1:30). When David speaks with that kind of resolve, even when he is at death's door, his enemies had better take care.

David's response was quick and overwhelmingly powerful. First he had Solomon set upon his own mule, the traditional mount of Israelite royalty, in a very public and dramatic demonstration of his transfer of authority. Solomon was to be led to a stream in the Kidron Valley where he would undergo ritual purification. David then instructed:

> "There have Zadok the priest and Nathan the prophet anoint
> him king over Israel. Blow the trumpet and shout, 'Long live
> King Solomon!' Then you are to go up with him, and he is to
> come and sit on my throne and reign in my place. I have
> appointed him ruler over Israel and Judah."
>
> (1 Kings 1:34, 35)

There is no doubt that Nathan and Zadok carried out this command with a great deal of satisfaction. These, the heads of the two Israelite institutions that stood before God along with the king, the prophets and the priests, knew very well that Solomon was God's own choice for the succession; indeed, in orchestrating David's response they had bravely risked it all in support of Solomon. So they measured out the sacred olive oil, originally mixed by the hands of Moses himself and carefully kept for centuries within the Ark of the Covenant, oil that had fallen over the head and shoulders first of Saul and then of David. The oil poured from the hands of the prophet of the living God and His high priest signified God's presence, God's Spirit, specially given to the chosen king. Thus Solomon was entered into a singular and intimate relationship with God, His intermediary among the people. To be king was to be God's own regent, ruling in His stead among His people; God's shepherd, to faithfully tend the sheep of His pasture.

All this, of course, was far too much for Adonijah, his petty attendants and their empty ceremonials. When news that an anointed Solomon sat enthroned on David's throne reached his festive hall, there where a new court gloated over their easy and therefore insignificant elevation, the bravado was transformed into cringes of fear. It was Joab who first heard the horns that heralded Solomon's ascension: "What's the meaning of all the noise in the city?" (1 Kings 1:41) he asked. But when the trumpet calls were followed by the devastating news that Solomon had taken the throne, Adonijah's court rose in alarm and fled for their lives.

It is not just CEO's and kings who must consider the issue of succession. It is important for all leaders, at all levels, to carefully oversee the appointment of a successor, if their legacy is to endure. How many of us have arrived as the new leader, uninformed of our predecessor's intent and often finding an Adonijah seeking to garner the reins to himself. For a new leader to be a success he has to absorb the values and goals of the institution, and to do this he needs help from the people. To just sit back and "see how he does" is to undermine the new leader's authority and risk the success he is brought on board to produce.

In David's case, the problem was that he had almost waited too long to install his chosen successor, though he had just enough time to salvage the situation. What a difference it made that he was still there to hand his steed to Solomon, to lend his awesome presence to the scene, and to authenticate Solomon's authority as he stepped forward to sit upon so august a throne. It was equally important that David was there to guide his successor's crucial first steps, to place the cornerstone of the house Solomon would be charged to build.

This story is also a lesson in the value of ceremonial ritual, rooted in real history and authentic symbols of authority, in establishing an heir or successor. The king's mule, the oil of anointing, and the glorious throne all served to solidify Solomon's position. Sacredly guarded, and brought forth at a crucial point in Israel's history, they exerted a commanding influence on the mind of the people, indeed on the mind of Solomon himself as he received the living legacy of his father.

> *What a difference it made that David was still there to hand his steed to Solomon, to lend his awesome presence to the scene, and to authenticate Solomon's authority as he stepped forward to sit upon so august a throne.*

These artifacts served to link him inexorably to a past, and to the principles and purpose that flowed from it.

Handing over the reigns of power requires a thoughtful and deliberate approach. Perhaps it will be just a solemn ceremony, like the passing of flags by which military command is transferred and sealed. Perhaps it is the presence of past CEO's to honor the new leader and enter her into their fellowship. The particulars depend on the organization, the heritage, and the culture. What matters is the nature of the statement being made and its impact on those who participate and observe.

Finally, we see again that it was David's loyal friends and companions who upheld his shaking hand and prompted his action at a crucial juncture. Nathan, Zadok, and Bathsheba, these are the heroes as the curtain falls on David's amazing life. The difference between them and Adonijah, Joab, and Abiathar lies at only one point. For it is not ability, not experience, not position that separates the champions from the scoundrels; it is the heart that makes the difference, then and now, the heart that distinguishes between faithfulness and treachery, truth and facade, purpose and petty opportunism. A great chasm lies between these descriptors; on one side stand the eagles, while on the other side the vultures circle.

And so the curtain finally falls on the astounding life of David, King of Israel. It is at Solomon's side that we last observe him, the son chosen by God to complete the work first commissioned through a shepherd boy. In Solomon, David received back what he had lost in his other sons, a legacy and a promise for tomorrow. He could not undo the fate of Amnon and Absalom and Adonijah, but he could pour himself into this one son, a man after his own heart and a true king for his people Israel. It is with satisfaction, therefore, that we read this solemn charge by which he at last surrendered his kingdom:

> When the time drew near for David to die, he gave
> a charge to Solomon his son.
> "I am about to go the way of all the earth," he said. "So be
> strong, show yourself a man, and observe what the Lord your
> God requires: Walk in his ways, and keep his decrees and
> commands, His laws and requirements, as written in the Law of
> Moses, so that you may prosper in all you do and wherever you

go, and that the Lord may keep his promise to me: 'If your descendants watch how they live, and if they walk faithfully before me with all their heart and soul, you will never fail to have a man on the throne of Israel.' "

(1 Kings 2:1–4)

Imagine all the advice David might have given: details regarding military tactics, financial secrets, pointers on handling the neighboring kings. Instead he offered something so much more precious; he pointed his son in the direction of true strength. "So be strong," he commanded. But how greatly David's conception of strength differs from ours today, and yet his words are just as true now. "Show yourself a man, and observe what the Lord your God requires: Walk in his ways." This is what it means to be strong: to submit to a higher truth, a higher cause, a higher authority. To hold precious the legacy of the past and walk humbly before the face of the living God. Resolve is born in a faith that looks beyond itself, its problems and its opportunities, to the God who rules over kingdoms and even history.

> *This is what it means to be strong: to submit to a higher truth, a higher cause, a higher authority. To hold precious the legacy of the past and walk humbly before the face of the living God.*

David had reigned forty years over Judah and Israel before dying peacefully. Here are the words of Scripture, describing the final trumpet blast calling him home:

Then David rested with his fathers and was buried in the City of David.

(1 Kings 2:10)

Short and sweet, a wonderful epitaph. He *rested*, his work done fully and well, *with his fathers*, at home with those who had gone before, those with whom he had kept full faith, *and was buried in the City of David*, a legacy that bore his name. Should not we too seek such a monument on which to hang our names for those to follow? For David did not leave just cold walls of stone and empty towers. He left behind a dream, and a purpose countless generations have been inspired by. May God Himself bless the faithful labors of those who give their hearts to leave such a legacy, great or small, for the sake of the flock with which they are entrusted.

It may seem sad or anticlimactic to see David pass on from this life with so little apparent fanfare. Yet he had something more, something even better, and with it he was finally able to make his rest in peace. Here, really, is the last stroke of the pen regarding this man after God's own heart:

> So Solomon sat on the throne of his father David, and his rule
> was firmly established.
>
> (1 Kings 2:12)

EPILOGUE

Like Morning's
Light

כאור בקר

David is one of the greatest men who ever lived, probably the greatest man in the Old Testament. In him we see ability and energy coupled with a noble and human spirit. How many other great men and women do we feel such love for? How many executives, great or small, inspire such a glow in the hearts of others. But in David we see something that is more than great, something good. We see love in him and so we love his heart.

In David's story we have witnessed an entire career. We think back to the sweet days of preparation, "The Lord is my shepherd . . . I will dwell in the house of the Lord forever." David's apprenticeship was a fine one, and yet only a point of departure. It prepared him to be a hero, gave him an identity amid the crowd, but it also ushered in challenges greater than Goliath, many of which he was less than prepared for. It was the trial, suffering, injustice, and danger of these days of challenge that honed his heart and made him something more than just a hero. What God forged in David's heart became a vision for an entire people; in that vision multitudes would find their identity.

We will never be able to forget the great failures that marred David's record, and yet it is not these that sum him up. Like most great men and women David was at his best in times of trouble and danger, when the sheep were there before him in need of his guidance. Can any of us rise higher than David did in his act of mercy and faithfulness at the cave of Adullam? Surely that was his greatest moment, the highest point his heart ever reached, higher even that the quick triumph of faith that slew Goliath. *For the heart of the executive shines brightest not when it reveals its own identity, but when others find theirs in it.*

David's story reminds us that there is really nothing new under the sun, that our challenges are no different in character than those faced in earlier generations. Calling out from the very first days of recorded history, the tenth century B.C., David's tale rings as true as if it happened only yesterday.

This is history recorded for a purpose, indeed for a variety of purposes. For that first audience, the children who heard it on their fathers' knees or when the priests read it out before the congregation, David marked out the dimensions of true kingship in Israel. But there is a message for us today as well, a message given quite deliberately to *us* and with just the same intensity. For in the life of David we see the outline of true leadership for our day, for every day, leadership that is sponsored and approved by the Bible itself and pleasing to its Author.

We have listened in on David's final charge to his successor and son, the very King Solomon whose name would become synonymous with wisdom and glory. But David has a charge for us as well, a charge for all those in our time who would seek to follow in his steps. It is found in the twenty-third chapter of 2 Samuel, which sets forth the very last recorded words of David, King of Israel. And there we read this message:

> *When one rules over men in righteousness,*
> *when he rules in the fear of God,*
> *he is like the light of morning at sunrise*
> *on a cloudless morning,*

like the brightness after rain
that brings the grass from the earth.
2 Samuel 23: 3, 4

This is David's message specifically for us. Does it sound too lofty? Then consider what you see around you in the workplace. If there is one thing our experience today makes clear it is that there is room for dreaming among us. David is a poet, but there is reality in his dramatic vision, there is a purpose and a principle that he commends to us. As is so often the case with David's poetry we must see as well as listen to these words: *light breaking through over new morning, like brightness after rain that brings grass from the earth.*

Let's start with the issue of purpose. What is the leader to bring about? What is successful leadership? It is seen when hard, barren ground issues forth in life, because light has shined upon it. This is our calling and our opportunity as leaders and executives, to illuminate dark places where men and women are found, to inspire hope and energy in those who have known neither, to offer love and meaning to those who have long settled for much less. *"Like the light of morning . . . like the brightness after rain."*

How exalted and far off such words can sound to our minds trained to dullness! And yet what is it that stands between us today and the attainment of something of this dream? It is the failure of our hearts. It is the want of leadership and true leaders, those who "rule over men in righteousness . . . who rule in the fear of God."

This, then, is the ultimate lesson in leadership that David has to offer. It is the principle writ large in his own life, both in triumph and despair: Do right and fear God. For we are neither autonomous nor alone; we stand before the reality of a truth by which our works will be judged.

In his own words, then, we may build upon this one great statement to summarize what David learned and what he teaches. In so doing we find four core convictions that enabled his astonishing career. The first, as he himself has insisted, is this: *God is sovereign.*

This, you may respond, is simply a religious belief. What would David say to that, but that our understanding of God is at the center of our beliefs about all other things. We have simply not grasped David's approach to leadership unless we gained this insight into reality. His view is summed up by simple words of Psalm 14:

> *The fool says in his heart,*
>   *"There is no God."*

Here is the height of folly, he says, to look around you and see no pattern in life, to gaze upward and see nothing in the stars but points of distant light, to look upon yourself and see nothing more than a machine and a vehicle for earthly attainment and satisfaction. David looked upward and saw more than a heavenly dome, gazed deeply into himself and saw the image of God. Writing in his psalms, he directs us to this:

> *The heavens declare the glory of God;*
>   *the skies proclaim the work of his hands.*
> *Day after day they pour forth speech;*
>   *night after night they display knowledge.*
>
>   Psalm 19:1, 2

> *Where can I go from your Spirit?*
>   *Where can I flee from your presence? . . .*
> *For you created my inmost being;*
>   *you knit me together in my mother's womb.*
> *I praise you because I am fearfully and wonderfully made;*
>   *your works are wonderful,*
>   *I know that full well.*
>
>   Psalm 139:7, 13, 14

David's own view of life was rooted in a conscious awareness of God's rule over all things:

> *The Lord is in his holy temple;*
>   *the Lord is on his heavenly throne.*

He observes the sons of men;
   his eyes examine them . . .
For the Lord is righteous,
   he loves justice;
   upright men will see his face.

Psalm 11:4, 7

David's awareness of God's presence did not make him afraid, but rather it instilled profound respect and a sense of responsibility for his own actions. God was a polestar for him, a steady guide by which David assessed his own life and actions.

It is impossible to underestimate the significance of this for David's career; apart from his faith in God there simply would have been no career. Think back to his first great triumph of courage, the victory over Goliath. What was it that inspired such valor but his confidence in this: "This day the Lord will hand you over to me, and I'll strike you down." Particularly in his times of despair, trials that doubtless would have finished off most people, David drew strength from his knowledge of God and with that strength he stood firm.

The Lord is my light and my salvation—
   whom shall I fear?
The Lord is the stronghold of my life—
   of whom shall I be afraid?

Psalm 27:1

David's awareness of God thus provided him with both a sense of responsibility and a capacity for hope amid darkness. Indeed, we may well chart the ups and downs of David's career by the vitality of his prayer life. It was God Himself who inspired David, so that he might inspire others. As David himself observes with joy:

You are my lamp, O Lord;
   the Lord turns my darkness into light.
With your help I can advance against a troop;
   with my God I can scale a wall . . .

It is God who arms me with strength
and makes my way perfect . . .
he enables me to stand on the heights.

2 Samuel 22:29, 30, 33, 34

There, in his own words, is the secret to his success.

The second key conviction that guided David's career was this: *The leader's success is measured in terms of his effect in and upon the people who follow.* This does not minimize the importance of being a competent leader in every way possible. David was renowned as a military leader and strategist, and many were inspired to his cause out of sheer confidence in his ability. And yet, especially over the long run, David's legacy was born out of the love and trust he earned in the hearts of others. David's own ability was never enough to overcome the obstacles he faced; it was through the commitment and loyalty that he deliberately inspired in others that he accomplished his aims and then preserved them.

> *David's legacy was born out of the love and trust he earned in the hearts of others.*

We think particularly of the later heartbreaks that marred his reign: Apart from the support of loyal followers, David would have toppled from his throne. But the same was true at the start of his career. How quickly he gathered adherents when he was forced to flee Saul's palace. Think of the personal loyalty of those who stuck with him through years of living in deserts and caves. Think of how Saul would have greatly rewarded anyone who betrayed David. And yet no one did. Here is evidence of a profound and valuable loyalty.

David's failure to nurture loyalty, particularly in his own household, was disastrous; his failure to devote himself to the shaping and training of young leaders nearly cost him his crown, and greatly tarnished what might have been his golden years. Even this exception to David's normal emphasis on personal bonds of loyalty, therefore, proves the point well.

We have noted the importance of friends at several points in David's career, and this too is a striking lesson from his life. First and foremost there was Jonathan's wonderful camaraderie, the paragon of faithful friendship which strengthened David's shaking hand on more than one occasion. Jonathan loved David as himself, more than his own royal status and more than his own career. That speaks volumes about Jonathan himself, and about the kinds of friends a leader should seek. But it also reveals much about David. It begs us to ask the question, *"Who has seen in me something they love more than their own ambition?"* Do you have friends and colleagues who would put your needs above their own concerns? If the answer is no, it is most likely because nothing compelling, nothing passionate, nothing purposeful has been seen in you. David loved his friends, wept over the fall of his enemies, stood erect before the storms and trials. He honored many and therefore feared few.

David was always, at heart, a shepherd, and his life was given to the sheep. This is where we first got to know him, on the green hills about Bethlehem where the young man was learning how to be a king through his service to the sheep. He understood what it meant to rely on another, and for the weak to rely upon him in return. "Blessed is he who has regard for the weak," he sang (Psalm 41:1). Therefore the rod he bore was wielded for the sake of the sheep, even as he had learned from the example of his God:

> *The Lord is my shepherd, I shall not want.*
> *He makes me lie down in green pastures,*
> *he leads me beside quiet waters,*
> *he restores my soul.*
> *He guides me in paths of righteousness*
> *for his name's sake.*
> *Even though I walk*
> *through the valley of the shadow of death,*
> *I will fear no evil,*
> *for you are with me;*
> *your rod and your staff,*
> *they comfort me.*

Psalm 23:1–4

Here is found David's entire philosophy of a servant leadership that saw both the means and the ends encompassed in the sheep themselves, the object of all his attention. In this way he built not only a city but a people, not just a short-lived cause but a vision that spans the ages. What we see in David is what Jesus sets forth as His measure of true greatness:

> *David loved his friends, wept over the fall of his enemies . . . he honored many and therefore feared few . . . David was always, at heart, a shepherd, and his life was given to the sheep.*

"If anyone wants to be first, he must be the very last, and the servant of all" (Mark 9:35). David, for all his flaws, comes out very near the head of such a list.

The next characteristic of David's approach to leadership is the sense of purpose which marked his actions. This is his third great conviction, *that leadership feeds on the vision of something great.* David knew where he was going when he set out. Rooted in his personal faith and in his identity with his people, David's purpose shaped his actions rather than the other way around.

Again, the first signs of this occurred as young David stepped out to face Goliath. "Who is this uncircumcised Philistine that he should defy the armies of the living God?" (1 Samuel 17:26). This is what sent him forth, heedless of his own life. This is what made him a dangerous change agent in the court of Saul, and it was this too that later provided David with the means to unite the contentious tribes of his newly forged nation. But it was in that crucial moment at the cave of Adullam where his focus on something higher than revenge, more meaningful than personal safety, led him to forge his own values in the hearts of so many others.

> *Leadership feeds on the vision of something great. David knew where he was going when he set out; his purpose shaped his actions rather than the other way around.*

"The Lord forbid that I should do such a thing to my master, the Lord's anointed . . . 'From evildoers come evil deeds,' so my hand will not touch you" (1 Samuel 24:6, 13). It was that sense of purpose, born of faith, that was able to conquer even hatred and fear, that more than anything else won the people to David's cause. In him, they saw not just short-lived success but a lasting peace, a hope for the future, and a city to bear his name.

Fourth and finally, David stands as a timeless testimony to this great lesson: *Leadership, like greatness, is born in the heart.* David was great for what he loved and for what he hated. It was his heart that held him fast in times of trouble and his heart that brought him triumph. This too is God's great message through David for every leader who seeks His approval: "Man looks at the outward appearance, but the Lord looks at the heart."

How poorly we understand this today, as our hiring practices, our leader development plans, and our personal improvement programs attest. Ours is a generation infatuated first with the mind, and then with the working hands. Yet both the mind and the hands are under full control of the heart. Hushai versus Ahithophel, Jonathan versus Joab, David versus Saul—what was the difference? If you look back you will find that the latter in each case stood taller and possessed, on the whole, a better mind and better skills. But it was Hushai's heart that won the day over Ahithophel's treacherous mind, Jonathan's love that lives on while Joab's lust rots in the grave, David's passion which overcame Saul's mere ambition. It is in the heart that every battle is won or lost, and so the heart is always primary.

David understood this well, and when he forgot, the result was always disastrous. On the whole, however, he guarded the springs that fed his heart jealously. In many of his psalms David talks with God about this war within his heart, and his prayer for a God-pleasing heart was frequent, as seen in Psalm 86:

> *Teach me your way, O Lord,*
> *and I will walk in your truth;*
> *give me an undivided heart,*
> *that I may fear your name.*
>
> **Psalm 86:11**

How often he asked the Lord to examine his heart, to instruct him in the things of life:

> *Search me, O God, and know my heart;*
> *test me and know my anxious thoughts.*

See if there is any offensive way in me,
   and lead me in the way everlasting.

                         Psalm 139:23, 24

Self-knowledge is a crucial step on the path to greatness, yet few dare to walk for fear of discovering something horrible in themselves. David, in contrast, became familiar with his failings, as Psalm 51 attests:

Have mercy on me, O God . . .
For I know my transgressions,
   and my sin is always before me . . .
Surely you desire truth in the inner parts;
   you teach me wisdom in the inmost place . . .
Create in me a pure heart, O God,
   and renew a steadfast spirit within me.

                         Psalm 51:1, 3, 6, 10

It was after seeing himself in the light of God's presence, that David gained the humility to ask for grace, to plead for wisdom:

Show me the way I should go,
   for to you I lift up my soul . . .
Teach me to do your will,
   for you are my God.

                         Psalm 143:8, 10

David dared to bring his impure heart into the presence of God's light, believing that God would make it whole. It was also in the presence of God that David learned to love with an unbounded heart.

But I trust in your unfailing love;
   my heart rejoices in your salvation.
I will sing to the Lord,
   for he has been good to me.

                         Psalm 13:5, 6

How priceless is your unfailing love!
Both high and low among men
*   find refuge in the shadow of your wings . . .*
For with you is the fountain of life;
*   in your light we see light.*

Psalm 36:7, 9

In the final analysis we are what we love. Can it be that what we amount to today is nothing more than money, status, admiration, comfort? Sadly, for so many there is nothing more than these. But David's love was

"Man looks at the outward appearance, but the Lord looks at the heart."

for his God, for his people, for a dream that shines on still. His love was who he was, what he became, a man after God's own heart. And so he leads us still.